Alistair Cooke enjoyed an extraordinary life in print, radio and television. Born in Manchester in 1908 and educated at the universities of Cambridge, Yale and Harvard, he was the *Guardian*'s Senior Correspondent in New York for twenty-five years and the host of groundbreaking cultural programmes on American television and for the BBC. He was best known for his weekly BBC broadcast *Letter from America*, which reported on fifty-eight years of US life, was heard over five continents and totalled 2,869 broadcasts before his retirement in February 2004.

Geoff Brown began writing about cinema at Cambridge University. He has been film critic of *The Times* and has contributed to many publications, including *Directors in British and Irish Cinema* (associate editor) and the magazine *Sight and Sound*. He currently writes on classical music for *The Times*.

Alistair Cooke at the Movies

Edited by GEOFF BROWN

PENGUIN BOOKS

PENGUIN BOOKS

Published by the Penguin Group
Penguin Books Ltd, 80 Strand, London WC2R ORL, England
Penguin Group (USA) Inc., 375 Hudson Street, New York, New York 10014, USA
Penguin Group (Canada), 90 Eglinton Avenue East, Suite 700, Toronto, Ontario, Canada M4P 2Y3
(a division of Pearson Penguin Canada Inc.)
Penguin Ireland, 25 St Stephen's Green, Dublin 2, Ireland (a division of Penguin Books Ltd)
Penguin Group (Australia), 250 Camberwell Road, Camberwell, Victoria 3124, Australia
(a division of Pearson Australia Group Pty Ltd)
Penguin Books India Pvt Ltd, 11 Community Centre, Panchsheel Park, New Delhi – 110 017, India
Penguin Group (NZ), 67 Apollo Drive, Rosedale, North Shore 0632, New Zealand
(a division of Pearson New Zealand Ltd)
Penguin Books (South Africa) (Pty) Ltd, 24 Sturdee Avenue, Rosebank,
Johannesburg 2196, South Africa

Penguin Books Ltd, Registered Offices: 80 Strand, London WC2R ORL, England

www.penguin.com

First published by Allen Lane 2009
Published in Penguin Books 2011

1

Typeset by Rowland Phototypesetting Ltd, Bury St Edmunds, Suffolk

Printed in Great Britain by Clays Ltd, St Ives plc

978-0-141-03606-9

www.greenpenguin.co.uk

Contents

CONTENTS

CONTENTS

REPORTER

PEOPLE

List of Illustrations

Introduction

He helped enormously to further English understanding and admiration of the United States, and in doing so he has exposed English apathy and snobbishness in a way that made the air vibrate. I thank him for his fund of anecdotes, for his sparkling parting shots, for his bold penetrating criticisms. His voice has been like a whiff of oxygen in an ether of carbon dioxide.

At a glance, a British reader might date this tribute to Alistair Cooke to his relinquishment of his BBC *Letter from America* broadcasts in 2004, after almost sixty years. But it's not so. G. Allen Batty's fan letter to America's most famous ambassador-at-large was published in the *Listener* magazine in April 1937, following Cooke's departure from his first sustained freelance job, as the BBC's film critic. On 8 October 1934, long before the wider world knew him from his *Letter* broadcasts, his television series *America* or his introductions to *Masterpiece Theatre*, Cooke had sat down at the microphone to give his first BBC talk, broadcast live. He was twenty-five and cocky, fresh from a glittering, cocooned university career at Cambridge, Yale and Harvard. His film stint wasn't without controversy, but, like Mr Batty, the BBC knew they had found a perfect radio voice – fluent, conversational, a voice you wanted to listen to. He continued these film broadcasts fortnightly, with summer breaks, until 1937, when he left to live permanently in what had become his promised land: America. Settled in New York, he continued film reviewing on radio stations until the Second World War, when the reporting and interpreting of real lives, real dramas, finally took priority.

Alistair Cooke's baptism as a film critic has not been entirely forgotten: through his long career he often drew upon his film knowledge and friendships with Chaplin, Bogart and others. But his film reviews of the 1930s – sparkling, quirky – have largely slumbered unseen. In 1971, the reissue of *Garbo and the Night Watchmen*, the enterprising book of reviews he edited in 1937, brought eleven of them back, among coverage by eight other critics. The present collection aims for a much bigger survey, drawing on both British and American radio talks, various magazine writings and Cooke's first steps into criticism from his student years at Cambridge. To round out the picture of Cooke at the movies, the anthology then progresses to Cooke the reporter, documenting Hollywood stories and personalities mostly for his BBC listeners and the *Guardian* newspaper (he was its American correspondent from 1946 to 1972). Finally comes Cooke the portrait artist, capturing in words (mostly in celebration) selected friends and Hollywood personnel. The selection span stretches from 1928 to 2003: an astonishing seventy-five years.

He had first approached the BBC for work in July 1931. An eager, ambitious Cambridge postgraduate student, he grandly announced that he was prepared to give talks on theatre and literary criticism, read fiction and poetry, write review sketches; it was quite a list. Cinema wasn't mentioned, though he'd long been a fan and in his early teens had spent many hours in a Blackpool gym hoping to become Douglas Fairbanks. For the Cambridge student magazine *The Granta*, among other roles (he was eventually its editor), he wrote cinema reviews in the self-absorbed, clotted undergraduate style of the time. In the summer of 1932, out in the real world, his first job was reviewing films for two months for *Everyman*, a gentle cultural weekly.

A Commonwealth Fund fellowship then transported him to America for the first time, for theatre studies at Yale and Harvard. He also spent time studying American speech, a sport and passion that led to lasting friendship with the philologist and buccaneering journalist H. L. Mencken. But cinema was never forgotten. In 1933, after planning the first of many long car trips exploring the continent, he baited the *Observer* newspaper in London with the prospect of Hollywood interviews, beginning at the top with Chaplin, though none of his candidates had yet been approached. The *Observer* bit, the interviewees bit, and Cooke found himself ferried round

Hollywood by studio limousines for a string of serious interviews. Cameraman Lee Garmes surprised him with the news that the luxurious foliage of *Zoo in Budapest* was whipped up in the studio; Katharine Hepburn, on the set of *Little Women*, surprised him with an ice-cream, a 'Good Humor' bar. A six-part series, 'Hollywood Prospect', appeared in September and October, with a smaller sequel in 1934. At this point Cooke was no journalist, and not much of an interviewer, though he thought enough of the soberly written encounters to propose repackaging them as a book to T. S. Eliot at the publishers Faber and Faber.

The excursion's one concrete, unexpected outcome was Chaplin's friendship. Alistair's charm and intelligence struck home. He became an intimate, at dinner, work and play. That enchanted summer, joining Chaplin and his new amour Paulette Goddard on their yacht, the *Panacea*, he put his new 8mm movie camera to work, shooting what became a little film, *All at Sea*, long thought lost, but recently rediscovered among Cooke's effects. The camera caught Goddard's beauty, a harpooned shark, the Pacific's sheen, Chaplin's lightning impersonations (among them Garbo, the future Edward VIII, Janet Gaynor and the Greek god Pan) – and AC himself, sleek and gangling, accidentally swiping Chaplin's face with his pipe. The pair's friendship deepened during 1934 when Cooke, on a second visit to California, worked on the script for a film about Napoleon long rumbling in Chaplin's mind, as well as a short burlesque planned to support what eventually became *Modern Times*. Shortly before, in April, through fast manoeuvring and a successful test in London, he had secured the BBC niche he had long wanted, as the Corporation's new film critic. He was replacing Oliver Baldwin (the son of Prime Minister Stanley Baldwin) – relieved of his post after he gave a withering public speech attacking Corporation bureaucracy. That summer, letters to Cooke's future BBC employers announced his address as 'c/o Charles Chaplin Studio'. They must have been suitably impressed.

In later life AC often depicted these trips across a country striving to fight free of the Depression under the recently elected President Franklin D. Roosevelt as the major turning point in his life. Driving from coast to coast, he saw the whole of America, and the American spirit, and loved them both. Yet once he returned to England for a job sitting in the dark, his broadcasts never suggested that here was a man wasting his time. Beforehand, he'd told BBC executive Lionel Fielden that there'd be no film fan chit-chat, no barren debates on 'Are the movies worthwhile?' or 'Should film stars marry young?' The only broadcasting film critic in Britain, he took his assignment seriously. He often saw films several times, and invited industry experts to join him for general talks about cinema's nuts and bolts – Cavalcanti from the GPO Film Unit talking about sound, Hugh Stewart (a Cambridge friend) on editing. He constantly pressed for extra slots, and in 1935 sought a trip to the second Venice Film Festival. Request denied, executive Charles Siepmann said, 'much as I should like to provide you with an Italian holiday'. At the same time Cooke spread his wings outside the BBC: writing quarterly film columns for *Sight and Sound* magazine, published by the newly formed British Film Institute; giving lectures; deputizing for Graham Greene on the *Spectator* when Greene needed time off for a film script. Since the bulk of the releases in Britain came from America, no doubt AC reasoned he could always keep in touch with his new love through celluloid.

Viewed retrospectively, the opening paragraphs of his first broadcast in October 1934 read almost like a *Letter from America*. As so often, he's describing a New York scene – Broadway's riot of electric lights. He's precise, vivid, personal; and he's drawing us in. It's a magical moment. But also deceptive: for one of the fascinations of these early broadcasts is their glimpse of Cooke in transition. The easy flow of language is there, the striking phrases, the intimacy of address – but it took the grind of daily journalism in the 1940s and the freedom of his *Letter from America* assignment to bring the nonchalant Cooke style to its peak. Here you can still spot the clever Cambridge graduate, reclining in adjectives, sprinkling talks with Eng. Lit. references certainly above some listeners' heads.

One name evoked is I. A. Richards, the Cambridge English Department lecturer who had galvanized many students' minds in the 1920s, AC's included, by subjecting literary texts to rigorous scientific and psychological scrutiny – the new art of 'practical criticism'. In a wicked review written for the *Spectator*, Cooke interpreted MGM's musical *Born to Dance* as life getting its own back on Richards – and any other intellectual too busy analysing to enjoy a film that an untutored audience would appreciate instinctively. AC himself could analyse, yet he always set himself up as a critic apart from those 'double-domed' intellectuals from Hampstead who'd run to anything with subtitles, even Edmond T. Gréville's *Remous* ('this whimpering, fish-like film'). Always, his keen eye for the phoney, the meretricious and the pompous stopped him in his tracks. Director Josef von Sternberg's stifling artifices irked him no end; so did the mannerisms of René Clair. As for the Soviet strivings of Grigori Kozintsev and Leonid Trauberg: 'For *The New Babylon*, I wouldn't swap one of my home movies.' That was his one-line review.

The few foreign films AC championed tended to be realistically inclined, such as the 1933 German film *Flüchtlinge* (*Refugees*), which he called, rashly, 'just about the most exciting film there has ever been'. He championed realism in Hollywood, too. Though he damned and ridiculed much studio product, he gave loud support to Warner Bros.' gangster dramas, Fritz Lang's *Fury*, Frank Capra's populist comedies: films demonstrating a cinematic vigour and a social responsibility that he rarely found elsewhere. Certainly not in British cinema: that was seen as a desert, except for isolated features and the documentaries produced by the talents clustered around the producer John Grierson. Like his *Spectator* colleague Graham Greene, Cooke stood out as a refreshing maverick in the critical climate of the time in Britain – neither a populist hypnotized by a film's publicity nor a precious worshipper of montage and all the accoutrements of Film Art.

He was also a maverick in the way he conducted his reviewing. Most people handed the critic's job, then or since, would pounce on the dedicated press screenings; pounce on the hospitality drinks, too. Cigarette in mouth – you could still smoke in cinemas then – AC often saw his films at public screenings, working an audience's reactions into his reviews, from overheard comments to overheard snores. His fascination with public opinion, an audience's private psychology and what we'd now call 'the viewing experience' was unique among Britain's film critics in the 1930s. In the same spirit of enquiry, he would sometimes alarm his BBC minders by springing listeners' polls upon them, canvassing views about this and that. 'I'd like to know on a postcard,' he said, 'how many people who have seen *Man of Aran* found the shark scene a strain on their eyes'. And that was in only his second talk.

At the same time he proudly paraded his own opinions, inserted frequent personal digressions and did everything to make his criticisms mischievously individual. Not for Cooke the rounded assessment, the listing of pertinent names, the outline of the film's plot. Sometimes he seems more jazz musician than critic, riffing blissfully on a far-distant theme. The extreme example is his coverage of MGM's *A Tale of Two Cities*. Starting from the shock of seeing Ronald Colman clean-shaven as the hero Sydney Carton, he spins into a rhapsody of regret for the influential Soviet manner of shooting feet, limbs, human bits and pieces, rather than the full face. Dickens is nowhere; nor, indeed, is there any proper evaluation of the film.

This was enlivening listening for many – one of the reasons why the BBC kept renewing his contract (at the time the usual span of a BBC critic's life was a year). But it clearly irked others looking for a plain man's guide to a film's pros and cons. In 1936 a rumpus was stirred over his comment on 22 November that moviegoers outside London would be better off reading a book than seeing the fortnight's new general releases. Previous suggestions in sunnier months that listeners go biking, or find their drama working as ball boys at the local tennis club, had passed unnoticed. This time a campaign was waged. The popular magazine *Film Weekly* opened its pages to letters of complaint about AC's 'peculiar' opinions and 'contrary' manner from readers and some obviously solicited industry figures; even Douglas Fairbanks Jr, then working in London, chipped in. A deputation from the Cinema Exhibitors' Association met the BBC; the BBC stood by its critic's independence, though it allowed that this one comment had been 'too sweeping'.

Throughout the rumpus Cooke fought his corner hard, defending his right to express 'disinterested personal opinion' and his general support for the mainstream. 'Though Hollywood needs smacking all the time,' he told *Film Weekly*, 'Hollywood is my baby and I'll defend it till death do us part.' But even before the arguments flared, both sides at the BBC were thinking about parting company. At the beginning of 1936, J. M. Rose-Troup, the new Director of Talks, had been a Cooke booster; now he considered him a little too cavalier, too princely. Cooke himself was always hunting for wider horizons. His London broadcasts for NBC during the crisis of Edward VIII's abdication had finally led to enough guarantees of American work to make moving across the Atlantic practical. No more BBC bureaucracy. Better pay. No more memos informing him that his schools broadcast of 27 November 1936 would be shared with the writer and naturalist Henry Williamson, 'who will talk about squirrels for fifteen minutes'.

For close listeners of his broadcasts, the move overseas couldn't have come as any surprise. Step by step in these reviews you can see his emigration approaching. Indeed, it wouldn't be fanciful to view AC's moviegoing as a significant influence on shaping his love for America. In his ordinary childhood in north-west England, in Salford and Blackpool, his mother and headmaster warned of cinema's vulgarity and vile propensity for ruining minds, but Alistair still kept heading into the dark. Douglas Fairbanks's athletic adventures taught him to relish American pep, optimism and good cheer. Talkies, he found, dashed silent movies' visual subtleties and diluted the appeal of another of his screen favourites, the dapper sophisticate Adolphe Menjou. But talkies featured Americans talking – talking often in slang, often with humour, using terms and inflections that AC had begun noting with zest during his student years in America. 'When will Hollywood begin to send us films entirely in English?' one good lady wrote to him over Christmas 1934; 'They all speak that dreadful American.' Cooke grabbed every chance to encourage his listeners to respect and enjoy the words and accents that many in Britain were hearing for the first time. And he refused to allow America as a country to be always tainted with Hollywood's sins, informing listeners that 'Hollywood is about as characteristic of America as, say, Blackpool Pleasure Beach is of England.' As a Blackpool lad, he would know.

Numerous other passions and hobby-horses are reflected in his film reviews beside the diverse glories of America. A former theatre student, he loudly trumpets cinema acting as its own, special skill. A hypochondriac fascinated by medical science, he lingers over any film featuring doctors, test-tubes and operating rooms. He also lingers, we'd better face it, over a string of beautiful women. In his very first talk he declares his old love for the lissom Loretta Young: not in hope of reciprocity, but in I. A. Richards's tradition of exposing those personal quirks that can secretly shape somebody's critical view. He also looks fondly upon Myrna Loy, Carole Lombard, the French actress Annabella and Geraldine Fitzgerald, heroine of one of the few British features he favoured, *Turn of the Tide*. A few comments about ladies' attributes may now seem outrageous but, as his period vocabulary on matters of race and colour reveals, AC was a man of his time – an Edwardian man, with the presumptions that entails. In a *Guardian* article in 1969, he chose Ava Gardner as the most beautiful woman he knew – 'a continuous enchantment', he wrote, from whatever angle or posture. But he never reviewed her films. The divinities he kept facing on the screen were Garbo and Marlene Dietrich. Neither really appealed. Meeting Garbo finally in 1952, he found her frozen, tongue-tied. Loretta Young, the lady often met in films 'lying crushed and frail in an emotional pause', was never encountered, except perhaps in his dreams.

Cooke's final broadcast as the BBC critic in 1937 suggested that he was fed up 'playing with life' and looked forward to facing the real thing. Nonetheless his criticisms continued from New York. Aside from broadcasting back to Britain in the BBC's series *Mainly about Manhattan* (1938–9), there was his WEAF programme *A Critic on Broadway* (1937–8) and, on WQXR, *The Stage and Screen* (from 1939). Since he was known as a radio critic, radio criticism was the work he could easily get. Yet once again, you never sense dissatisfaction. In a January 1938 lecture to the critics and educationalists of the National Board of Review, he singled out radio as the best hope for direct, independent criticism beamed at the widest audience possible. It was the country in microcosm, he said: an audience made up of 'plumbers and priests, housewives and taxi-drivers, professors and cops, convicts and mannequins, of anybody who leaves his radio on while he eats or reads or nods or washes his hands'.

Nor was it just expediency, surely, that led him to an association with the Museum of Modern Art's newly flourishing Film Library, where he researched Fairbanks's life and career for a popular film series and a book, *Douglas Fairbanks: The Making of a Screen Character* (1940), and gave extraordinary lectures in a film study course run by MoMA and Columbia University. Students could not have been expecting what Cooke offered: elaborate probes into audience psychology, practical criticism exercises, aural identification tests, details of his astigmatism and taste in colour (pastel grey preferred), even the sensitivities of women's bladders. He told his students in January 1940 that he saw about twenty-four films a week.

In a letter to MoMA's Ron Magliozzi in 2001, Cooke recalled the prevailing atmosphere during his Fairbanks researches. 'It was a nervous time for an expatriate Englishman. The war was on and the little that was happening was going badly. By the time *Fairbanks* came out, Britain was bracing against invasion and the Blitz.' Not yet an American citizen (that came late in 1941), he offered to return to the UK, but the British authorities told him to stay and continue with the general reporting he was now doing, both for the BBC and the London *Times*.

Though the war closed off his critic's niche – decisively after Pearl Harbor – Cooke the reporter never stopped returning to the movies for stories, colour and social commentary. Publicized and disseminated across the planet, Hollywood and its movies proved a natural resource for the quick, memorable image that every reporter needs. Sentencing eleven Communist Party members, Judge Harold Medina, Cooke told his *Guardian* readers in 1949, looked like 'a cross between Adolphe Menjou and the White Knight'. The boxer Randolph Turpin, in 1951, faced his opponent Sugar Ray Robinson with the implacable manner of 'Boris Karloff wheeling into the petrified drawing-room'. Seventeen thousand spectators in the shrivelling heat of the 1969 United States Open golf championship recalled 'gun-bearers in some preposterous DeMille epic panting obediently after the old sahibs'. Beyond these incidentals, AC always kept his eyes and ears open for Hollywood's absurdities, misdemeanours and crimes, from a Humphrey Bogart court case of 1949 to the Hungarian bauble Zsa Zsa Gabor, robbed of her jewels in 1970 by men wearing pointy shoes.

But the movies were far more than a source of fun to Cooke the reporter. Movies and American society went hand in hand. In the 1940s he saw Hollywood straining to face up to the changed conditions of wartime. That battle done, he reported on the war between Hollywood and television, both as an observer and a TV practitioner (from 1952 he had a perch there too, hosting CBS's cultural series

Omnibus). Year by year, almost, he saw Hollywood shrinking. Hollywood's showmen might thrust Cinerama and 3-D on the world, and dangle the allurements of drive-in theatres, but audiences, stars and genres steadily decamped to the box in the living-room corner. Writing in 1962 for the *World Book Year Book*, Cooke could see scant hopes for artistic vitality or commercial success from future American movies. Television, in his eyes, had bankrupted Hollywood, made it a failing industry. Fifteen years later, he was reporting on the video-cassette, feared by Hollywood and television together.

A more penetrating and darker gloom penetrates AC's post-war reporting. The political crises of the 1930s had only peeped into his film reviews; now there was no avoiding his own Cold War fears and the general national panic about 'reds under the beds', so harshly exploited by the House Un-American Activities Committee and the ranting Senator Joseph McCarthy. Though a correspondent for the left-leaning *Guardian*, he jumped to no quick conclusions reporting on the Alger Hiss perjury trials of 1949–50, and gave those Hollywood talents who fell foul of HUAC no automatic support. He deplored the effect of the industry's blacklists on those who held 'mildly radical political opinions', but hard-core Communists 'enlisted in an international conspiracy' remained for him a genuine menace. Treason was treason. Against this background, his *Guardian* coverage of Soviet leader Nikita Khrushchev's famous and disastrous visit to Hollywood in 1959 might seem unsuitably light-hearted. But nervous black comedy lies behind the jokes. And the following report on the film *On the Beach* makes scarily clear the depth of his concern about the blast that could annihilate the world and the civilization in which he had taken so much delight.

As the century advanced, and Cooke with it, he found less in the film world that he wanted to report on – less certainly that he could view with pleasure. Always a 'conservative liberal', his conservative side finally triumphed with the advance of the 1960s' youth revolution. Throughout the 1960s and 70s, in his annual arts reports for the *World Book Year Book*, AC decried the violence and pornography he saw disfiguring what had been his favourite popular entertainment. He reeled at the prospect of 'Andy Warhol's movies of junkies with pimples on their rump'. Nor could he smile upon *The Godfather* or

Taxi Driver, noting with alarm the audience response of greeting each murder, each rain of bullets, with 'whoops and cheers'. 'Films with gut grab', a Hollywood producer called them; AC hated the concept, hated the phrase. But there was more to this horror than an aesthete's wince. He had lived through the 1920s and 30s, seen fascism rise; his driving fear was that the permissive society might bring the wheel turning again, towards state censorship and repression. 'The first guarantee of liberty,' he wrote in 1967, 'is the willingness not to demand too much of it. The fly-wheel of liberty is responsibility.'

For solace, understandably, he increasingly returned to the films and habits of the past. In that area at least he could practise the appreciative criticism he had grown to cherish – a lingering legacy from his first Cambridge guru, the gentlemanly Professor of English Literature Sir Arthur Quiller-Couch. When a Hollywood legend who took his fancy died, Cooke was ready with his memories and crisp summations, some for the *Guardian*, others for his BBC broadcasts. For his 1977 book *Six Men*, he added personal recollections to obituary material on Humphrey Bogart written twenty years before. For the Chaplin memoir, he wrote his fullest ever account of the charmed period in 1933–4 when their friendship was at its closest, the years before he had found to his discomfort that he didn't like *Modern Times*.

In later decades AC continued his film memorials, but had to take into account that the world was now younger, and memories shorter. 'Does the name of Ronald Colman mean anything to you?' he asked a television producer, in her early forties, in the 1980s. A thoughtful pause followed. 'He was, was he not, a United States senator?' His own memories never left him. Asked by MoMA's Department of Film and Media in 2001 to suggest a film for a Cooke tribute, he came up with Lubitsch's *Trouble in Paradise* (duly shown), with *Double Indemnity* and DeMille's *The Plainsman* as runners-up. It's moving to find him in 2003 near the end of his life – and at the end of this book – remembering for the last time young Katharine Hepburn on the *Little Women* set, and that Hollywood visit of 1933 when the ball started rolling.

Collating the best of Alistair Cooke's trips to the movies over seventy-five years has been an exhilarating, often challenging, transatlantic task. Thanks to the *Guardian* and *Observer*'s joint online archive, researching his British newspaper articles proved easy. Not so the reviews from his 1930s film talks, pulled together and extracted from multiple sources, including typewritten manuscripts, the BBC's scripts, the cut editions printed in the *Listener* and the versions in *Garbo and the Night Watchmen*. Preparing his broadcast talks for publication, Cooke would generally leave them unaltered, except for 'a little trimming and polishing'. Given the avalanche of new material uncovered, a little more trimming and polishing was sometimes necessary. But my goal was only the sensitive manicure I felt AC himself would have applied had he revisited these children from his past – if I have felt it useful to add background information for the reader, I have done so in passages at the start or the end of the text, indicated by paragraph symbols. And every labour was sustained by the belief that this anthology didn't simply open a window on to cinema's past. Here was also important new evidence of the passions, motivations and dazzling talent of one of the twentieth century's most original and remarkable chroniclers.

Geoff Brown

In the old days you went into a bare room where sometimes a screen clattered down before your eyes. The lights clicked out, the film flickered in, the projector buzzed, spluttered, and the screen was dark again. Somebody clapped and somebody hissed. The lights went on again and a cracked slide was pushed horizontally across the screen. It told about a corset store round your corner, or it apologized for the wait. Sometimes the manager came on. Then the lights went out again, there was a happy cheer, and we were watching moving pictures . . .

'Death of a Clown', American radio broadcast, WEAF,
15 September 1937

CRITIC

A cinema critic is very much in the position of Matthew Arnold, who having first written out for himself what he believed poetry was, and what he believed it wasn't, suddenly found himself confronted with Byron, who fitted none of his prescriptions. Arnold had the critical common sense, and enough healthy suspicion of his own motives, to accept Byron and remark simply, 'In poetry, we must take what we can get.' Now Myrna Loy has no place in my scheme of international cinema. But I'd accept her just the same. If she'd accept me.

The Cinema, BBC, 16 September 1935

'Too Utterly Utter': Reviews from *The Granta*

¶ Cooke contributed to *The Granta* throughout his Cambridge years, 1927–32. He began with caricature drawings, progressed to parody articles, theatre and film criticism, and spent his last year as the university magazine's editor. Fellow critics included Michael Redgrave, the intellectual all-star Jacob Bronowski, future documentary maker Basil Wright and William Empson, the brilliant poet whose writings continued to percolate in Cooke's mind decades later, even when writing Marilyn Monroe's obituary. Period features in this brief selection from his reviews include the undergraduate writing style (facetious and strenuous), the knowing Eng. Lit. references; a fascination with Marlene Dietrich and a reverence for Adolphe Menjou's dapper performances in his silent films. More particular to AC was his marked aversion to the French director René Clair – then the intelligentsia's idol.

*   *   *

Love and Learn

6 November 1928

This film puts criticism to instant and agreeable rout. Is not the plot preposterous? Are not American judges revealed as incredible nincompoops? Is not the daughter's device to unite her unhappy parents an impossible artifice? But then, is not the whole picture a box where sweets compacted lie, and Miss Esther Ralston the most delicious of delicacies?

The answer to all these questions is the word – yes. And whether two people can undress and sleep in the same room without being aware of each other's presence, we hold, with Sir Thomas Browne, but a wavering conjecture. Enough that all the players act with just the necessary exaggeration and inconsequence to make questions of probability irrelevant. Superlatives are called for and you may take your choice from the language of the Girnhamite behind me who pronounced this film to be 'too utterly utter'; from that of her friend who declared it 'topping'; or from that of the undergraduate on my left who said it was '— marvellous'.

My own opinion is that this is a very delightful film, which demands a zest for fancy rather than fact. It has no concern with reason. If it had one would ask Miss Ralston to act – a churlish request in the face of her pretty termagant tricks.

¶ *Love and Learn*. USA, 1928, Paramount; d. Frank Tuttle. Esther Ralston, Lane Chandler, Hedda Hopper.

'Girnhamite' was a slang relic of Josephine Elder's 1926 novel *The Scholarship Girl at Cambridge*, set at the lightly fictitious Girnham College.

Men Call It Love

16 October 1931

This is a worthy Menjou plot, but they must be 'directing' him more vulgarly than usual, he is being used as flavouring to a dish of infidelity. *Fashions in Love* showed him ageing but consummate, and helped to charm by what disappointingly appears now an assumed French accent. His close-ups were haggard and shocking, because you felt him trying to keep his job, the mask is cracking and we saw the sweat behind the tricks. Here poise is abandoned, he has gone horribly just back-porch poppa; he now appears in crisp tweeds and, apostasy, is disposed to genial acknowledgement, over drinks, of his conquests. So that you must be prepared for the loss of gallantry, of style, of a woman's man, a fastidious libertine, avuncular in an ambassadorial way to men, but condescendingly biding time till a woman was there to be charmed, supervised and, with the ultimate sigh, taken. From Menjou to disreputable commercial traveller is no joke. It so insults his heroines. Whereas formerly we wondered if these trusting, eager little wives would be worthy of his fine, scrupulous sophistication. But some things remain – he still wears his clothes (even a dinner-jacket), he is still too wise for this world, and he still bows.

¶ *Men Call It Love*. USA, 1931, MGM; d. Edgar Selwyn. Adolphe Menjou, Leila Hyams, Norman Foster.

Fashions in Love (1929) was Menjou's first talkie.

Morocco

6 November 1931

There was only one *Blue Angel*. We may pray that Mr Wallis has booked *Dishonoured*, and for no less than a fortnight. Certainly, we can only hope that we shall soon come to talk of this one not as a film but as inferior Dietrich. For it has no quality, not even qualities: no unity, except of obtuseness and a dismally reverential production, and no 'moments'. And the photography had one stultifying trick of tracing her carefully through distant objects with a moving foreground of palms, table-tops, chairs, bed-rails.

With such superior and undeniable queens as Dietrich and the Garbo, the story should seek simply to point their fascination. The dénouement of this just debased her to what Menjou (not, regrettably, himself) called the rearguard, to one of the touchingly loyal but contemptible women who go off, with each move of the Legion, 'after their men'. We had to laugh at this fine-limbed, prouder Tallulah shaking off Fifth Avenue shoes into the sand and stumping off into heat and snow; we had to laugh to hide our baffled and unsheddable tears – we had not expected such suburban tricks. But it was thrilling to have her beginning raddled and slowly guess, through a gradual crescendo of better days, the next step towards the final, consummate Dietrich; so that, although she keeps her style in rags, we began to ache for the civilized, fastidious beauty that we might have been given had the film lasted another half-hour: were ready to stand on our seats and cheer the last, blinding shot.

¶ *Morocco*. USA, 1930, Paramount; d. Josef von Sternberg. Marlene Dietrich, Gary Cooper, Adolphe Menjou.

In 1968, Cooke paid tribute to the idiosyncratic stage actress Tallulah Bankhead in his *Guardian* obituary: a frail and lovely hellcat with the eyes of a sleepy leopard and the tongue of an asp.

Le Million

20 November 1931

Having a general prejudice against French film technique, against angles as points of rest, against the artistic pretensions of half-lights, against 'character' shots, used sentimentally to make tedious melodramatic plots seem like 'slices of life', and against René Clair in particular, I have no right to say much about this film, except that it is generally admired by the intelligentsia, that it is supposed to be a witty brief chronicle of the French mind, that it is better than *Sous les toits de Paris*, which drove me last term to an unforgettably early dinner in one of our large sordid eating-houses.

Next week we are blessedly to receive *City Lights*.

¶ *Le Million*. France, 1931, Films Sonores Tobis; d. René Clair. Annabella, René Lefebvre, Wanda Gréville.

Westfront 1918

4 March 1932

In the libraries of the American companies there must be a formula: home and beauty, dalliance, Came The Call, tinny uprights and black silk stockings behind the lines, poignant parcel from home, the attack, then noise, just noise, and stark piles of bodies, and intermediate enlightening captions ('Cut off!'). Pabst, on the contrary, is not out to tell you, with a gluck in the throat, about the universality of clean limbs and dirty minds. He is interested in a fairly common story and tells it with that peculiarly steady German watchfulness. The picture has every ingredient of the dimmest American glory-ride. He doesn't presume to differ with anyone about right occasions for sentiment.

But, unlike DeMille, he happens also to believe in them, and reveals his intelligence at the moment he is revealing the sentiment. For your own self-respect, you'd be a fool to laugh. Instead, you are wiser to follow the camera belittling, from above, the soldier as he goes downstairs after leaving the faithful wife.

The actual sequences tell you everything. You can follow, and grow anxious about, the way they're cut off; the tone (photographic) of the first half-hour is like nothing before; there is no protesting how harrowing it all is – the three minutes of the dressing station suffice; there are two fine German performances, in their timeless inflexible way, from the husband and his mother, and a quick, lovely bit of acting from the French girl; and the psychology of 'Kiss her or I'll shoot', and of the singing Bavarian's slyly appraising his accompanist's alertness on the mouth organ, is inevitable and immediately moving.

¶ *Westfront 1918*. Germany, 1930, Nero-Film; d. G. W. Pabst. Fritz Kampers, Gustav Diessl, Hans-Joachim Moebis.

¶ Alistair Cooke broadcasted as the BBC's film critic from 8 October 1934 to 28 March 1937. He spoke for fifteen or twenty minutes, and gave around fifty-six talks, supplemented by one-off programmes and items in schools broadcasts. Initially he planned to alternate 'review' talks with 'topic' talks, but the distinction gradually blurred. He also planned to bounce ideas off various experts, some linked with film only in Cooke's mind – such as the adventurous literary academic I. A. Richards, or Charles Fox, author of *Educational Psychology: Its Problems and Methods*. Reviews of London's new films were balanced with reviews of general releases: in this way many films were covered several times. He also wrote about them in *Sight and Sound* and, during January 1937, in the *Spectator*.

Picking favourites that year for his *Garbo and the Night Watchmen* collection, AC snipped most of his choices from much longer, discursive scripts. I have followed his lead, though the first BBC talk is reproduced complete. The selection's most serious omission is the sound of AC's voice. 'I have that first recording, by the way,' he wrote to the writer and journalist Tony Aspler in 1975, 'and the few times I've heard it I've alternately squirmed and laughed out loud at not only the Oxbridge accent, but at the fatal Oxbridge vocabulary.' The particular sound of Cambridge men, he told students in America in 1939, resembled 'hysterical daffodils'.

*   *   *

A Critic's Testament

The Cinema, BBC, 8 October 1934

This day last week I stood for the last time on Broadway, very forlornly watching, in the middle of a blaze of gyrating lights, one particular sign flashing out R ... O ... B ... E ... R ... T ... – black-out – D ... O ... N ... A ... T ... I recalled Mr Donat as a hard-working young actor at a provincial repertory company theatre playing weekly leads opposite a hard-working young actress, Miss Flora Robson. I should probably have gone on to muse with much pathos about the uncertainty of human fate, and so on. Luckily for you I did not. Instead I longed to see *The Count of Monte Cristo*, about which I had heard fine things.

But I had made a firm resolve across the continent – after mad little dashes to see the newest films – to resist any further indulgence in New York. I had resolved rather proudly that instead I would spend a last evening taking a walk through cool, lovely Central Park; that I would spend the last afternoon in taking once more the ferry to Staten Island and again looking across the magnificent fairyland that is New York; and that when dusk came I would go to the top of the Empire State Building and feel for the last time the healthy superiority of being higher in a building than anyone else in the world. Naturally, I stayed in bed late, had to spend the afternoon checking my luggage, and spent tea-time desperately wondering how I could find a good excuse for rushing away to a movie. But in Times Square I said, 'I will resist this one.'

Two years in America had not extinguished in me, you see, the well-known English principle that what is uncomfortable is good for the character. I looked to my right and noticed *Of Human Bondage*, which thankfully I had seen. By this time I was a glutton for piety and I decided also to resist *The Merry Widow*, which I had also seen. In the end I began to look for ways of sneaking into a movie house. I was being temperate for two reasons – I had lately seen too many Big Pictures; secondly, I was hard up. After a little burst of sympathy with myself on this account, the devil didn't desert me. Two minutes later I was paying 25 cents – half the usual charge – at a newsreel theatre. It was cheap and it wasn't a big picture. I now believe that newsreel theatres exist for no other purpose than to ease the conscience of people who are trying to reform. So I went in, with that very temporary, hopeless virtue that Mr and Mrs Mark Twain must have felt after an expensive first year of marriage when they agreed violently to cut their expenses and Mark Twain wrote to a friend, 'We find we can economize on two things – our subscription to *Harper's* magazine, and monograms on guest towels.'

I tell you this anecdote because I think you should know what sort of failings you are going to have to prepare yourselves for. A film critic should be a man who can't stay away from films or a man who never goes at all. I leave you to guess to which class I belong.

And I think before we settle down for the winter you should know some of the oddities and difficulties of my position. To those of you who know and are charitable I must offer my apologies. But many more of us, I think, are not aware just how feverishly some people hang on these harmless words ready with a pen, paper and the blank form of a libel action. Such devoted listeners, I am told, are usually interested parties – say a producer, a director, a casting manager, the officials of theatre circuits. To these I must recite my little declaration of independence. Which goes like this:

I declare that I am a critic trying to interest a lot of people into seeing, a few ambitious people into making, interesting films. I have no personal interest in any company. As a critic I am without politics and without class. I swear I am committed to no country, no director, no star, no theme, no style. For a film hero I am prepared to take John Barrymore, George Robey, a battleship, Mickey Mouse or an Italian straw hat. I hope that everyone who wants to make a lot of money in films will make it, that every girl who aches to become a star overnight will become one. I hope a little more fervently that any man or woman who can make an interesting film will somehow, somewhere, be allowed to make it.

My malice extends only to those who have a dull talent and continue to exploit it, whether they live in London, Hollywood, Moscow, the African jungle or behind the sets of a musical comedy. All hail, therefore, Amkino, Fox, Gainsborough, Gaumont-British, Paramount, RKO, Ufa and Universal. Metro-Goldwyn-Mayer, long may your lion roar. Greetings of equal warmth to the Hollywood Academy of Motion Picture Directors, the London Film Society, the Edinburgh Film Guild, the Merseyside Workers Society, and all users of 8mm home movies. For Victor Fleming, Alexander Korda, Pabst, Eisenstein and Eddie Cantor . . . a sincere cheer. These are my respects. And now I hope I may not be misunderstood when in the future I find fault with the works of any of these institutions.

A month or two ago I had an earnest letter asking me rather gravely what I was going to do about politics. Like most other people I am just now much more anxious to know what in the next few years politics is going to do about me. Happily, I can only repeat that as a critic I can *have* no politics. But my correspondent was not beside the point. He went on to say, 'What, for instance, will be your attitude to *war* films?'

Well, it would be very coy of me to talk about photography, about cutting, about technical details of acting and at the same time profess a vast, naïve ignorance of the forces that more and more will make or destroy our lives. I know, for example, that very many of you sincerely believe that wars, however hideous, are still the most straightforward way of settling international quarrels. And I also know that very many of you find it daily harder to believe that wars are conducted by disinterested parties for noble reasons. I don't see how you can contrive to squeeze in a compromise between these two honest attitudes. And it certainly isn't my business to try. But however weak or however decisive your opinions may be, usually they are formed in a more random way than most of us would care to confess. On this topic, for example, a firm militarist may be made by some personal experience of physical heroism, by a cartoon in *Punch*, by a politician's remembered speech. And for all I know Mr Archibald MacLeish's recent article in the American magazine *Fortune* on the sale of armaments may have a profound influence on European politics, may, in fact, save several million necks. And nowadays, much more than newspapers, much more than books, the most popular, and I believe by far the most powerful, opinion machine is the cinema. The story-film is a machine which manufactures for us attitudes, sentimentalities, disguises, through which we can hope to escape the real difficulties of our private lives. And no effort of the imagination could create more vivid ready-made opinions about international affairs than the newsreel. Because it is a visual thing. You see a photograph and you are tricked into thinking you have seen some part of the actual facts. But it is only a fact some hectic cameraman has selected. And sometimes the false selection of incident is not the conscious work of any man: it may be in the angle at which his camera was tilted. A scene of a riot, or an accident, or a parliamentary session abroad can, of course, very sharply puncture a legend. But it can also inflate one. It would be nice to know just how fearful a bogeyman Napoleon would have seemed to the inhabitants of the south coast of England if they could have seen him in the newsreels.

And even in the story-film itself, the feature picture that seems so guilelessly, so comfortably far away from these grim realities, there is constantly an implication it is impossible to overlook. I mean a political, a social one. A film directed by, say, Lubitsch, is a film created by the society in which he lives. And those who saw a single film of his before he went to Hollywood will not need to search very far to discover where Mr Lubitsch learned to represent that very ritzy sort of poverty in which Miriam Hopkins and Gary Cooper basked in *Design for Living*.

And yet, however much I might want in private to rage or protest or moralize, these actions have nothing to do with criticism. As a moralist I could be shocked. As an educationist I might lament that the subject was not elevating. As a businessman I might feel glum that the seduction was clumsy and therefore bad box-office. But I am not a moralist, an educator, a businessman. I am merely a critic, and I have to try and decide whether Miss Harlow's smiles and pouts were performed expertly enough to entice Mr Gable away, and whether in deserting his Texas farm for Miss Harlow he was being wicked, obvious, tactful or just plain cynical. So if a film comes from Elstree and is full of propaganda for, let's say, social slavery, it is not for me to say that such propaganda is shocking. It is simply my job to try and describe how tellingly the propaganda has been done. And similarly, if a film from Russia teems with propaganda for Communism, it is entirely impertinent for me as a critic to say whether

Communism is a good or a bad thing. I have to say if the story, the direction, the acting, are likely to move you to believe for the time being in the propaganda. If they don't, the film is trivial. If they do, it's probably a good film. And there goes one of two words I have been trying all along to avoid using: the words 'good' and 'bad'. Which brings us to the question of praise and abuse.

To say 'this is a better film than that' is practically a useless remark. It's a roundabout way of saying, 'You listen to me – I'll tell you what's what.' And critics are a roguish race who have developed with considerable cunning ways of telling you just that. When you see on the cover of a book, 'A remarkable book . . . magnificent in its delicacy, its sweep, its power . . .' and similar quotations, you know that the man who said that didn't have time to think. Otherwise he would have been able to tell you *why* it was remarkable, and not just behave as we all did *creditably* at the age of twelve and leave the poor book with an elaborate tick in the margin, which merely says, 'I approve; others do likewise.' In short, a critic should defend and explain his *opinion*, not *himself*. Yet to do this, I suppose he had better know himself very well indeed, say about half as well as his friends know him. I think he will then decide – and at first it's an awful shock – that his job has actually very little to do with liking and disliking. As I see it, a critic is firstly a person who sees differences where other persons are liable to see only similarities. He has to distinguish things that look the same. And there is perhaps only one occasion when he should heartily condemn. That is when he strongly dislikes a film, thinks he knows good reasons why, and is sure that the film is likely to set a fashion in dullness.

You will want to know how this works out in practice. Well, take a film I like and one I dislike. The film I like is of a certain type – a murder mystery. It is called *The Thin Man*. But it is for once so much better than its type that it becomes a remarkable film. The film I dislike (which is called *The Fountain*) is a type I much prefer to murder mysteries, but this example of the romantic film is very much worse than its type and in one thing – its dialogue – sets a new fashion in pretentiousness. I believe that it is my duty to you to review at greater length *The Fountain* than *The Thin Man* because most of you will see *The Thin Man*, will see a murder film fairly rattling with detectives and thugs made into a gay, neat comedy. But *The Fountain* may be copied and imitated and a new fashion in boredom may catch you unawares. The pretentiousness lies in its slow, bemused stretches of dialogue. It is the sort of film in which the feelings of the characters, especially of the man and the girl, are represented as being so noble, so fine, that it seems to hurt the author to reduce them to the vulgarity of mere words, and when he does get them down and you hear two people in love, you look around the theatre and wonder if any of these ordinary nice people like you and me have ever aspired to this lofty highbrow business of being in love. In the end I decided that probably half the audience I sat with had known this emotion, this relationship, and had somehow been able to speak it out simply, and probably at this very second hundreds of young men in England are saying 'I love you' without grimaces, without dictionaries, and without assuming that doggy look which the film actor thinks denotes spirituality as well as the more material quality of conquest.

So for these reasons I shall talk mainly about films I *like*, about scenes I like, about bits of acting, story and direction I like. Because I think you bore people less by talking about things you like. A film you like, as also a person, may become, if you will make the effort, something you understand. Unfortunately abuse is much more attractive, much more dramatic, than praise. And many critics anxious to cut a figure in this world like to have lots of things around to dislike. I plead guilty to this failing and though I promise to abuse nothing – sometimes my temper is liable to get the better of me.

But on the whole I shall try and keep religiously to a sentence I am just writing on the table with my thumb. This is it . . . *I mean what I say*. Please don't try to seek implications. Don't say, 'Well, of course, he's soft-pedalling there . . . he really means he hates her.'

After these rather solemn promises I come to the most ticklish part of this critic's testament, I mean my confessional, the personal whims, prejudices you'll have to keep an eye on. There is only one major one. And because it is common to all critics and I dare say to all men and women, I mention it here. And also because I have never seen any critic confess to it. It is a particular warning about the criticism of actresses. There are lots of reasons why I should like an actress. But if not the chief one, I'm sure the first one is – because she's a woman.

This is something outside the control of criticism, education, intellect, what you will. I will in the future give you very plausible, very responsible reasons why Miss Nastasia Vine's performance was, just a little, off. The real reason will be, probably, that her features, her colouring, her eyes, aren't the sort I like.

Two or three years ago the world could be divided into two classes, those who liked Greta Garbo and hated Marlene Dietrich, and those who liked Marlene Dietrich and hated Greta Garbo. There were numerous variations and subdivisions, as of people who thought a lot about Greta Garbo and didn't think at all about Marlene Dietrich. But this was the issue. Then in another year Miss Dietrich was for the time overshadowed and the choice was between Katharine Hepburn and Garbo. And this will always go on.

I hear some of you say that a critic should be above such sensual competition. But even a critic has a heart. Or had one before he became one. And though I solemnly swear to take no new lights of love, I can't abruptly get rid of all my old flames. Their impression is there, even if I've done with them. I believe it my duty to tell you, for instance, that until very recently I was in love with Loretta Young. Now, please . . . there's no point in snorting, or saying 'Tut-tut', or even, I'm sorry to say, in applauding loudly. It just happens that my peculiar chemistry and Miss Young's peculiar chemistry seem to click, I hope. And I shall probably be abominably unfair to the rest of the cast in her pictures. Another way you can tell my personal feelings about an actress, and so learn to ignore them, is when I'm specially catty about her. This will almost certainly mean she *was* a flame but now I feel for her only that slight contempt, that abominable faint pity one triumphantly feels for people one did love but now loves no more.

This is something I'm not ashamed – in fact I'm very relieved – to tell you. There is no way of being above it. Everybody has a face, a person they instinctively grow fond of, often in reckless opposition to their reason, even their eyes. I have heard of only one man who conquered this romantic privilege. There was a time not so long ago when a famous American dramatic critic, who had married a celebrated actress, wrote in reviewing a play she performed in, 'When I married Miss — she gave her profession as that of actress. I saw nothing in last night's proceedings to justify the description.' Ten days later they were no longer man and wife. Even then, I leave you to puzzle out whether this was honesty or spite.

And now, having said all this, I'm going to ask you not to hold any of it against me. I have tried to put before you the severe limitations of a film critic, and to say (for my own guidance as well as for your reassurance) what he should *not* pretend to be. You may feel, therefore, that I'm going to behave very nicely and nobody is ever going to be outraged. But of course, they are bound to be. And it may often be my fault. Only I take no responsibility if, when I say that Miss Hepburn's hair was a little untidy in these scenes, I should the next day receive a cabled suit for slander from the Master Barbers' Association of Southern California. Because it's humanly impossible to work out a plan of dealing with a million or two men and women and then to live precisely up to it. If I could always keep to my purpose, if I could always know exactly when I wasn't just praising, or abusing, or airing a prejudice, I should be . . . well . . . I should be Shakespeare or Goethe. On the contrary, being me, I can only ring a bell or, better, have someone in the studio blow a whistle, every time a prejudice comes along that I know I have.

As for all the unconscious prejudices, confusions, all the times when I'm not sure whether I'm feeling like myself or more like somebody I'd like to think I was, or like someone I admired felt – these you'll have to put up with. But please *pity* your new teacher and remember they are much more of a burden to him than they'll ever be to you.

Coronation Equals Big Scene

The Cinema, BBC, 22 October 1934

Mr von Sternberg approaches all his films with an *awful* reverence, with enormous solemnity. You feel that whether you like it or not – what's worse, whether it's appropriate or not – Mr Sternberg is going to make an epic of it. If somebody asked him to make a picture about Little Miss Muffet (with, of course, Miss Dietrich swimming around gorgeously in luscious bowls of curds and whey), I have the uncomfortable feeling that every time Miss Muffet winked you'd be likely as not to hear the Brandenburg Concerto. Mr Sternberg always announces the mood he has chosen and bullies you into taking it. Now, as making drama is a business of making you anticipate one mood and then giving you another, continually defeating the way you would sentimentally like to write the story yourself, it follows that Mr Sternberg has, so far as I can discover, no sense of the dramatic at all.

In *The Scarlet Empress*, for instance, there is to be a wedding. Without thinking about it, Mr Sternberg decides it must be a crisis, because . . . well . . . because it's a *wedding*! Luckily, here, he's right. Miss Dietrich is being married to an idiot. And all of us are rightly revolted that so much beauty and grace should be wasted on someone who is not the handsomest man in the film. But later the main interest of the film simplifies itself into one question . . . is Miss Dietrich to be made Empress, or isn't she? Once you know she is, you can pick up your hat and go home, as I'm happy to say when I saw it many people did. But Mr Sternberg, king of sentimentalists, has another kind of arithmetic. He says . . . Coronation Equals Big Scene. So for fifteen minutes bells chime, white horses clatter through marble halls, and Beethoven and several thousand extras are called on to make you aware of the importance of the event.

Somebody says, 'So, why see it then?' There is a 'but', and a big one. He will spend ten minutes trying to impress you with the grotesqueness of his heroine's surroundings. He will make his camera float up tables of exotic fruit until a grape is more fascinating than the emperor himself. He will make people sit, not in chairs, but in gargoyles straining to look like chairs. For clocks he wouldn't dream of having a clock: he has a dozen mechanical gnomes beating gongs with little hammers. But then, a few minutes later somebody performs a perfectly ordinary gesture, dusts a chair, takes out a handkerchief, and *this* becomes grotesque. Once I remember stopping in Victoria at a coffee stall on the evening after a day I had spent at the funeral of a friend. The man behind the counter sliced my sausage rather badly, and as he handed me my hot dog said quite casually, 'He's been fairly squashed, hasn't he?' That's not a grim or a terrifying remark. But because I had been to a funeral it became so, and the little man behind the counter was a frightening figure. Mr Sternberg tries to be powerful and strange and ghoulish, and is none of them. And then somebody lights a cigarette and because they are doing it in a morgue it becomes a grotesque gesture. What makes effective Miss Dietrich's decorating the officer who has given her her child is the fact that she is doing it *there*, that a human being is doing something normal in the middle of a nightmare. Another time Miss Dietrich swings a handkerchief, taps a musical box with her finger, and though Mr Sternberg has meant these details to be dramatic they are intensely, oddly charming. Such moments in a Sternberg film are worth the usual ninety minutes of people doing ordinary things in ordinary places.

¶ *The Scarlet Empress*. USA, 1934, Paramount; d. Josef von Sternberg. Marlene Dietrich, John Lodge, Sam Jaffe.

Film – Past and Future

The Cinema, BBC, 5 November 1934

One listener asks, 'What will happen after we get the stereoscopic movie?' And I hope that two other correspondents speak for thousands when they ask, in effect, 'What happens to old films?' Is there no storehouse for them or permanent library? Why must we be condemned to seeing fifth-rate films which happen to be new instead of old films which happen to be first-rate?

One of the more illiterate things about the film industry has been the pretence that it has had no history. A performance of a play on the stage must always be a single theatrical event. Whereas the cinema's unique pleasure should be that you can as often as you like see precisely the same performance as you saw ten years ago. It is certainly very sad to hear talking airily about the power of pantomime a new generation that never saw *The Gold Rush* or *The Kid*; and it is embarrassing to know that thousands of film fans feel they should show their discrimination by admiring Conrad Veidt in *Jew Süss*, when they will probably die without having seen him in the days when he was really acting as he is never going to act again – that tremendous, unforgettable performance in *The Student of Prague*. But apart from the financial risk a manager would run in trying to popularize an old silent film, there are practical and profound difficulties that belong to the cinema as a form of entertainment and as a form of art.

The cinema is liable to become a completely different art overnight. Only five years ago, to be able to see a bad film in which people could be heard speaking and whistling and slamming doors was fascinating enough to tear most of us away from very many better films where you only *saw* doors being slammed. You may say that sophistication has gone queerly askew when it can prefer *Broadway Melody* to *The*

Virginian. But I have no doubt that sometime next year or the year after we are going to sit enthralled while forty pink legs and green shoes swing out rhythmically into the audience and we all instinctively duck our heads and whinny with pleasure. I don't know how you begin to analyse novelty. We are all pretty relentless about finding out new sources of pleasure. I suppose human beings have always hoped that whatever else you could use up – like petrol and pencils – pleasure was inexhaustible. And until the scientists have learned to breed babies who already know that boredom is essential to the pattern of even exquisite pleasures, there is nothing you or I can do about it. The best you can do is to accept fundamental changes and not pretend they are only growing pains. You are always being told that the cinema is in its infancy. I should say that its chief trouble is that it has already died two deaths and the third is slated for somewhere around 1936.

If you walk up the Charing Cross Road you will come to a news-theatre where the items are placarded outside. At the bottom of the list is the line 'NEWS', and then in brackets '(BLACK and WHITE)'. That simple sign means that in another three years there will be a better chance of your going home and finding Garbo nursing your baby than that you will ever again see *The Front Page*, *Westfront 1918*, *M*, *The Deserter* or *Trouble in Paradise*. And then, round about 1940, by the time we think we are pretty clever at analysing the emotional effects of colour, the flat, two-dimensional screen will vanish for ever and only the knowledge that we are sitting in Sheffield or Dover will prevent us from rushing up to the stage and shaking hands with a non-existent Gary Cooper and trying to make a date with an ethereal Margaret Sullavan. Then, years later, when all the movie theatres are empty or have been converted into showrooms for smart two-seater shopping models of transatlantic aeroplanes, we shall switch on our wireless and see the first night of a New York revue, the last night of a national gathering in Manchuria.

And when your children are your age there is a more frightening possibility still – that when there are no more film stars and no more actors at all, young artists will dictate to Nature the latest models in blondes by pricking pins into pieces of sound and image track celluloid, and painting in not only the eyes they like best but the accent that most charms their ear. I stop casually at 1960 merely because my time is almost up – but I see no reason why in fifty years or so forlorn young men who are members of the New Hygienic Pygmalion Society shouldn't be marrying the images they painted on a piece of film and having lots of gay, lovely children with skin smooth as celluloid. In fact, it seems to be a race between the people who do research in films and the people who do research in poison and disease-germ gas. *I* hope the film people win. But then I'm a film critic and naturally prejudiced.

Tarzan Meets Schubert

The Cinema, BBC, 19 November 1934

Tarzan and His Mate is a preposterous story that only in one place and one character gets in the way of the excitement. Maureen O'Sullivan doesn't know quite whether to treat Tarzan as Herbert Marshall or as Pluto the pup, and seems to be wondering whether she's really in the jungle or is only a professional actress brought in to strengthen the cast of a film about, say, Aran. Which gives her joint escapades with Johnny Weissmuller a sort of Our Gang look. But some of the fighting scenes with the jungle are so brilliantly cut – cut just in time, you might say – that you are sure the cameraman is by this time thoroughly swallowed and digested. And Johnny Weissmuller's fight with a crocodile and his swimming underwater are as luscious photography, of that filtered, limpid kind, as we have had since Lee Garmes made *Zoo in Budapest*. In fact I can think of only one omission that makes that comparison feeble – Loretta Young isn't in *Tarzan and His Mate*. Anyway, I don't suppose many of you have ever been lying around an ocean bed when Johnny Weissmuller was swimming up above. If only for this unique pleasure, anyone who isn't afraid to enjoy his senses should make a point of doing it now.

I don't imagine, either, many of you are in the habit of climbing on to the roof of a hospital's operating theatre and watching proceedings from that tricky angle. And *Men in White* tends at times, whenever it can't think up a new bit of story, to climb back on to the roof and meditate on the neatness of the patterns you can contrive out of men in white and tables and walls in black. But it's a rare thing in adaptations from stage plays – and this is one – for anybody to look at the story and try and tell it by other means than acting as you see it from the third row of the stalls. Because you're closer and a camera can

23

help you look for a few sharp seconds longer on a rubber glove, a sterilized apron, the washing of hands, those uniforms and instruments *become* actors and you pity the girl they are being used for much more intimately than you did in the play, where everyone was a little too inclined to pity himself. And about the film there is a kind of terror the play couldn't give you – the clean terror of bandages and shining knives, a more visual contrast between messy, untidy lives and the tidy means of healing them. The story is as carefully sentimental as the play, however, and if your admiration for doctors is a melo-dramatic one here you can cry and feel martyred along with the rest of the hospital.

Composers in films have their own venerable tradition. The legend is that no musician is really a musician until he forgets what two and two make and begins to leave his hat around. It's a pity that Schubert's charm, in the very agreeable *The Unfinished Symphony*, should be rooted in this particular bed of roses. Because even apart from the fact that he writes music when he thinks he's writing arithmetic, and apart from his habit of feeling his hat all the way round to make sure of the brim, Hans Jaray *has* a charming manner, charming enough to scare Gary Cooper or Leslie Howard into thinking it's going to be impossible to be a successful film actor if all you have is good looks, acting ability, and a British English or an American English accent. Hans Jaray is, like all the Schuberts we have seen or shall ever see, petulant, plump, very modest, rather simply gallant and writes his music mainly as an accompaniment to his love affairs. I should have been thankful for just one scene showing him working from nine till twelve straightening out some stiffish bit of orchestration. But no – Hollywood and Elstree are agreed that musicians are impractical, childish people, that the cabinets of England meet only to arrange some scandalous marriage, that everybody before 1800 always wore fancy dress and laughed whether there were any jokes about or not, that – as the new film *Caravan* exhaustively demonstrates – the people of Central Europe, again in fancy dress, spend all their days and nights singing and dancing and drinking in an orgy of gaiety. In *Caravan* they are so gay that, believe me, it hurts. If, however, you can forget or ignore these treaties and conventions, and if the music of Schubert means to you your childhood, or pleasant Sunday evenings or any other period of your emotional history, then you are likely to enjoy *The Unfinished Symphony*. If you are fond of Schubert's music not so much as a memory teaser but in a musical way – I'm not so sure.

¶ *Tarzan and His Mate*. USA, 1934, MGM; d. Cedric Gibbons, Jack Conway. Johnny Weissmuller, Maureen O'Sullivan, Neil Hamilton.
Men in White. USA, 1934, MGM; d. Richard Boleslawski. Clark Gable, Myrna Loy, Jean Hersholt.
The Unfinished Symphony. UK, 1934, Gaumont-British; d. Willi Forst, Anthony Asquith. Hans Jaray, Marta Eggerth, Ronald Squire.

Remember the Writer

The Cinema, BBC, 17 December 1934

Hollywood is a place where energy is respected and its officers, what-ever they cannot do, can take enormous time and trouble to find out who in the civilized world knows most about the Hanging Gardens of Babylon (if Mr DeMille is making a film), or who knows what sort of lamp-posts they have in Constantinople. Some of us unfortunately have that brilliantly perverse sort of memory which recalls that croco-diles used to swim along only the *left* bank of the Nile, and that Egyptian schoolboys weren't allowed to visit Cleopatra until they were prefects. But on the whole Hollywood is fantastically accurate in such matters. Well, six months ago there was published a long-hidden manuscript by the most popular author England has ever known. And sixty-four years after his death Charles Dickens found himself America's best seller. Hollywood sooner or later pleaded to reflect his glory. And so in the early summer there arrived in that sun-drenched town a very distinguished, a very respectable English author who knew a great deal about Dickens. He was there to write the scenario – that is the description of the scenes and the dialogue – for a film of *David Copperfield*. He soon set about his job. He worked conscien-tiously and hard for a day. He produced the first 'treatment' of one scene. A day or two later, standing in the office of a studio executive, Mr Hugh Walpole – that was the author's name – looked down on to a table, recognized the manuscript of his treatment, and saw written calmly and forcefully across the top of his work the single word: 'Lousy'.

Mr Walpole has confessed that after twenty-five years of writing for reading he has now to learn as a child would learn how to write for the screen. And he has evolved an excellent first rule: he says, 'I have learned to say "I see" before each sentence.' We assume too often that the two things can be done by the same man. There's really no reason why a great novelist should be even a fairly good writer of scripts, any more than he should be good at ping-pong. I have walked along the corridor of a Hollywood studio and passed doors that had inscribed on them the names of four or five American novelists with international reputations. They all came, wrote and were massacred. Their wordy, niggling scripts were taken by some alert little man, who probably earns about $30 a week, and made to read and sound like a recognizably good film. This alert little man is usually somebody you have never heard of, and I'm sorry to say you never will hear of.

So I beg you, in practically my final good turn of the old year, please remember the writer. Even if all your senses are working overtime to take in the charm of Katharine Hepburn, or Norma Shearer or Gary Cooper – remember that Nature gave them something, which is what they are in private life. But to this natural beauty or poise or voice, three men brought all their talent to bear – a director, a cameraman and a writer – and composed the thing you worship. Somebody often so unlike that witty, handsome, civilized creature on the screen that when you meet it the next noon sitting in a restaurant with its red and pouchy face, supported by its undistinguished hand, you think you've stumbled by mistake on to the star's idiot twin.

Here Comes Arthur Edeson

The Cinema, BBC, 17 December 1934

If this were a just world you would have seen outside the Regal Theatre two weeks ago a stream of bright lights saying 'Arthur Edeson' – in tiny lights, 'photographed' – in big lights again, *'Here Comes the Navy'*. And underneath you would have seen: 'ably supported by James Cagney, Pat O'Brien and Frank McHugh'.

This film is never for a moment hard to look at. Arthur Edeson has composed his pictures not for the sake of art, not for the sake of any frivolous idea of symmetry he read about in a book, not for the sake of pleasing anybody who once had to cut a Russian short. He puts his camera where it can best tell the story. And when there's good dialogue and good acting – and there's a lot of each – he doesn't try to wave to you with a filter from behind to tell you that he's still about. But the rest of the time he sees the film – and it's an exciting way of looking at an open-air film – as a story happening inside a newsreel. When Pat O'Brien walks towards you from away along the deck you think you are seeing a newsreel. It's an added shock and pleasure, therefore, when he suddenly breaks into a dialogue. You have the feeling not only that Pat O'Brien is a real person, but the new, warm feeling that perhaps our admirals and politicians are too.

I always feel that a newsreel, far from enlivening the appearance of famous people, helps generally to make them respectably and unforgettably dead. Most of the newsreels of the royal wedding were very dull. Dull, of course, because the weather was unkind; but dull really because the scenario, so to speak, the plan of making the films, was resourceless. A distant procession, a lot of cheering, a peal of bells, a still of Westminster Abbey, a picture of two women using mirrors as periscopes – that was the limit of their invention. Into this hackneyed pageant Paramount threw a small human bombshell. You remember, all of them showed the Duke of Kent standing on the balcony patiently waving and waving to the crowds. But Paramount – who did much the best record of the wedding – had a telephoto lens that was lucky to seize one glorious moment, when the Duke stopped waving and gave a polite but genuine and mighty sigh. When I saw it every bridegroom in the theatre sighed in unison. And for, I think, the first time in a newsreel I felt that a famous person had forgotten he was being watched; I felt that he had done something vivid and natural, and had broken triumphantly through the silent impersonality of the newsreel technique.

The effect is less, but not less pleasing, with Pat O'Brien. If you are tired and spiritless, I shall not be recommending anything quite so hilarious for a long time as this tonic film. From the first blast of the navy's football song, through the racy impudent dialogue, to the no-nonsense heroism at the end, it is gloriously and commendably American. Incidentally it is as good an advertisement of the American navy as any American could hope for, and should therefore be particularly popular along the Pacific coast.

We can perhaps admire a little more dispassionately a long sequence in the middle of the film of battle manoeuvres. Here Mr Edeson and the soundtrack excel themselves. There are, for about four minutes, resounding cannonades, photographed from the end of the barrels (I hope Mr Edeson is still alive); photographed from inside the shell (I hope Mr Edeson has been since straightened out); photographed from the detonator (we all hope that Mr Edeson is now quietly resting with a laurel wreath in bed). If this were a newsreel you would be shown a picture afterwards of a grimy, smiling cameraman being congratulated by the film company's director. But as it's only a story film apparently it's all in the day's work.

¶ *Here Comes the Navy*. USA, 1934, Warner Bros.; d. Lloyd Bacon. James Cagney, Pat O'Brien, Gloria Stuart.

Arthur Edeson photographed many Warner Bros. films, including *Casablanca*, and the silent films of Douglas Fairbanks.

The Royal Wedding. UK, 1934, British Paramount News.

The newsreel featured the Duke of Kent's marriage to Princess Marina of Greece on 29 November 1934.

Refugees

The Cinema, BBC, 17 December 1934

The Board of Censors has not given it a licence. It is a German Ufa film, photographed by Fritz Arno Wagner (who did *M*), called *Refugees*. The LCC has seen it and approved; so it is being shown in London at the Curzon. It's very hard to see who is going to take insult from it. Unless it's Hans Albers, whose tremendous performance, I am sure, could not be repeated by another living actor. I have managed for ten weeks to avoid superlatives, but now I am breathing down on you and saying out loud this is just about the most exciting film there has ever been. And I can think of no reason why it should be banned in the provinces. I appeal to local and county councils and censorship bodies to see that your county shall have the chance of seeing this quite magnificent film. It is one to lose and exhaust yourself in. It depends on the anxiety that the audience is feeling, and unless you are a monster of callousness I don't suppose it makes a second's difference whether your sympathy is being entreated on behalf of Poles, Chinamen, Germans or Alaskans. They'll get it just the same.

It is simply about some German refugees who are being kept as Russian citizens in neutral territory. They want to get back into Germany. If they are seen they will be shot. They work and mutiny and work by night to repair a railroad track. Then . . . do they escape? You must go and find out. Fritz Wagner's camera – it is not only a spectator looking on, but one of the refugees themselves – noses everywhere you want to be and nowhere that you needn't be. It is made with that tireless German sincerity – I am talking about film-making – that takes account of all sorts of irrelevant incidents happening outside the story. This at once reassures you that the story is happening in the middle of real life, and keeps you champing with anxiety and impatience to know the worst. But chiefly Wagner's camera and that precise, athletic, German acting of Albers' makes this as good a film as I have seen this year.

¶ *Refugees (Flüchtlinge)*. Germany, 1933, Ufa; d. Gustav Ucicky. Hans Albers, Käthe von Nagy.

Wary of any film propaganda, the British Board of Film Censors had refused a licence to this early product of the Nazi regime. The London County Council's approval allowed for a London run, but despite AC's enthusiasm no wider British distribution followed.

The Merry Widow

'Films of the Quarter', *Sight and Sound*,
Winter 1934–5

The Merry Widow is Mr Lubitsch's essay in the new Thalberg genre
– the opera film. As such it is only in the acting – what we shall soon
be calling the speaking-intervals – more resourceful than *One Night
of Love*. But as a film directed by Lubitsch it is a portent. Mr Lubitsch
has been careful in his last three films to exercise his suavity in milieux
where such dexterity would pass for wit. No director has been more
apt to choose characters and situations at exactly the strength of his
style. They are as glib, mischievous and amusing as he. But *The Merry
Widow* is too good a book, its story takes uneasily to satirical turns,
the '90s was an epoch to enjoy or despise, not to snigger at. And the
Lubitsch box of tricks is trivially and self-consciously spilled. No
conclusion could better reveal a manner outworn than the end of this
film. The elegant jewel-box thrust desperately into a prison cell is as
frantic an end as a romantic film could have. Here it is a sign that
Mr Lubitsch has exhausted one manner and must now choose – the
dilemma was once Herr Lang's – to abandon his box of tricks and
begin again with human beings, or else to fritter away an excellent
small talent in more and more mechanical parodies of it. The fade-out
was once Mr Lubitsch's invitation to the audience to share his *moue*;
it is now an interval between a jest and an episode.

¶ *The Merry Widow*. USA, 1934, MGM; d. Ernst Lubitsch. Maurice
Chevalier, Jeanette MacDonald, Edward Everett Horton.

'That Dreadful American'

The Cinema, BBC, 14 January 1935

My first letter of the New Year was from a lady who indignantly asks, 'When *will* Hollywood begin to send us films entirely in English? They are getting better, but there are still a lot of films it is impossible to understand. They all speak *that dreadful American.*' That is not the end of the good lady's very self-possessed abuse. But it's the essence of it. And against the chorus of listeners who have written cheering postcards about *The Thin Man*, there rise two complaining voices which protest, 'You didn't warn us that it was in a foreign language.' I am grateful for that last remark, because though it means to be sarcastic it is actually a guileless statement of fact. Perhaps I have taken too much for granted. I should therefore blame myself for not warning you that American films are often in American. I am certainly not going to blame America for sending us films in its own language. At least not until we are all agreed that René Clair simply must be stopped sending us films in French.

One way of learning to enjoy foreign films is – if I may make so bold – to learn the language. But for every thousand of us who sometimes have had to wrestle with French verbs or German nouns I suppose not two of us make the effort to study, oh . . . say, American prepositions, to say nothing of American manners. I don't say in order to see an American movie you should. But I do say that before you pass an opinion it is a necessary effort, an effort simply of courtesy.

I am greatly indebted to one friendly correspondent who assures me he is a 'strongly traditional' and, I should add, an admirable Englishman. He points out in *The Thin Man* a merit I have seen or heard nobody else mention. Let me remind you of the scene he is writing about. It's the one in which the wife (Myrna Loy) and her ex-detective husband are the hosts at a very rowdy and casual party which includes detectives, a lawyer, a few journalists, a young university student, a few ex-convicts, a fashionable divorcee. There is a chorus of drunks limply conducting a carol with any article of fire-irons they can find. A fat man is howling for a long-distance call. There are three or four people chasing each other. You have to assume that at least a dozen wine glasses will be broken, tables scratched, that cigarettes will by this time be quietly punctuating the pattern of every strip of carpet, lace and cushion in the room. The atmosphere is so compelling, in fact, that Myrna Loy is moved to fling her arms round her husband's neck and confess weakly, 'What I like about you, darling, is – you have such charming friends.'

Now this is what my correspondent says: 'However congenial or revolting the whole group seems to you personally, there is one astounding fact about that party. It is the way it is conducted. Can you think offhand of any English couple you know who, faced with that motley crew, wouldn't have given in, refused to serve people drinks, turned somebody out, felt their indignity wounded, or had a bitter quarrel about it afterwards? On the contrary, the good temper, the easy flippancy, the quick, alert manners, the indifference to the good looks of their household; above all, the smooth indifference to this howling mix-up of social classes – all this was taken so much for granted that in the middle of laughing I nearly forgot to notice it. But now I should call it – and I'm choosing my words carefully – a quality of breeding that probably no other race possesses.'

Well, that's a thought for the week, all right. At a later time I shall try and suggest why it is possible in America for social classes to mingle freely and vitally and yet without sentimentality – the reason is in the language. But for the present I pass on to you this correspondent's letter with a little signature of applause. And I ask you when next you see an American movie to look on it as something entirely foreign and to like or dislike it by the standards it sets itself, not by ones you would apply to England and English people. And when you hear an expression that seems a little odd to you, don't assume it was invented by a music-hall comedian trying to be smart. It was probably spoken by Lincoln or John Paul Jones. Remember, even if you had been living 300 years ago you might have used it. And when you hear a strange pronunciation, remember you are not hearing a chaotic speech that anyone has deliberately changed. Suppose, say, it is Franchot Tone – you are hearing almost an historical voice. For though it is the cultivated speech of a New England gentleman of 1934, it happens in essentials also to be the cultivated speech you would have heard in London over 200 years ago. When you hear somebody call somebody else a 'stool-pigeon', don't think it's another word for idiot. A stool-pigeon is a profession as authentic, if not as respectable, as a solicitor or an insurance agent.

Now suppose, you say, I should like to be able to understand better the American language, how can I go about it? Well, begin humbly by borrowing, buying or sneaking – I nearly said 'snitching' – Mr H. L. Mencken's classic and simple book called *The American Language*. And when that has opened your eyes to the extent of a permanent goggle, see if this world of stooges, and hamburgers, and corn on the cob, of sophomores and hillbillies, where people go haywire and pass the buck, isn't a new and a more understandable place. I can promise you that if you then see again *The Thin Man* or *Blonde Bombshell* you will have a new experience that, as the American cigarette advertisements say in their easy Elizabethan way, is an experience 'that will surely please'.

¶ *The Thin Man*. USA, 1934, MGM; d. W. S. Van Dyke. William Powell, Myrna Loy, Maureen O'Sullivan, Nat Pendleton.

AC's comments triggered a joint broadcast with NBC on 'English on Both Sides of the Atlantic' (25 March 1935), later printed with footnotes in the *Listener* magazine. Speaking about Max Reinhardt's planned Hollywood film of *A Midsummer Night's Dream*, AC warned the great German theatre director that accurate Shakespearean accents and pronunciations would only be obtained if he sacked every actor except James Cagney and sought his cast among Americans living in the mountains of Kentucky.

Sound Unrefined

The Cinema, BBC, 28 January 1935

In the far-off days of 1929, you may remember, we simple people used to sit and watch images on a screen. And if we heard anything apart from our neighbour's comments it was an orchestra or a gramophone or, I'm afraid, an organ trying to provide music to fit – Sousa for the newsreels, Tchaikovsky for the love scenes, the Moonlight Sonata for quiet robberies. Then sound came in. And cinema artists good and bad scrambled to use it. Or rather what they scrambled to do, in a fit of relief, was to replace the cinema orchestra. Once they found that doors would slam, they were delighted to show lots of musical comedy managers losing their tempers. People picked up things for the joy of letting you hear them being put down again. But this couldn't go on for ever. And besides, a man signing a cheque sounded like an Alpine climber scaling a particularly treacherous boulder. So when the first mad era of backstage musicals was over they thought again. The second thought, whether for better or for worse, was simply to use lots of dialogue after the stage model and then to put a microphone in front of it. And that is roughly where we are today. It is an odd fact that even quite intelligent directors have not yet thought of selecting what sound to put with the picture, though they would be appalled to let the camera show you every unnecessary bit of the story. The camera still goes on selecting, recalling, emphasizing, delaying, but the microphone is there all the time. A film opening in Piccadilly Circus may show you only three shots – one of a bus, one of the clock, another of the statue of Eros – but you may be sure that you'll hear a confusion of all the sounds that were about. A motor-horn and a taxi-driver's stray remark might give you a much more vivid notion of Piccadilly Circus than a medley of all the street noises. This is the curious misfit of selected image and unselected sound.

Continental Snobbery

The Cinema, BBC, 11 February 1935

Lots of people still want to ensnare me into hoisting flags and joining in international squabbles. Well, quite quietly, I should like to repeat what I said in my first talk in October: 'I am committed to no country, no director, no theme, no style.'

The average film made in France is rubbish. So is the average film made in Russia, Germany, Mexico and England. There is about ten times as much rubbish made in Hollywood as anywhere else. For the same reason also, it's ten times safer to choose a Hollywood film if you are faced with a choice, because they naturally make about ten times as many agreeable films as any other film centre. This means roughly that in fat years Hollywood produces about a half-dozen excellent films. Please note I say the average Hollywood film, not the average American film – for Hollywood is about as characteristic of America as, say, Blackpool Pleasure Beach is of England. Over here we know all the reasons why Elstree does not spell England. The reasons are at everybody's doorstep – the milkman, the postman, the people you meet in the streets, the games you play, the books you read. But people who waste expensive ink in the newspapers denouncing bad Hollywood films somehow have the curious idea that every film which crosses the Atlantic bears the blessing of the White House. I should guess, without any actual proof, that in newspapers and social life films and film stars are treated to more space, more fuss and more unthinking praise in the Old World than in the New, where intelligent people are in the habit of regarding them as a necessary and sometimes amusing evil. I offer you this kind of preconception as the lowest stripe in the army of film fans.

One stripe higher only is the person who is learning, with some complacency, to take account of European films. This is, of course, an admirable ambition. But it very often becomes translated into a witless following of whatever is made in the more intense and whispering corners on the Left Bank of the Seine. A film made, say, by a doctor in Prague has for many eminent English people the immediate thrill of an undiscovered Gauguin, of something they assume must be a sincere and literate work. When the film turns out to have all the exotic delicacy, the sweep and imagination, of a Brussels sprout, nobody is caught out saying so. When René Clair recently gave us *The Last Millionaire*, his last, and worst, film, the gravest of our morning papers lifted itself on to one elbow and said the film was 'very Gallic'. It forgot to tell us that it was very bad Gallic.

Well, France has recently sent us two curiously awful films: *Remous* and *Marie – Hungarian Legend*. *Remous* is about a husband, an architect, who, in an accident on his honeymoon, becomes permanently paralysed from the waist down. The film goes on to show you the wife taking a lover, a handsome athlete; then standing in bitter remorse before her husband, who promptly goes away to shoot himself. Now disability is the sort of problem that when it faces two adult, likeable people in real life, forces them to a blunt, but effective alternative: they can choose to do something about it, or do nothing about it. The architect and his wife did not choose to do either. They drift through a series of well-lit and inarticulate close-ups pretending the situation doesn't exist.

It doesn't matter, for the quality of the film, whether the architect becomes a person to admire or pity. It does matter that he should become a person to be interested in. That way, the problem could have been a real problem, and the pity could have been deepened. Instead the director concentrated the relationship on the one plane which didn't matter any more – the physical plane. The film meanders to its resourceless crisis in a night-club scene where a girl comes to the architect's table and asks him to dance. Grimly he shows her his stick – the audience is shown that stick all through the film. Accidents may be shocking, but they are not all equally good material for tragedies. And there is actual proof – if I may say so with delicacy and respect, there is President Roosevelt – that no foible of personality, no energy of intelligence, need be sacrificed to a personal tragedy of this sort.

To redeem this whimpering, fish-like film there might have been some technical fluency. A famous critic who festooned this work with all the orchids from a flower shop wrote: 'Technically the film would leave any British producer gaping if he had the mentality to gape.' I'm afraid it's only an exchange of verbal bombs, but I shall say it just the same: technically, this film should leave Alfred Hitchcock feeling like Shakespeare. Technically, it was not even workmanlike. There was, true, a studied artiness about its living rooms. But somebody had evidently told the director it was very dashing to move your camera away from your actors before you fade on a blank wall, and then fade in again on a different blank wall. Most of the time the camera is being swung about waggishly in this way. Except when it's interrupting each episode to show you a few square feet of the roaring, pitiless ocean – that ocean they used to show you in the early Westerns as a cosmic hint that Time, in case you'd forgotten, still had that dramatic habit of going on, and on, and on.

The second film features an old flame of mine whom I'm not yet quite certain whether I've survived. This should be the more reason for being easy on it. But if there is showing anywhere in England a more mawkish and inexpert film than *Marie – Hungarian Legend*, I hope I may never see it. *Marie* is out to tell you, in its symbolic, folksy way, how April showers come about. It gathers us all round the schoolroom fire and tells us how Annabella – late the divine – was indiscreet and unlucky one evening under an April tree; how she was subsequently driven from village to village until her child was born; how when she died and went to a golden kitchen as tasteless and tinselled as the heaven in the film *Wonder Bar*, she looked down and saw her daughter about to repeat her slip. So she lifted up her pail of soap-suds and poured it on the village. And saved her daughter.

Now that we know how girls go right, there is no need to dwell on a film made with every shop-worn continental trick, and the same nauseous, hopeless self-conscious striving for pity as *Remous*. Of course there are hundreds of sillier films than these being shown all over the country. But they are probably just the ordinary bad Holly-wood and Elstree films which nobody sane would hold a brief for.

¶ *Remous*. France, 1934, H. O. Films; d. Edmond T. Gréville. Jean Galland, Jeanne Boitel, Maurice Maillot.

Marie – Hungarian Legend (Marie, légende hongroise). France, 1932, Films Osso; d. Paul Féjos. Annabella, Germaine Aussey, Simone Héliard.

AC's delicate reference to Roosevelt, wheelchair-bound by polio, was most unusual for the time. Following the President's lead, the media generally kept his disability well away from public scrutiny.

Strictly Confidential:
Broadway Bill to Win

The Cinema, BBC, 11 February 1935

Frank Capra, a lively little Italian-American, made two years ago a delicious comedy called *Lady for a Day*. The critical tributes he received were so extravagant that many people expected he would settle down to becoming the sort of hopeless director who is damned with the label 'competent'. Instead he went away and made another comedy, *It Happened One Night*. And now he has ignored the applause for that and turned out a third film, better, I think, than his last. It is called *Strictly Confidential* [US: *Broadway Bill*].

It is a story that came in almost with the movies themselves. About the businessman whose heart is, so to speak, in horses, and who couldn't wait to go off and win the Derby . . . here it's the Kentucky Derby. But the story is made to matter and to seem the one we have all been waiting for because Frank Capra has in comedy the gift that Pabst has in tragedy: he believes in his stories. Which is half way on to making *you* believe.

He achieves this by first respecting every character that comes into the film. Characters do not merely appear or find themselves thrown in to fill up the background. However small and fleeting their impression is to be, Capra sees that it is a precise and picturesque one. In the films of von Sternberg, you can feel the director's control working from outside the picture, pushing a character here, arresting a gesture there. In *Strictly Confidential*, what you can feel working from outside the film is Capra's affection – not only for Myrna Loy and Warner Baxter, but for the darkie stable boy, for the colonel, for his gloomy companion, for the whole Higgins household, for the feedman, even for the crooks themselves. And nothing could be more typical of the way his affection and quiet realism can disperse a looming cloud of sentimentality than in a scene at the end where a horse is being buried. An open-air funeral around a beloved dumb animal sounds like an unfailing recipe for nausea. But Capra's camera shows you each group of heroes and villains casually and mildly. He has had the inspiration to photograph the scene in a high wind. And it is the wind that comes along to make everyone blink slightly, to turn Hollywood actors into ordinary people who have to hold on to their hats. It's the wind that makes the funeral seem trim, refreshing and quite unfussily sad. The story is blessed too with dialogue from that gay, kidding writer Robert Riskin. This is so genially and rapidly spilled that in the three times I have visited this film the audience has been hardly aware of an excellent wit smiling all around them.

¶ *Strictly Confidential* (US: *Broadway Bill*). USA, 1934, Columbia; d. Frank Capra. Warner Baxter, Myrna Loy, Walter Connolly, Raymond Walburn, Clarence Muse.

Women in White

The Cinema, BBC, 11 February 1935

If you have an hour to spare sometime you may get an honest laugh from watching and hearing Charles Butterworth in *Forsaking All Others*, a cheerful, shall we say an amoral film, that seems to be the polite way of talking about a story with no morals at all. To make up for this you might see *The White Parade*, which has morals enough and to spare. It's Hollywood's tribute to women in white. It shows a group of just ordinarily pretty American girls, a group such as you might see on the river at Northampton or on Rose Day at Vassar, all getting ready to sacrifice themselves – not to anything worse than death, but to medicine itself. You see these disturbingly decorative nurses walking spickly up gleaming corridors, holding test-tubes, bestowing on their patients the wit, loving care and glimpses of beauty that they'd have you believe belong in an American hospital. Apart from making me nostalgic about my own appendix, now interred in Connecticut, I found *The White Parade* a film to laugh or to cry over. But I couldn't quite manage a sneer. It's one of those embarrassing films whose moral is nonetheless true for being homely. I only hope for all our sakes that more girls like that will find their rightful calling.

¶ *Forsaking All Others*. USA, 1934, MGM; d. W. S. Van Dyke. Robert Montgomery, Joan Crawford, Clark Gable, Charles Butterworth.
The White Parade. USA, 1934, Fox; d. Irving Cummings. Loretta Young, John Boles, Dorothy Wilson.

Proving the Twentieth Century
Doesn't Exist

The Cinema, BBC, 25 February 1935

The Count of Monte Cristo is made by Rowland Lee with the endearing naïvety that makes his melodramas so charming. When a man betrays by his general laziness in moving around ideas that he doesn't know the twentieth century exists, he's probably a dull dog as well as a hypocrite. But when, with his eyes wide open, he deliberately *asserts* that there is no twentieth century and gets excited about proving it – then there's an interesting film on hand. There've been several films about lately that are not hard to praise because they deliberately yawned at sophistication and went away to perform, and believe in, quite childlike illusions. The director of *Mrs Wiggs of the Cabbage Patch*, for instance, deserves praising for not caring whether his audience laughed at his material or not. In the same way, you'll recall that Rowland Lee was once more interested in lighting the neck of – yes – Loretta Young than in minding whether you laughed at *Zoo in Budapest*.

And again he has done something for Dumas and trick-less romance that better men daren't attempt. *The Count of Monte Cristo* shows you corpses being thrown into the sea and disentangling themselves from the fauna. It shows you villains stroking their chins and being foiled into their cravats. Best of all, it introduces you without even a blare of trumpets to a very handsome, dashing young man who threatens to take over the comeliness and the nice satirical gift of the cavalier Barrymore of twenty years ago. My lords, ladies and gentlemen, I give you Robert Donat.

¶ *The Count of Monte Cristo*. USA, 1934, Reliance; d. Rowland V. Lee. Robert Donat, Elissa Landi, Louis Calhern.

As a student AC had become modestly friendly with Donat during the actor's stints at the Cambridge Festival Theatre. Years later, he told Donat's biographer Kenneth Barrow: 'We were taken then with his youthful, innocent bounce . . . I never thought of him as a great actor, but he undoubtedly emerged and shone as a star: "star quality" being, to me, the undefined capacity to make people never take their eyes off you' (*Mr Chips: The Life of Robert Donat*, 1985).

The Symbol Called Garbo

The Cinema, BBC, 11 March 1935

I am aware that any hopes I may have of fame might rest on worse claims than the single sentence – 'the man who went to sleep in two Garbo films, stood twenty minutes of *Queen Christina* and yawned through the others'. There, the wretched truth is out. And I'm not apologizing for the intimacy of this confession. Some months ago I said that when a man is criticizing an actress the most practical criticism he can offer you is to warn you of his personal tastes. Acting very rarely goes to the head. It hits you in your nerves or in the pit of your stomach. And when a woman is acting, it strikes most of us, heaven help us, hard on the left side of the chest. Or not. Well, Garbo strikes me not. I'm ashamed, but I feel I have a mischievous advantage over most of you. I can admire odd gestures, take to pieces certain tricks of her listening and walking at the moment that I am watching them. When most of you, of course, are falling sobbing into the aisles.

This time I am given an unusual boldness by a significant incident that happened the night I went to see her latest film, *The Painted Veil*. During the 'interest' film, I found myself sitting next to a gentleman with white hair and a distinguished profile. When the Garbo film had been unrolling itself, as the French say, for about twenty minutes, I began, as usual, to feel very lonely. At this point, the gentleman on my left breathed a deep assent. I imagined that some old personal experience of his was being finely illumined. I tried unsuccessfully to search for profundities in *The Painted Veil*. But upon his sighing becoming louder, I turned decisively and faced my venerable neighbour. He was in a profound sleep.

This not only confirms my opinion that *The Painted Veil* is a very dreadful film. But it raises awful questions. It raises one almost as terrifying as the dread legend I saw last year titling an article in a fan magazine. It said, 'Is Baby LeRoy through?' Those of us who take our cinema seriously are almost prepared to band ourselves into an international police force to see that this young man is saved from entering the anecdotage of his career at the age of four. But if Garbo is beginning to wane, that is something that is going to affect several million people who have never been inside a cinema in their lives. For Garbo has long ago passed into a region beyond that of actresses. She is the unapproachable goddess of the most remarkable and widespread mythology in human history. The fame of a Greek goddess was restricted to a population of something less than the population of Hampstead. Garbo yields in the matter of being the best-known person in the world to only one human being. Will Rogers has said it neatly: 'The Zulus know Chaplin better than Arkansas knows Garbo.'

But to be the most famous woman in the world is not only a social responsibility. It is at the same time a social revolution. Some time ago *Vanity Fair* published a set of photographs of film actresses under the heading 'Then Came Garbo'. It showed portraits of Joan Crawford, Tallulah Bankhead, Katharine Hepburn and several others before and after Garbo had drooped those eyelashes over Hollywood. The top set of portraits was a collection of fuzzy heads, odd strings of pearls, occasionally a dimpled cheek. It showed a set of young women graded between the buxom and the perky and the wilfully coy. Their expressions extended from kindness to one downright grin. The bottom set of pictures looked like a set of pictures of the same girl. Every face seemed to be sucking hard at its cheeks, to be curling its upper lip, to be straining to sweep its chin with its eyelashes. The only face that did all these things with a bored and magnificent accomplishment was the original – the Garbo's. And yet, my point is that there *is* no human original. Someone in Hollywood had a conception of a face and a symbol. A quiet, rather gawky girl arrived from Sweden. And on the screen became that symbol.

Hollywood has never made an effort to discover the particular human being that was Greta Gustafsson. Somebody saw possibilities of simplifying that complex creature, of reducing it to the proportions of a gigantic sullen doll. And they called it Greta Garbo. As they planned, she has become every man's harmless fantasy mistress. By remaining a fiction, created by celluloid, photography and make-up, she remains the safest and most easily disposable of sirens. By being worshipped by the entire world, she gives you the feeling that if your imagination has to sin, it can at least congratulate itself on its impeccable taste. She is secure in her position not because she is beautiful – if that means anything at all – but because she is a super-human symbol of the Other Woman.

For once, Hollywood was inspired. It did not perform its usual operation of grooming an actress out of her humanity into becoming a prosperous abstract noun. It took an interesting and intelligent woman and made her into nothing so trivial as a mere dramatic convention. But for the first time, with genius, it turned an actress into a social convention. And to convince anybody who was wondering, in the silent days, if after all Greta Garbo was only flesh and blood, there was the final exoticism of a foreign, low voice to make it clear once for all that Woman – especially the woman in this case – is always a mystery.

In *The Painted Veil* you don't believe that Garbo is Herbert Marshall's wife. I'm not suggesting that there's a sordid detail Mr Somerset Maugham had missed. But she's simply something dropped from heaven, a visitation to grace for an hour or two the humble, befuddled life of a hard-working doctor. Herbert Marshall is one of those remarkable Hollywood scientists – the type includes medical students, research biologists, inventors – whose claim to the Royal College of Surgeons would be the odd one that they dress meticulously and can never get any work done because they are so busy picking up new jobs in China. The whole story of *The Painted Veil* is as comically conventional as this character. But through the mess of fervent fidelities and infidelities strides the gleaming figure of Garbo. She starts off actually as a home girl, a girl who loves her father, and he loves her. Which sounds like the end of Garbo indeed. But soon she's in the East and able to pick up what look like odd towels and sling them round her head to defy you into saying you've never seen a more gorgeous hat. Which I haven't. She spends the rest of the picture striding through rooms looking glacial and tremendous. If you want to know what clothes your fantasy life is wearing this spring, well here's an orgy of them.

¶ *The Painted Veil*. USA, 1934, MGM; d. Richard Boleslawski. Greta Garbo, Herbert Marshall, George Brent.

¶ Around March 1935 AC mulled over his progress and the secret of a good radio voice in an undated letter to an unspecified BBC executive – probably Charles Siepmann, the Director of Talks until June 1935 and Cooke's main BBC champion at the time.

*　　*　　*

'I'm Enjoying It Immensely'

I'm enjoying it enormously . . . I feel I'm able now to convey the tone and the effects I want, and I more and more realize that quite apart from whatever quality one's writing has, to broadcast as just oneself requires a deal of experience of acting. Somebody – I think it was [Lionel] Fielden – asked me some time ago if I knew of anybody young to do books, and I now know that however clever the young man might be, an awareness of himself – the psychological effects of his tones, his delays, inflections – is necessary if wireless talks are to become pleasant and revealing and human things to listen to with us. Unfortunately, most good critics here have never done a minute's acting. Hence, the terrifying shock of Chesterton, the ogre of Delafield, the egg-in-the-mouth pomposity that issues from people who in private life are really charming but have no notion of projecting their personality through the highly artificial medium of a microphone . . . I wanted to reassure you that I really watch each talk as it comes from the womb, that I haven't the slightest intention of taking them for granted and slipping up on you.

¶ The protean author G. K. Chesterton had recently taken part in a programme debating whether parents were fit to bring up their own children. The 'ogre' is novelist E. M. Delafield, author of *Diary of a Provincial Lady*.

Hollywood Virus

The Cinema, BBC, 13 May 1935

There should be no reason why a mature director should not work as conscientiously in Hollywood as in Prague or Berlin. He will meet on an average more distinguished and intelligent writers, novelists, artists in Hollywood in a week than he will meet in any European capital in a year. This is, I assure you, statistically true. But I never yet met anyone who went to Hollywood to *do* his thinking. Most of the famous novelists, critics, sociologists, playwrights are indeed delightfully accessible, touchingly informal. Because it's quite evident that they are taking a busman's holiday. They all relax their standards unselfishly for the good of the party, and are prepared for a few sunny months to give Hollywood the benefit of any artistic doubt. But when they decide the party's over and it's time to work, somehow they can't get back. The joints creak just a little from story conferences. They are mentally muscle-bound from lying in the sun. And one tends to say to oneself that it is very churlish to fight for one's personal convictions with so many lovely and disarming people around. And the result is that often very grave, very distinguished men begin to beam with tolerance. They have been injected with Hollywood's virus to mankind, Delayed Adolescence. The end is the day when you no longer want to know how people live and behave, but when you want to be reassured and to pass on that reassurance to others around you. It may be the beginning of a charming man, but it's the end of a creative writer or director.

The Lives of a Bengal Lancer

The Cinema, BBC, 27 May 1935

Here, like it or not, is real film acting – from two actors notably, Franchot Tone and Gary Cooper. In *Maskerade*, Paula Wessely was often wasteful of her effects in the speed of her walk, the flamboyance of her gestures. These, I am sure, are delicious on the Viennese stage, but they're not much use when the camera can only take in a face, one arm and a shoulder blade. I'll clear my throat and try a simple definition: the body is the unit of stage acting; the face, neck and shoulders are the unit of film acting. I'm not saying this should be so – because I happen among other things to admire Sir Cedric Hardwicke's posture, Katharine Hepburn's walk, Lee Tracy's hands and practically the whole of Loretta Young. But actors are being directed at present to act in that small, rigid frame. Gary Cooper has other qualifications than a pleasant, wry face, and Franchot Tone other qualities than a fine New England voice. But here it is enough for Mr Tone to move an upper lip or contract his forehead. For these small gymnastics are the whole apparatus of film acting.

The Lives of a Bengal Lancer is about the fineness, comradeship, the loyalty, the bravery and almost everything else you care to throw in – of Gary Cooper, Franchot Tone and Richard Cromwell. The first half-hour is taken up with elaborate and nervous explanations of how it comes about that three men with American accents are children of the British Empire and find themselves in a British regiment. We're all delighted – we're simple folk – to know that Gary Cooper is really a Canadian, a Scottish-Canadian at that. That Franchot Tone has lived most of his life in Cheltenham and Oxford, and that it was the merest whimsy that makes him talk the way he does. And that Richard Cromwell, the forlorn – and I may say awfully cute – son of British parents has somehow gone to America with his mother, and because his father was in India he just couldn't get out of America in time to talk like you and me. What I – a niggler in these matters, I admit – am still wanting to know is why a Scottish-Canadian talks the purest Montana . . . but we'll let that pass. The next hour of this film demonstrates the difficulty of being a good officer, a sensitive father and a good husband all at the same time. It's out to warn you, is *Bengal Lancer*, in Aubrey Smith's words, that 'when that sort of man goes to India, it's the end'.

The film's artfulness lies chiefly in the way Franchot Tone has been used to keep cynical people in their seats in odd moments when they might be wanting to get up and walk out. Whenever the bravery is getting a little unnecessary, Franchot Tone is there to say they know it's silly but it's awful fun. Whenever the preaching's getting a little square-jawed, he's there again to say quietly in a corner, 'There's an awful lot of speaking minds going on around here.' This clever trick is the one in which Mr Noël Coward is already a past master – loading a film or play with double-bluff so there are several ways of taking it and keeping your intelligence at the same time. I am sure that *Lives of a Bengal Lancer* is having a direct success with thousands of people too kind to attribute motives of any sort, let alone cunning, to film people. But unconsciously, too, it satisfies almost as many of us – because we can get excited, and yet there's always Franchot Tone and his intelligent sly sneers to help us keep our self-respect.

¶ *The Lives of a Bengal Lancer*. USA, 1935, Paramount; d. Henry Hathaway. Gary Cooper, Franchot Tone, Richard Cromwell, Sir Guy Standing, C. Aubrey Smith.

The 39 Steps

The Cinema, BBC, 24 June 1935

After all the trumpet flourishes, I went to see Mr Hitchcock's new film, *The 39 Steps*, believing, as I had no legal right to believe, that I was about to see a masterpiece. From time to time Mr Hitchcock's talent seemed to be getting under way, but then I felt he had gone back to his notebooks and decided to include this little trick here, that funny line there. Somewhere I had blamelessly read that Mr Robert Donat was performing in an English idiom the kind of flip, cocksure comedy that Mr Clark Gable does so well in the American idiom. When the movie was over I had sadly to confess that Madeleine Carroll and Robert Donat as the English equivalent of Claudette Colbert and Clark Gable were handsomer, but as either comedy actors or human beings were seventy marks short of the comparison. If only, one feels, they would break down and forget to be a little lady and a little gentleman, their comedy would have had the chance of fluency.

It would also have had the chance of looking like something they enjoyed doing. Miss Carroll looked cold all the time. I don't mean she has a chill English beauty, I mean that literally she looked as though she were feeling a draught; and Mr Donat looked terrified, not so much by the thought of a murder but by the much more terrifying thought of his next line but one. For short stretches – the train ride north, the scene at the end in the theatre – this is an accomplished film, but the main criticism must be that it is a patched and uneasy joke. Mr Hitchcock seems to have had in his mind many of the moments in the film long before he had the story itself. And having found the story he then nailed on the jokes, amusing bits of camerawork, elaborated bits of 'business' left over from *The Man Who Knew Too Much*. I would not willingly persuade anybody to stay away from a film by one of our two English directors who have graduated to a personal style. Though it is in the worst and most serious sense a tricky film, it's a failure that not more than a dozen directors in the world could have made. If you can catch on to the refined accents early enough in the film, you may go far towards enjoying it.

¶ *The 39 Steps*. UK, 1935, Gaumont-British; d. Alfred Hitchcock. Robert Donat, Madeleine Carroll, Godfrey Tearle, Lucie Mannheim.

Goin' to Town

The Cinema, BBC, 24 June 1935

Mae West's latest picture, *Goin' to Town*, is smooth, artless and shamelessly self-assured. She makes a play not only for the rather incredible English earl in the piece, but for everybody in the audience who came hoping she had grown more refined. The gentlest protest from a lover, a stranger, a rival, is the cue for her to hurl into the audience a monstrous hint that no lady would have the wit to think of. By this time we needn't worry about Mae West's progress. She will not progress, or change. So now that the first delighted shock is over we can settle down to expect from her an extremely artificial comedy with conventions to be tolerated. The only times in *Goin' to Town* that the film is boring and rather embarrassing are when the audience is asked to believe that she could for a second take love seriously. But there are other unexpected times when she watches herself making her jokes, watches you receiving them, and her subsequent satiric emphasis in an occasional good-humoured smile or roll of the hips is good enough to make you think you are watching Groucho Marx in skirts. There's no more that can be profitably said about this picture. Mae West, like George Arliss, is to be liked or left alone.

¶ *Goin' to Town*. USA, 1935, Paramount; d. Alexander Hall. Mae West, Paul Cavanaugh, Ivan Lebedeff.

'Delicate' Play and Indelicate Movie

The Cinema, BBC, 24 June 1935

Suffocated by the weekend papers, drunk with adjectives which I suspect were written by quill pen on parchment, I feel it my duty before we leave each other for the summer to comment on what I might call the reflex comforts of being a dramatic critic. Wherever you turn nowadays, you'll find sprinkled through theatrical notices waggish asides, amused sneers about the 'world of celluloid', the 'movie mind' and other neat generalities. Nothing can be done, however, about weekend literary gentlemen who look upon culture as a means of protecting us all against the vulgarity of tramlines. If a man insists on getting to Devon by stagecoach in 1935, nothing is going to stop him, except possibly the stagecoach.

What is contemptible about these manufactured quarrels is the entirely unearned prestige which a theatre critic will attribute to himself when he has finished the unpleasant task of looking at the cinema. Before he starts on the comparison he knows he is going to find the cinema cheap, loud, vulgar and illiterate. He knows he can publicly proclaim his relief on being able to fall back on a theatre that has – he assures us – delicacy, dignity, taste. I said that quarrels between the stage and the screen are manufactured, because they have no quarrel with each other. A king may look at a cat – and perhaps envy it its suppleness and grace. Regarded as artistic products, however, the cat and the king have not the slightest advantage over each other. They have only different functions.

The latest concession of one of these gentlemen is that the cinema 'at its best is only approaching the level of Marlowe: it is not yet in sight of Shakespeare'. This is one of those splendid, vague sentences that cannot be argued with because they wouldn't descend to such menial considerations as proof, or definition of terms. How, in the names of Einstein and I. A. Richards, you go about equalizing the effects of an Elizabethan writer of blank verse tragedies in five acts with the effect of a modern European telescoping time and space with a camera in an hour and a half – this is one of the mysteries of the higher criticism that must remain decently buried. But I should be obliged to receive by return of post a list of those plays written since the war, exhibited in London, which are within howling distance of Marlowe. I may be obtuse, but I don't recall having seen in Shaftesbury Avenue or elsewhere the work of any authors of the past forty years which can compare favourably, as adult and literate writing, with William Shakespeare. I imagine that the number of plays aesthetically at the level of the film *Getting Gertie's Garter* must vastly exceed the number of plays at the level of, say, the films *The Student of Prague*, *The Gold Rush* or *The Front Page*.

I have reversed Mr St John Ervine's treatment and looked at some current plays. Eighty out of every hundred films are materialistic, sentimental, crude in their idealism. But for two or three minutes in each you will find an admirable gesture, cut, glance or other piece of sharpened realism. What the films are not, however, is what I have painfully discovered nine out of ten current plays are – pretentiously coy, building whole situations on scruples which everyone in the audience knows died a clean and unregretted death with the crinoline.

This spider-like invention, spinning fake manners, fake dignity, fake affection out of the tail of your writing, is a talent the cinema is too hard-boiled and too contemporary to attempt. At its worst the cinema is a record and a recreation made with the public eye that for better or for worse the twentieth century and the camera have given us. It is a record made, not out of one man's imagination, but by at least three or four men together. It has to be written, directed, photographed and cut. The working conditions of the theatre, as practised in the West End, belong admirably to a spacious age of leisured liberalism. The working conditions of the cinema belong to our day and age – to the committee of experts willing to sacrifice dignity to the machine. 'The beauty of the machine,' said the late T. E. Shaw, 'is that it teaches you how unimportant you are' – a sentence that could hardly have come from the lips of a fashionable West End actor. The cinema, at its worst, may deal with its issues loudly, familiarly and crudely. But nine times out of ten its issues are alive today. Whereas for what are called delicate plays, in which, as Mr Nathan says, the repressed young wife will at the end of the second act throw herself into the arms of any male character who can play the piano, provided only he was gassed in the last war – in this sort of thing many serious people see only the criminal waste of the audience's leisure, the deadness of the issues.

I suppose the ultimate choice for the mass of the population between the cinema and the theatre is whether you prefer to hear a bricklayer and a taxi-driver talking about collective security, or two duchesses discussing the way Oscar Wilde used to part his hair. I must confess to being for the taxi-driver every time. And there is this week one film which, possibly highly inferior as a literary product to the 'delicate' plays which purge a West End audience, is so vital a piece of journalism, that as a twentieth-century artistic product it seems to me to relegate those plays to the family album.

G-Men is a picturization of the Kansas City Massacre. James Cagney is a law school graduate who on the impulse of a sentimental friendship decides to join the government agents – the G-Men, recently empowered by Congress to fight gangsters with their own weapons. The sentiment is of the homeliest, the love interest a favourite Hollywood gambit, but the argument of the film passes away from the dialogue and plausible situations into the actually visible conflict of this man's daring against that man's cunning, in the tension created by competing toughness, quick wits, gunfire. In this sort of film nicety of acting and photography matter only when they begin to be obscure in point, or less than competent. What matters is a double-edged integrity in the director: fidelity to the material, to the incident, the characterization, the social problem; and a technical responsibility to keep the tenor of the film level. Both of these Mr William Keighley demonstrates with the hurrying competence of a man too sure of himself to dally over his jokes.

Preceding *G-Men* at its London performance was a prologue in which one Gordon Fellowes gave a lurid account of gangsterdom and equally lurid thanks for being in a safe country. The effect was to simplify by sensationalism nothing less than extremely tricky issues of the government of forty-eight states. Excellent things might have been said in that prologue. It could have pointed out that the government of the United States is a federation of forty-eight sovereign bodies, none of whom can arrest a man who committed a crime in another. It could have recalled that there are as many criminals going unhung in Europe as there are in the United States, which is several times the size of Europe, with more and equally independent governments. These things were not said. The prologue stressed the accident of criminal liberty, and could do nothing better than viciously persuade complacency in us who live on an island one-fifth the size of Texas.

¶ *G-Men*. USA, 1935, Warner Bros.; d. William Keighley. James Cagney, Margaret Lindsay, Ann Dvorak, Robert Armstrong.

St John Ervine's views of cinema were expressed in his weekly column as the *Observer* drama critic (23 June 1935); writing in the Summer 1935 *Sight and Sound*, AC placed them on a level with 'a medieval baron discussing air-conditioning'. Mr Nathan is George Jean Nathan, the corrosive American drama critic. Mr Fellowes had recently published *They Took Me for a Ride* and *Insurance Racketeers*; he was a British insurance investigator with American experience of fraudsters and 'men who would not hesitate to take human life'.

Abyssinia

The Cinema, BBC, 16 September 1935

There is one movie showing in London which in the last month or two it has become almost a political duty to see. It is called *Abyssinia*, and is made by a Swiss – Mittelholzer.

In the midst of a thick wash of speculation and conflicting descriptions, this picture is as clean to memorize as a seagull; here is visible and memorable proof that no single adjective will do to dispose, according to the colour of your political prejudice, of a country which can contain so much casual disease and so proud and fine-treading an aristocracy. It is not a neat or a noticeably unified film. The director has obviously had great difficulty taking some scenes and they are left in as records of hard work rather than of good material; much is left in that would have been smoothed out if a third person had done the editing. But – and even with the fine aerial section omitted (the best wide-aperture photography I have ever seen in a travel film) – it remains a remarkable progressive sketch of the manners, rule and life of the country. Perhaps, on second thoughts, the disjointed strips of panorama that get in the way of the exposition are no less than a symbol – I left the theatre with the despairing idea that in such a country good intentions are manageable just as long as the land is unbroken . . . but that you're never certain, in one of your civilizing moods, of not coming on a sudden deserted empire of heat and precipices – a war in the Grand Canyon could be no more hopeless. Here is a film with no grooming, no story, no acting. It's just a rough diary snatched from somebody's travels. But even without much care in the editing it seems to justify a movie camera long after you can remember the best film of the year.

CRITIC

¶ *Abyssinia*. Switzerland, 1935, Praesens-Film; d. Walter Mittel-holzer.

Mittelholzer was a Swiss aviator and explorer. The film documents his flight in 1934 from Zürich to Addis Ababa in Abyssinia (now Ethiopia). During the summer of 1935, Mussolini amassed troops on the Abyssinian border; on 3 October, two weeks after AC's talk, the troops invaded.

The March of Time

Sight and Sound, Autumn 1935

By the time this note appears, *The March of Time* will be about to burst into at least the London theatres. These observations are made on the specimen *March of Time* which its sponsors in this country, Radio Pictures, showed a week or two ago to the press. They are spontaneous and unconsidered, and must be revised when it is possible to see the thing regularly as a monthly feature. Meanwhile, the impact of this newsreel on this country suggests some astonishing and some ominous consequences.

It is odd that the most realistic documentary group in England, the GPO unit, our only sentient turners of history into news, should suddenly, by the production of a handful of fine American journalists, be left stranded; should suddenly appear as conscientious dramatizers of platitudes; should turn into a group of gentle academes roaming England with a camera and finding only what the already completed scenario had arranged for them to find. This is so monstrous a reaction that I am sure I am wrong. But my first vivid impression after seeing *The March of Time* is that men whose first and acute interest is the growth of fact into news have at every turn triumphed over men whose first interest is the technique of cinema. The men who have something to say in any art are not necessarily its professional practitioners – though *Time* assured itself of cameramen who have been at their trade for most of the past twenty years. It is to be hoped that documentary groups will not feel obliged, after the popular success of *The March of Time*, to search out that to ridicule either in the material or its technical method. These tracings of the origins of events, this view of news as conceived incident rather than as columns of accidents, is elaborate enough. But the aloofness, intelligence and apt irony, which for the past ten years have made *Time* so pathetically superior to any other newspaper or magazine in English, here make *The March of Time* the first adult newsreel. Admirers should be reminded that such results are not the happy picturization of a flip sense of news. *Time* has a research staff of such size and thoroughness that when vouching for its foreign correspondence one is constantly, hopelessly, reminded that the Soviet correspondent of our own immortal *Times* writes from outside the Soviet, from that Ruritanian hotbed of rumour – Riga.

When this newsreel was first mooted *Time* spent endless money and trouble and two years of experiment before the thing seemed a feasible proposition. As in their weekly collection of foreign news, the filmed *Time* is admirable by the amount of concealed research, chasing, cabling, digested history its slickness represents. But let us pray that no British company will now have the bright thought of imitating it before they have assured themselves of a staff, a vast library, years of experiment, a news service in most cities of the world and that unique combination of shock tactics and fundamental taste which is, I suspect, *Time*'s secret. Let all other film companies give pause before the horrific example of the *Daily Express*, which, having once read *Time*, now reads like the office boy's idea of *Time*.

¶ *The March of Time*. USA, 1935, March of Time.

The newsreel series continued monthly for sixteen years; in 1938 AC was brought in to record a separate commentary for the British release versions. On 7 July 1951 he reported on the newsreel's impending closure in the *Manchester Guardian*: '*Time* Marches – Off. From Cinema to TV'.

Mark of the Vampire

The Cinema, BBC, 30 September 1935

Some of the cinema's most distinguished names have had the ambition
to do no more than make one great and shocking thriller, and then to
die prosaically in their beds. The first film that was a film, *The Cabinet
of Dr Caligari*, was one. And *The Spy*, *M* and *The Testament of Dr
Mabuse* are the classic work of no hack, but of a great German, Fritz
Lang, and his wife, Thea von Harbou – surely the most cheerful
marriage of wits in the film industry.

The only native director in Hollywood with a gift and a pride in
this sort of thing is Tod Browning. And now his *Mark of the Vampire*
has been generally released. I should again warn you that this is the
sort of thriller which outrages half the audience, the sort of thriller in
which the wandering ghosts that have caused you so much agony turn
out to be Uncle Fred in a pillow-case and an eiderdown. But this, I
think, is a very intellectual objection. It's odd to notice people reduced
to paranoia by the film complaining as they leave the theatre that the
public hadn't ought to be cheated that way. 'After all,' Uncle Fred can
rightly complain, 'I did sicken you at the time.' And though these
vampires move in a world that we know is made up of black cloths
and smoke blown into the lens of the camera, to a simple soul like me
it looks like a graveyard. And that's bad enough. Mr Browning has a
great feel for knowing when to track his camera, when to whirl it up
to the object you are seeing in the distance, and when merely to look
at a passing ghost out of the corner of his eye. He respects a vampire.
And the respect passes into excitement because it passes into his
editing.

There is one trick that is worth pausing to relish. It is to let your
camera wander amiably about, with a roving enjoyment, at the back

of the neck of the character you are following. And then instead of seeing, with that character, what is inside the door on your distant left, there is a direct cut to a still picture of three living corpses standing beautifully grouped just inside the door itself and peering serenely at you. This second shot has no movement at all. It arrests your blood-stream without warning, you suddenly feel that even the inconsequent camera itself is being watched. The effect is a very horrible and pleas-ing tingle. Such tricks as these encouraged in the audience the supreme reward of a thriller – some screaming and one fainting fit. If you want to feel deliciously unwell, I recommend *Mark of the Vampire*.

¶ *Mark of the Vampire*. USA, 1935, MGM; d. Tod Browning. Lionel Barrymore, Elizabeth Allan, Bela Lugosi, Lionel Atwill.

Garbo and *Anna Karenina*

The Cinema, BBC, 14 October 1935

I am told there's a movement now to find the Garbo ageing, to ask that she should be given a rest, to look about for another goddess. This is embarrassing for me, because having always gone out or gone to sleep in the Garbo pictures, I am now converted by *Anna Karenina* into the most prostrate and awed disciple. And the only excuse I can find for this backsliding is that the Garbo must be approaching her maturity. There is a great deal of nonsense talked about maturity in acting, especially the maturity of actresses. An actress is usually said to be mature at the time when her daughters threaten to take over the parts she made her name in. But Garbo's maturity is not the maturity of her career, but the maturity of her outlook. That bold, fine disdain has given way to a sort of amused grandeur. Most people are grand, or not, about the eyes, and amusing – certainly most revealing – about the mouth. Since Garbo's most seductive gift was her mouth, you can imagine that the new combination is irresistible. The old brazenness has gone and with it that rather tiresome challenge of the bold, bad woman. It's frightening now to reflect that Garbo's 'appeal', as it was called, was the commonest of romantic conventions – the worldwide convention of the 'come-hither' look. She managed, because she is a supremely beautiful woman, to raise it into a religion. And in *Anna Karenina* she raises it to a philosophy.

For people who like to be made uneasy by the plot, who like to worry whether the villain will be done down in the next quarter of an hour, this film will be a disappointment. For the most modest claim of a philosopher is to guess about the last step soon after you've taken the first. And in the first five minutes of the film, when the smoke artfully provided by the train clears away and reveals the Garbo's face, you might just as well pick up your hat and go home if you can't guess the end. Before she has even chosen her lover, her look tells you that it doesn't much matter who he is, such affairs are bound to go the same way home. From our point of view, it could very well have been almost anybody but Fredric March. He brings to this very pre-war, elaborate Russia the manner of a West Point cadet entraining for a junior prom, a manner that singles him out for more than his share of protection. And he gets it. They all get it. For the new Garbo grandeur, this tolerant goddess, wraps everybody in the film round in a protective tenderness. She sees not only her own life, but everybody else's, even before it has been lived. This fatalism has happily passed over into her technique. And since the plot is now much ado about nothing, the chief excitement is to watch how perfectly she sees backwards, like a perpetually drowning woman, not only her life but her part. And her gestures, the way at one point she takes Fredric March's arm in the box; the way she looks down at the baby of a young friend; the way she picks up the field-glasses to watch March fall from his horse; the way – years ahead of the acting textbooks – she hides a broken moment not with a cute nosedive into cupped palms, but with the five inadequate fingers of one bony hand – her gestures, too, have the same tender calculation, the same anxiety to treat people with perhaps too much care at the moment, because she knows what's going to happen to them later. Tenderness is a prickly word, but it's nothing short of tenderness that has happened to the Garbo. She has suddenly and decisively passed out of her twenties. She no longer brightens to exciting, or handsome, or new people. And this calculated gentleness, a gift usually of women over fifty, is an overwhelming thing to watch when it goes with the appearance of a beautiful woman of thirty.

It's no use to talk about the others or even much about the direction, which like most of Clarence Brown's work is very conscientious and crassly unobservant. It provides mouth-watering, classic Metro backgrounds for Garbo to move against, and when any one of a dozen people threatens to get in the way he is briskly and reverently swept into the nearest convenient corner. Basil Rathbone keeps up a steady electric hum as a refrigerator, chilling us all with his clockwork unconcern for other people's moods. But when anybody else looks up or down, laughs, asserts, boasts or begs a favour, their well-meaning acting gets referred back to the way Garbo looks at people these days, the way she implies that the least you can do for people in this stupid, brawling world is to keep them warm and give them a share of comfort before the end comes.

¶ *Anna Karenina*. USA, 1935, MGM; d. Clarence Brown. Greta Garbo, Fredric March, Basil Rathbone, Freddie Bartholomew.

Coalmining in Hollywood

The Cinema, BBC, 14 October 1935

Black Fury is the final name given to a radical and sombre piece about coalmining, which Paul Muni, at one stage of the Hollywood softening, cynically suggested should be called *Coal-Diggers of 1935*. By all the laws and customs of the colony, a Hollywood film about coalmining should have been indecently bad. It should have been hearty and reassuring where some painful and blunt legislation was called for. It should have mussed up with sentimentality a problem that, like all workers' problems, cannot be solved by a nice smile and a pat on the back. Quite remarkably, *Black Fury* is none of these things. I am a stickler for movies being movies and not re-baked plays. But l can truthfully say that while several Russian workers' epics have been visually more thrilling in stretches, there has been none as memorable as a sketch of workers' lives. The film is a distressing, brilliant sketch of a strike of coalminers in Pennsylvania. It is written in a dialect that is beautifully earnest and, I have no doubt, fiendishly hard to understand here. But don't let that put you off. Don't, for truth's sake, get angry about Hollywood voices. These are very decidedly *not* Hollywood voices; they are the voices of Pennsylvania Germans, Poles, Irish. To an English audience the voices will be helpful mainly as a sort of harmonic scheme; the actual notes themselves will not come clearly. In this strange, inarticulate community Paul Muni is magnificently the simple Nordic immigrant, the honest, vain, confused simpleton who would and does get chosen as a radical leader and who finds himself deserted by his followers and left in the end, in one strong instinctive incident, to blow up the mine in sections as the police dare him to surrender. Again, the direction is ordinary, but concerned enough about the story not to wander off into trivialities.

The virtues of this film are in its complete acceptance of a simple community, in keeping faithful to its language at the risk of being obscure; in keeping faithful to the way the mothers and daughters look in those parts, at the risk of boring people who like to have at least a plucked eyebrow to fall back on. These virtues, I take it, belong to Michael Curtiz. And to the cameraman, Byron Haskin, must go a salute for some finely composed long shots which differ from Russian long shots in being under-lit from an accurate knowledge of the country and not from an earnest inability to use an open lens. If you like to be amused, if you are a tired businessman, if you like the movies to comfort you or make you long for a bedroom in white silk, you must at all costs avoid this film. If you can bear, for once, to see people moving about the screen who actually exist, in much more pitiful conditions, just 3,000 miles away; if you can bear to see a fine actor create an actual character rather than put on a piece of character-acting, *Black Fury* is worth waiting to see.

¶ *Black Fury*. USA, 1935, Warner Bros.; d. Michael Curtiz. Paul Muni, Karen Morley, William Gargan.

A Turning Tide

The Cinema, BBC, 28 October 1935

It has been a constant grumble of mine that British films have always done one of three things. They stayed indoors and tried to present an English newspaper office not as it is but as it might be if it were run by Clark Gable and Lee Tracy. Or they went outdoors and took charming, wistful stills of bridges and running brooks, and called it England. Or they went both indoors and out, sometime in the seventeenth century, and gave a clear romantic picture of the Hungarian view of English history – cardboard castles, a great deal of filtered cloud, a kingly wink or two, mention of the 'wenches', and bustling, patriotic laughter in the kitchens, where the lambs – the lambs of Old England – were being slaughtered.

Suddenly, with no advertisement, with no tolling of Big Ben, no premiere and square-jawed ladies from Mayfair pretending to be mistaken for Ginger Rogers, there appears a genuine English film, *The Clairvoyant*, full of English faces, English voices, and – a surprising risk – an English hotel. All of the year 1935. All talking and looking as they might talk and look any day this week in Leeds or Manchester or Sheffield. It is about a man who prophesizes a train wreck, converts his vision into profit as a music-hall turn, finds himself soon at the mercy of his gift, and in the end sensibly abandons it for the sake of sanity and Fay Wray. It has a sense of movement unusual in British films; and, what is more unusual, a sense of *tempo*, which is the business of arresting, delaying and playing about with movement. These and much else are remarkably to the credit of the director, Maurice Elvey. In two scenes, once on a train, then in the direction of the audience in a music-hall, he has done a quieter, more observant job than Alfred Hitchcock has done to date.

In the theatre scene, the high spot of the directing, an ordinary good-natured Londoner is gently barracking the clairvoyant, whose routine with his assistant has gone wrong and left him sprawling blindly about the stage. Suddenly the clairvoyant gets his vision and nervously tells the man to go to his wife. The little man looks suddenly interested, embarrassed, excuses himself and reaches down for his bowler hat. In this tiny scene Mr Elvey has performed a small miracle of observation. Four Londoners, four thumbnail sketches depending only on a certain grouping, on a few assorted syllables, remain as perfectly in my memory as anything in ten films I have seen since.

The miracle is not what Mr Elvey put into this. The miracle is that for the first time in the history of English cinema a cockney sketch was represented without a thunderstorm of jocularity and the waving of false moustaches. I had the feeling, again for the first time in a British film, that the editor and the continuity writers might quite likely know each other. There were no rhetorical dead-ends of dialogue with the cameraman then being called for to get on with the next sequence. And it has become a truism to say that since Claude Rains is the leading player, the clairvoyant, there is at least one brilliant, wide-awake performance. This film was out some months ago, but nobody seems to have seen it.

Another British film, just out, does not deserve the exploitation and the garlands or roses that it's going to get. *Turn of the Tide* is no more than an honest film about Yorkshire. But it is no less than this. And at the risk of seeming to join in the general chest-beating, I can say that it is likely as not to give you more pleasure than almost any film that has been made on this blessed isle. Where *Man of Aran* went to painful trouble to purify the ruggedness of the life on the island, *Turn of the Tide* is exhilarated to show its simple people depending on a bus timetable and a new suit. Perhaps it is a little too fond of the irrelevant good looks of some of the country, too fond of what might be called the momentary gape, which is also called the picture postcard. But it gains momentum in its story at precisely those points which some people are going to be embarrassed by. One of the ideals of these young fishing-folk lovers is to save enough money to buy a new boat. But, very pleasantly, another of their ideals is to have enough money to go to the pictures. There is never any attempt to give the story or the sentiments of the people a fake 'purity' or consistency. And also, it has some beautiful acting, especially by Geraldine Fitzgerald, who – as is right in this kind of film – never seems to be acting at all. After Hollywood has tricked out its sirens with the last secret of sex-appeal, along comes a plain girl in a woollen sweater, takes one frank look at a fisherman she loves, and leaves you swooning in your seat from excitement. Miss Fitzgerald is the most exciting thing I have seen on the screen for a long time; and I mean exciting as a woman simply.

When you can forget her there are several natives taking earnestly but not too well to being directed in a film. And there is a beautiful, slow-minded performance from a native who is also, and always has been, an actor of the first rank – Mr Wilfrid Lawson. Everybody talks more or less Yorkshire – Miss Joan Maude especially giving a valiant performance against every natural instinct. Leo Walmsley makes no mistake at all about writing Yorkshire all the time. All these virtues are organized by Norman Walker into a unity that is never a myth. Mr Walker has only another eight weeks to go before his anxiety can be relieved at having turned out the best British film of the year. The *most* British film of the year, of course, is *Sanders of the River*.

With *The Clairvoyant* and *Turn of the Tide* to pride ourselves on, you might think that the future of British films was set fair. But films, like buildings, are rarely the product of a period: they are the product of individuals who set the period. The honour for *The Clairvoyant* goes to Maurice Elvey and to Claude Rains. The honour for *Turn of the Tide* almost solely to Norman Walker. This should be insisted on in thinking over the news that has been vaunted in the newspapers ever since Mr Korda came back from Hollywood and announced that Elstree and Hollywood will draw closer, that there is to be a systematic exchange of stars. Everyone has assured us this will result in happier films all round. But if the British film chiefs have embraced the ambitions of Hollywood, there is one reflection that might be worth a moment's notice. It is simply this.

Whenever a Hollywood film company buys a play or an author, sets him working on a script, and the film gets written, cast, directed and distributed through the ordinary mechanism, the chances are a hundred to one against the result being a bearable film. The best

American films have been a constant proof that good work can be done in spite of the system that is supposed to simplify the making of good films. Lewis Milestone was thought to be reverting to his cranky Russian origins when he sacrificed a good part of his salary and took twenty-seven weeks to edit *All Quiet on the Western Front*. Walt Disney carried his unprofitable mouse twice across the continent before he set up shop in a garage, then in his own studio, and waited for the industry to come to him. Of the one talented comedy team working in Hollywood, Robert Riskin, the writer, has a small genius for naturalistic dialogue, and Frank Capra, the director, has an affectionate eye for American character; and because they can work hand-in-glove these men have been freed from restrictions of the system which would have killed their talent, and have turned out in three years the best three film comedies of that time – *Lady for a Day*, *It Happened One Night* and *Strictly Confidential*. And Charles Chaplin is the only man in Hollywood who can dare to spend four years writing, rewriting, making, remaking, one film, who will readily employ the janitor and odd friends to play parts Hollywood would entrust only to actors from a casting agency, who refuses to turn out a foot of film which does not satisfy himself and only him. These oddities, these rebels, have been so far the glory of the American cinema.

With this in mind, it would be rash to cheer the news that Marlene Dietrich is coming over, that Shakespeare is coming over, that we shall have more Americans in British films and more Britons in American films. The only possible result can be that British writers will hopelessly try to write American dialogue, which is the saddest sound the cinema can provide, unless it be an American acting an English clubman. And that Britons will be playing more and more of those vague Scottish-Canadian exile parts. And that messy, sentimental, confused, bastard child of the cinema, the Anglo-American film, will spawn over two continents.

From this confusion there is one way out. It is to respect an English writer's ability to write for English situations, English inflections. It is to respect that an Englishman who could write a tolerable American prose would be a more remarkable literary figure than Conrad. It has nothing whatever to do with the big drum of patriotism. It has everything to do with the carefulness of *The Clairvoyant* and the integrity of *Turn of the Tide*.

¶ *The Clairvoyant*. UK, 1935, Gainsborough; d. Maurice Elvey. Claude Rains, Fay Wray, Jane Baxter.
Turn of the Tide. UK, 1935, British National; d. Norman Walker. J. Fisher White, Geraldine Fitzgerald, Wilfrid Lawson, Niall MacGinnis.

Leo Walmsley, author of the original novel, wrote in his autobiography that he was pleased that AC mentioned his name, 'but we happened to miss the broadcast'.

Alice Adams

The Cinema, BBC, 11 November 1935

In all cinema there is only one spectacle more embarrassing than Harpo Marx meeting a lady. It is the spectacle of the heroine who *is* the heroine because she eats with the wrong fork. The big scene of the film is where she picks up a spoon when everybody else has picked up a knife, and retreats in tears to the hallway, where the son of the family, a moron if ever there was one, cuts off her escape and threatens to marry her. The formula was given local but permanent pathos in literature by the publication twenty-five years ago of a novel by Booth Tarkington, *Alice Adams*. The screen has been hankering after a full-length treatment of this sort of thing for just about as many years. And at last, by the simple process of recreating Alice Adams herself, the screen has got it. It has also been lucky enough to get its inevitable Alice, who has been in Hollywood for some time now working away furtively under the name of Katharine Hepburn. It's nice to have her coming out from behind that high-jumping and answering to her real name.

Alice Adams lives in a small wooden-frame house. By some talent or privilege which is not made clear, she manages to get to the parties of very social people who definitely do not live in wooden-frame houses. At one of these parties she meets the cheerful, if unimpressive, Fred MacMurray. He is very rich, socially very impressive. But he is also very attractive to Alice. The tragedy is already under way. By the time Alice sits with him on the porch and doesn't take him inside the house because she's ashamed to, you know that sooner or later he's going to *have* to come to dinner. Which he does. And the dinner is directed by the young George Stevens with such unblinking truth that it emerges from the rest of the film as a masterpiece of pain.

Katharine Hepburn has done nothing as good as this since the first, the charming, half of *Morning Glory*. She is badly let down at times by sudden air pockets that the film strikes when the director is dozing. Hollywood so rarely lets people cry: it sticks them weeping up against a window streaming with rain, and leaves them there as a symbol. But when she's left alone to act something and not to *be* something, she handles the character charmingly. She manages to laugh at the bewildered snobberies of Alice Adams and yet keep a clean and tidy person underneath. Dorothy Parker's remark, reviewing a play, that Hepburn ran through the gamut of human emotions from A to B – that was funny but untrue. It should have been from Y to Z. She knows those moments perfectly, the few seconds before you commit suicide, or fall in love or break off an engagement. But she's incapable of a build-up. She comes straight to the point, with a flash of the eyes and the nostril. I'm not complaining. Katharine Hepburn doing Y and Z is good enough to me. And even if they weren't, Fred Stone's performance as the father, and Ann Shoemaker's anxious mother, are both perfect.

Cinema fans of the left wing should be warned that here again is a director who doesn't want to take a lot of separate pictures of hands and wheels and faces and then assemble these images on a screen. He starts with the screen, like a comic-strip artist, and moves people about inside it. George Stevens is interested less in film than in the psychology of one family. And there are moments – when the father is recovering from an outburst of temper and motions his wife away from lacing his boots – there are moments which Stevens must have lived to know so well. There are many more which it should be your pleasure to discover. Lots of people can be confidently begged not to see this film. The sophisticated; the young intellectual who is embarrassed to discover that a kiss is a platitude; people who are constitutionally afraid of the obvious; the sixth form of schools, who have probably emerged from the Alice Adams stage of heartburn, and therefore have a profounder contempt for such antics than the rest of the world.

¶ *Alice Adams*. USA, 1935, RKO; d. George Stevens. Katharine Hepburn, Fred MacMurray, Fred Stone.

Dorothy Parker's A–B crack was prompted by Hepburn's Broadway performance in the drama *The Lake* (late December 1933), and quickly became an essential quote for Hepburn commentators. Cooke used it repeatedly.

'Our Common Language'

The Cinema, BBC, 25 November 1935

The one disturbing flaw in *The Clairvoyant* is Miss Fay Wray, who seems to be neither English nor American, but just a pale shadow of Everywoman. Now Miss Wray is, of course, an American. And a couple of years ago, she and Loretta Young both had charming, believable American voices. But she's stayed here too long, or maybe too solemnly. She has been at pains to acquire the English dipthong 'o' for the American vowel 'o'. She has taken, hesitantly, to the broad 'a'. Of course, the natural basis of anybody's speech is the organization of delicate sounds that an elocutionist thinks are improper. And the fundamental difference between an American and an English voice lies in the 't', the 'l' and the 'r'. Miss Wray was not born to say what the phoneticians call 'clear ls'. Any more than you or I were born to say 'dark ls'. And the American-voiced 't', what we sometimes stupidly hear in an American as 'd', is a unique and characteristic American sound. Miss Wray might as well try to change her looks and figure as try to change these. And she would be as ill-advised.

I am not saying these things about Miss Wray from any personal pique. I admire her likeable looks and acting enough to want her to keep her quality, which is that natural American combination of good sense and unaffected allure. But her case is the test case, the thundercloud on the horizon. For with the prosperity of our studios, more American studios are going to open up here. Miss Wray is the unlucky straw of fate. Two years ago, in *One Sunday Afternoon*, her voice was languid, warm, American; now she threatens to go the way of Loretta Young and become a vague, squeakily affected doll.

For exactly the same reason, Ronald Colman and Clive Brook have, as the years rolled by, stripped themselves of their character; they are now neither English nor American. Ronald Colman especially has grown into a buzz-saw hacking away at the soundtrack. He has, of course, the excuse of having lived in Hollywood about fifteen more years than Miss Wray has lived in England. He went to Hollywood as a very enviable type, as a romantic convention. He now talks like a committee for Anglo-American friendship. And his acting, instead of adding the precision of one to the fluency of the other, has lost all hope of either. We should watch out too for Herbert Marshall. In an indifferent film out this week – it's called *Accent on Youth* – he is given the part of an American playwright of a previous generation. To hear Herbert Marshall trying to warm to saying 'doggone' and 'oh boy! oh boy!' is the most heartbreaking sound in English history since 'When did you last see your father?'

In the present state of internationalism, there's no doubt that nations learn to respect and like each other as they learn to respect their differences of habit. Miss Wray and the coming hordes of imported Americans will do neither themselves nor their country a service in pretending vocally that they are just a different sort of Englishman and woman. They know how very foreign their nature and country are. We, alas, have a long way to go before we begin humbly to appreciate America as a foreign, non-European country. For this reason, the news that American studios are going to start English branches is the biggest threat to genuine understanding that the movies have made. It need not be. If Hollywood and Elstree will resist the cosy warmth of sentimentality, they can still offer a positive and valuable resistance to the dangerous rubbish talked in public by well-meaning gentlemen with knitting needles about the two countries bound together by – you know – our common language.

Edith Fellows: Small Genius

The Cinema, BBC, 25 November 1935

The big shock and pleasure of *She Married Her Boss* is the performance of a vile, irresistible little moppet called Edith Fellows. She has, it seemed, been acting in pictures for years, in *Jane Eyre* and *His Greatest Gamble*. But I get this from my *Motion Picture Almanac*, not from my memory. Whatever the effect may be on you, you ought to know she is no Shirley Temple. She is simply an actress. Or is likely to be. The camera to her seems to be just so much sunlight, except that she probably has to blink before the sun. She sits at a table, is invited to eat choice foods, rudely and without fuss refuses. She goes up to the first stranger that comes in and asks boldly and naturally, again without hysteria, what she thinks she's doing in the house. When a child actress is being what is called 'delightful', it is usually grinning or weeping with the camera about three feet away. And when it is showing its character, it usually glistens and stamps with rage. The small genius of Edith Fellows is that her tantrums have no temperature. She can keep ice-cold and yet show great variation of mood, a trick I'd always thought was the secret of actresses who played aged spinsters. She is a child to watch – for about another two years. Then, from the age of nine to nineteen, the acting coma sets in, and she can be left free to bathe in the sunshine until she decides to start being an actress again or, maybe better, to go in for bookkeeping or marriage.

¶ *She Married Her Boss*. USA, 1935, Columbia; d. Gregory La Cava. Claudette Colbert, Melvyn Douglas.

Edith Fellows retreated from Hollywood aged nineteen, but continued acting in theatre and television.

A French Film Director

The Cinema, BBC, 9 December 1935

In *La Bandera* at the Curzon the title and the dialogue may be foreign but the story is as homely as the screen itself. There's no need to ask why it's always three men who join the Foreign Legion, except that it allows more variations in the stooge, the dumb partner. In *Beau Geste*, if I can lean back so far, there was one silent partner; in *Bengal Lancer*, one small baby for the other two to get noble about; in *La Bandera*, the stooge cleverly pretends not to belong to the other two at all, skulking around as the villain instead, until the last few feet of film are giving out and he dashes in just in time to look down over his left shoulder as he shakes with his right hand.

But suddenly, adroitly, there comes a film of the Foreign Legion printed indelibly not on celluloid but on the lives of a half-dozen people; taken not against Hollywood canvas but against the firm, credible background of Spain itself. The story is trite enough, the acting is distinguished only as a comparative relief in understatement, all except Annabella, who is overstated to a degree, so that sooner or later even Gracie Allen would catch on to the idea that she is there to provide the love interest. So I take it that the positive merits of the film are in the watchful but undallying direction of Julien Duvivier. When the French cinema dies it might do worse than find his name written across its retina. Since René Clair bowed himself out of distinction with increasingly obvious gestures, there has been no one in France who could be graceful without taking on the aspect of a daffodil. *Lac aux Dames* was a film to preserve because it showed the most characteristic weaknesses of French direction. They needn't keep even all of it; there was one sequence that would do, what they tactfully call a 'sensitive' boy set alongside a plump, perky little girl, real enough; the progress of their emotional scrambling, their holding off with what Robert Benchley calls 'cricket trouble' against a background of coyly draped – believe it or not – fishing nets. If the film failed it could only have been because the fishing nets failed to cause the spring stir in interior decoration that was expected of them.

M. Duvivier is sensitive, too. And he's also a male with a gift of tenderness which he seems to accept in himself as something not to melt over. But if he has one thing more than another it is the practically unique power today of looking generously at beautiful scenery without bursting into sobs. There's a lot of filtering in this film, but it's not beauty seen through a Hollywood veil of tears; it's not an album of postcards, like Dreyer's in *The Passion of Joan of Arc*; it's not MGM's telescope; not Mr Korda's spectroscope. It looks like an exquisite newsreel taken away and baked brown to give you the feel of the air. And in dialogue scenes in the open air Duvivier has managed to improve on an inevitable alternative – that of taking no-nonsense pictures with the light behind you; or taking fantasy pictures, like Murnau's in *Tabu*, into the sun with a shaded lens. Duvivier shoots across the light with the sun just striking his lens. It is typical of his sensible realism that he doesn't bother to use Flaherty's effective refinement, that trick of taking all your pictures before ten in the morning or after five in the evening, which gives to trees and people in a single plane a lovely, unreal stereoscopy. I cannot recall a film with outdoor photography that so sensibly and movingly matched the emotional stages of the story. Up to the arrival of Annabella the film is a masterpiece. After that it's just another movie. But it has scenes – the arrival in the dormitory, the cabaret scene in Barcelona, where a mobile camera gives you the strange feeling that a delicate, alert mind is behind the camera easing you into every detail of behaviour; not, like the usual mobile camera, giving you the increasing fear that a hypochondriac is in full control.

¶ *La Bandera*. France, 1935, Société Nouvelle de Cinématographie; d. Julien Duvivier. Jean Gabin, Annabella, Robert Le Vigan, Pierre Renoir. The cameramen were Jules Krüger and Marc Fossard.

Ruggles of Red Gap

The Cinema, BBC, 23 December 1935

Ruggles has probably given more harmless people a blissful evening than any other single film of the year. It was so lazily easy to like, so free from startling queer detail. I suppose that's why it leaves behind the taste you get from a meal that's solidly according to the menu. If somebody had hidden one muscatel with the sole there would have been a moment's anticipation, a moment's excitement. But *Ruggles* was an anthology of every comic platitude there has been, from Lancelot Gobbo to Ronald Frankau. Even so, once you catch yourself in an audience with this film, there's only one thing that can happen. You either laugh or leave. It's like that record of 10,000 people singing the Hallelujah Chorus.

¶ *Ruggles of Red Gap*. USA, 1935, Paramount; d. Leo McCarey. Charles Laughton, Mary Boland, Charlie Ruggles, ZaSu Pitts, Roland Young, Leila Hyams.

Jimmy Cagney: The St Louis Kid

The Cinema, BBC, 23 December 1935

As far as I'm concerned, it's certainly the best Cagney film there's been. Its background is a stretch of road somewhere between Detroit and St Louis. And when I say 'background' I mean literally what you see over the hero's shoulder. The straight roads, the flat horizon, the filling stations, the trust bank, the diners – they are all so plain to see that *A Perfect Week-End* [US: *The St Louis Kid*] takes its place as one of the few regional comedies turned out of Hollywood, even though I'm sure the whole movie was shot between Hollywood and Pasadena. Mr Cagney and this time Mr Allen Jenkins are truck-drivers, which should satisfy everybody. What may annoy some people who think of Mr Cagney only as a natural tough is that in this film Mr Cagney's gift of not believing in anybody but himself is so technically polished, so charmingly played within his use of his fore-arm, his lower lip, the way he walks out of rooms, that it takes on an odd sort of pathos that he's not had before. It seems as odd in Cagney as humour in Beethoven. But that happened too, and the discovery of it in *A Perfect Week-End* is a precious thrill for everybody who knows James Cagney as one of the few technically perfect actors on the screen.

¶ *A Perfect Week-End* (US: *The St Louis Kid*). USA, 1934, Warner Bros.; d. Ray Enright. James Cagney, Patricia Ellis, Allen Jenkins.

Housing Problems

The Cinema, BBC, 23 December 1935

In fifteen minutes, two young directors, Elton and Anstey, crash cleanly through Eisenstein's bearded theorizing about the professional and the 'natural' player. They put a microphone in front of simple, gaunt wives who tell you how they sleep on Mondays, their husbands on Tuesdays, because one of them has to stay awake to beat the rats off the children. They move a camera with shameless curiosity through the slums and show you staircases propped with filthy cushions and the sticks of old chairs, torn wallpaper that literally throbs with roving lice. And against this daily setting men and women tell with dignity and interest their story. By the present system, *Housing Problems* will be seen possibly in film societies, only certainly by the employees of the Gas and Coke Company, under whose praiseworthy auspices it was made. But this film, unless our producers are shiftless knaves, must be bought at once by some big, and preferably prosperous, firm. Its point must be made in the same programme as the glamour of Shearer and Crawford. In a world of celluloid, the cinema can offer no saner justification than intrusions from the world of slummy unsocial fact.

¶ *Housing Problems*. UK, 1935, Association of Realist Film Producers; d. Arthur Elton, Edgar Anstey.

Fred Astaire on the Wing

The Cinema, BBC, 3 February 1936

John Grierson has just put out a new article. I don't mean a new documentary film for the General Post Office to be lucky enough to sponsor. I mean an article written with pen on paper, or possibly, if I know Mr Grierson, with pencil on pillow, but proving again that of all writers on cinema he is the only one who manages to make film jargon sound like a special clue to ordinary human wisdom. In the course of this essay, Mr Grierson starts to praise a new book, which tries to set down in cold print the emotional effects of fade-outs, close-ups, dissolves, wipes and the rest, a book which is trying therefore to write an anatomy of the cinema. Sighs Mr G: 'The curse of anatomy is that you must first kill the body you are going to work on. Cinema is no longer on the wing or caught in the bright flashes of occasional inspiration. It is on the cold and horrid slab in process of dissection as to viscera and nerve fibres, but the real factor in the situation is that the subject is stone dead.'

Well, now and then a critic escapes from his surgery and wants to chase his butterflies, or catch cinema on the wing, as Mr Grierson puts it, along with the rest of the world. There are films, and some of the greatest – especially in comedy – which release chiefly those energies that spring from benevolence. This is fine for families but bad for criticism. They seem too good to talk about. Whatever piece of life they take a look at they deal with so authentically and surely that it seems a clumsy retreading of the good ground to talk about them at all. Of such was *Alice Adams*. And so, I think, is *Top Hat*. There's no call at this time of day to pin Fred Astaire down to the mortuary table and start dissecting him. And I'm afraid *Top Hat* is the sort of film nobody wants to have analysed. It's not so much a film that, as we say in our lazy moments, *defies* criticism. It's a film that doesn't encourage it, though. It says, 'Go on, you criticize me and just see all the people you're going to pain.' I defy Mr Grierson or anybody else to catch hold of Fred Astaire once *he's* on the wing. Fred Astaire soaring up and down rooms is good enough for most of us, without making him unscrew his legs to see how they work. The only assurance you need in a musical is that those legs *do* work.

In fact, Mr Astaire probably wouldn't mind giving the rest of his body to the slab for dissection. For his legs can do most of the things you and I will need a harp and a fancy dress for. The dialogue is witty enough, but those legs are wittier. The new and funny Helen Broderick winks wickedly, but those legs wink wickeder. And so it goes. Looking back on it, I have just one grouch. I wish musical comedies didn't have to take quite so prosperous and Rotary a view of life. It hurts after *Alice Adams*. I for one shall enjoy watching Mr Astaire and Miss Rogers as a mere sailor and his girl in their next film. Even then, I suppose the battleship will have a scrumptious ballroom where all the real killing is done, and I expect the port-holes serve chocolate milkshakes at the drop of a hat. But there it is, you take what you get, especially as Mr Astaire and Miss Rogers are, from all accounts, not to be together again. I don't know why I'm calling them Mr and Miss. But Fred sounds all wrong. Let's hope when his present partner deserts him he'll call himself by his real name and make a new series of musicals, partnered as God meant he should be, by his first and oldest flame, Miss Minnie Mouse.

¶ *Top Hat*. USA, 1935, RKO; d. Mark Sandrich. Fred Astaire, Ginger Rogers, Edward Everett Horton, Helen Broderick, Erik Rhodes.

The book Grierson was reviewing, in *Sight and Sound*, Winter 1935–6, was Raymond Spottiswoode's *A Grammar of the Film*. Graham Greene, reviewing *Top Hat*, also compared Astaire to Mickey Mouse.

Coming to Terms with the Movies

The Cinema, BBC, 3 February 1936

Three items of news have come out in the last week or two that taken together make the cinema sound like the most calamitous social affliction since the Black Death.

The first is a sentence from an interview, on the celebration of his seventieth birthday, with a distinguished actor. In the course of a heartening passage about what he called 'the present generation of actors and actresses' (try and figure that one out), he said he had seen one or two cinematograph performances. He then concluded with the astounding remark, 'I don't think they do much harm, these cinema shows.' He meant of course that the movies have done little harm to stage acting. Which must be a fine thought for Eisenstein and John Grierson to warm their toes with. But perhaps he meant the movies have done no harm to people. Well, haven't they, indeed?

Last week, in this decent tolerant country of ours, a wife applied to a magistrate for a separation order on the grounds that her husband got up, went to the movies, took his midday meal, returned to the movies, came back to tea and went off to the movies again. That's the sort of conscientious schedule I hope some day I can keep. It's the life of any honest film critic. And some of us stay married. But not this poor man. The separation order was granted. And I for one am the sorrier for it. For who shall throw the stone when the third item tells us that a recent enquiry into who goes to films, and how often, discloses that of all professions the parson is the most regular film fan. Yet he usually seems to stay married better than the rest of the population.

What these three cuttings amount to is nothing very positive as signs of a social trend. They are casual reflections, though, of a state of things that most of us never knew existed. They go to show that most of us still seem to accept the cinema as a variation on golf. At least we seem a long way from accepting it as itself. The distinguished actor accepts it as a harmless child trying to imitate papa's mature and virile poses. The man now separated from his wife had already grown to accept it as a permanent drug, and he just about managed to keep his body going in between pipes. The parsons seem to have accepted it as a regular rest from social work. But there's not much evidence to show that we can any of us congratulate ourselves on having come to terms with the movies. And it's as much a personal obligation nowadays as it is to come to terms with peace and war.

The vast majority of adults in all countries seem to look upon the cinema as a kind of play where the seats are more comfortable for the money and you can see the actors better. I have no grumble, and shall do no crusading, with anyone who doesn't like the movies and comes right out and says so. But people are always writing to me reflecting aloud how wretched this is in the movies, how charming it was on the stage or bound in morocco. They don't reflect that maybe this inflection, that composition, the organized excitement of that movement, could never in a thousand years of Jessner or Piscator be put on the stage. Or that over a quarter of a century at least a couple of hundred movies could exist in only one place – a screen.

For better or worse, Mr Edison one night in New Jersey in the 1880s played a gramophone record and thought it would be nice to see what he heard happening. And he invented the movie. And when the movie started to compete with the theatre, it was as an entertainment, not an art. If more people read novels than go to watch water polo, it would be considered highly comic for novelists to say they do far better on dry land what polo players do in the water. But because the cinema has rifled the theatre box-office, it is threatened not with theft, which would be all right, but with abduction of the play and players. It doesn't need them. It never did. It needs a lot of photographs of people and places and a man with imagination and a pair of scissors. With these, that man may produce the effect of profound feeling. But great directors are not two a penny, and the average director has to rely on a good actor to make his points with speed and understatement. So he gets a special actor, and our own film industry could make laudable history by refusing to accept any actor, however famous, on the strength of his performances in the elaborate, overstated art of theatre acting.

Let no stage actor, however distinguished, despise an art of acting in which he would probably fail to graduate into the first thousand. Let any wife think twice before divorcing a lazy husband for seeing movies three times a day. Let no congregation whisper against its preacher for going off to see *Alice Adams*, for he thereby learns more about the authentic detail of the average working family than a month's slumming will teach him.

The movies offer you a two hours' close scrutiny of your fellow men and women. Whatever the plot says, whatever the author says, whatever social fact is being glossed over, the stance, the features and the voices of people give off their own evidence of character and philosophy which no scriptwriter, author and director can efface. At the worst you can notice rhythms in a whiff of smoke, in the flight of a bird, in somebody's mouth and smile, that you can get nowhere else. And sometimes the man with a movie camera saw these things first and organized them – so the whiff of smoke becomes a film on *Housing Problems*, the bird's flight becomes *The Song of Ceylon*, the mouth and smile become *It Happened One Night*. And if you don't like any of these, you know where Shaftesbury Avenue is.

Chaplin, Ancient and Modern

The Cinema, BBC, 17 February 1936

On Tuesday morning of last week one of those squat rumbling Channel steamers was chugging across the sea with strange passengers aboard. No stranger, perhaps, as human beings, than the daily crew of cigar merchants, wine tasters, ailing people going off to find the sun. But however queer they looked they had more things in common than a blustering wind. And though they spoke many languages, their profession was the same ... that is, if film criticism rates as a profession. They came from Berlin and Paris, Stockholm and Rome, from Holland, Belgium and Czechoslovakia – and it is possible that if there had been an outbreak of fire, there is not one practical sentence of English that they could all be sure of repeating. But as this boat pulled into our tight little isle, a German, a twinkling, inconsequential little man, cocked his head up at the moon – it was a good moon – and began to sing to himself. In a minute or two another man came up and hummed alongside him. Soon a small group of them, French and Austrian and German, had forgotten all about security by poison gas and encircling each other's country, and they were all leaning overboard singing hard and high and slightly out of tune. It was an old song, a song about the moon shining bright on a man with a bowler hat. And this curious crew of critics, who should have been fast asleep in Amsterdam and Prague before getting up to see their daily film, were coming to London for ninety minutes' entertainment. They had come to see how the moon was feeling, after twenty years, about the man with the still-unmended trousers. They had come to say whether Charlie Chaplin stood where he did in 1915, as the world's funniest and most famous man.

Five years have done a lot to the movies, but not so much as they

94

have done to us. Our hearts may go on beating on the left side of our chests, telling us all sorts of touching and heartening things. But our eyes take advice from none of the other senses. And one of the discouraging things about the movies considered as an art, one of the countless cues for the psychologist, is this optical sophistication that delights in, then wearies of, new conventions almost before the other senses have taken any account of them. And what chiefly makes cinema critics a restless and uncertain lot, a group of tipsters swapping guesses and hunches, is the knowledge that impressions begin to bore them before they have been absorbed.

Well, since 1931,* several things have happened. First, recording on the soundtrack is much clearer and more intimate. Musical scores can sound like a concert performance. What is more, and perhaps worse, they can be amplified to volumes of lushness unknown to any concert hall. Next, the trend especially in comedy has been towards the inconsequential, depending on a slow-timed inflection. There never was an era in the movies when genre work was less likely. We are on top of the players all the time. In 1931 Hollywood was editing a little more aloofly, less lap dissolves and angles, they had not begun to file away as useful tricks the devices that were basic principles to the Russians. Since then the move to merge the audience into the screen, to make the effort of looking on less and less painful, has gone along briskly. When Charlie Chaplin started making pictures we were normal men and women looking from a far distance at the antics of creatures jerking their sawdust hearts around in another, practically a puppet, world. Since then they have become more like us and move at the distance of ordinary conversation. We're no longer an audience, we're just pals.

In the early Chaplins, he looked like a normal man because everybody else looked insane. But since 1915 the camera rose from its bed and walked, we have been seeing eight more pictures to the second than we used, and though we are fooled the way we always were – the screen is still black half an hour in every hour – yet the action has slowed down and accepted us as a norm. All this has been fine for Myrna Loy and Greta Garbo and for Robert Riskin and Frank Capra.

* The date when Chaplin's previous film *City Lights* was released.

But it has made the Chaplin figure become increasingly grotesque . . . it has made the Chaplin talent *look* like a period piece even when his psychology and feeling were subtler than his contemporaries'. But all his films had a unity and a style because it seemed, as the years went by, that he wisely kept his art within the limits of its first technical shape. He triumphed by making no concessions – where other men kept their cameras still from lack of imagination, he kept his still from conviction, the conviction that the peepshow movie was the best for him. 'They are indecent because they have no distance,' he once said of the players in a typical Hollywood piece of two years ago. If, performing some gesture, the camera was forced to pan or tilt to take it in, he would prefer to send his camera back and keep it still, framing the whole act. And, in truth, that miraculously compact extravagance of mime could best be seen when you could see the whole figure. In light values, too, he kept on the other side of the Hollywood fence. Cartier-Bresson has excellently noted his 'bad' photography in a protest against the banal excellences of the latest Hollywood films; and indeed the 'funny man would dissolve in that suave lighting, which brings a Garbo to life'. And he had many unforgettable scenes, lit with exquisite understatement, providing an aura for his miming to etch itself in. As late as *City Lights*, the contrast with the current commercial film was startling. Where it was smooth, expensive, illuminated, his film was lit cheaply and vaguely in a world somewhere between Rembrandt and Hogarth, ready to move poignantly into one, to tear cheekily into the other.

Well, for the first time in Chaplin's history, we have a Chaplin film that looks and sounds as if it came from only one place – Hollywood. Prosperity has turned the corner and flashed its diamonds along Easy Street. And the street can't take it. Nor can the little man, who, suddenly caught by suave lighting, like a romantic aeroplane spotted by a searchlight, far from dissolving crystallizes out into something solid and functional. In *City Lights* the music, brilliantly amateur, snatched a little Tchaikovsky and Beethoven from memory and orchestrated them for a small-town band. In *Modern Times*, the themes are as good as ever but they have been orchestrated fatally by Mr Alfred Newman, United Artists' accomplished and probably inoffensive music master. And the product is a purring ocean of harmony, lush and symphonic. Whereas all that Charlie Chaplin needs is a tango band or a drunken cornet. For much of his charm is that air of a child honestly and successfully being the little gentleman. Give him a tin trumpet and the child's skill is more amusing . . . give him a grand piano and he is far from an adult.

Since he has yielded these twin integrities – the looks and the sound – he has yielded much of his strangeness. I am aware that this is possibly the most serious lament to make about a Chaplin film, and I have taken some trouble to verify my anxiety. Maybe, I thought, there never was a characteristic oddity and his movies flickered and 'rained' no more than anybody else's. In the last day or two I have seen again *The Cure* (1917), *The Pawnshop* (1916), *The Vagabond* (1916 – and some of it fresh as magic), *City Lights*; and with them Harold Lloyd's *Just Neighbours*, and Harry Langdon's *Saturday Afternoon*. The Lloyd was terrible, without character of any sort; he might have been any amiable young American. *City Lights*, the most relevant test, has long stretches of mawkish wistfulness that *Modern Times* has not, though it has its share. The swallowed whistle incident I found helplessly funny, funnier than anything in *Modern Times*. But the production had the Chaplin setting, the lighting of the streets, of the embankment; the brilliant orchestration of the boxing match with three or four dithering strings. And there was a form in it, and unflagging continuity.

Modern Times is inexplicably an anthology of gags rather than the progress of an episode. This again is a remarkable defection. For, as Paul Rotha has rightly insisted, Chaplin's continuity was always simplified by dint of great labour. I am personally so mystified by this sudden sprawling and redundancy that I suspect another, and a clumsier, hand has done it. Perhaps Mr Joseph Breen, the censor, may be the real villain, for practically as the film was catching the boat six sequences were ordered to be trimmed for ribaldry. It was charming, harmless stuff, and since it is unfair to Chaplin to lay at his door all the blame for not realizing the Chaplin myth (which I have tried to ignore), it is with relish that I single out Mr Breen, Mr Newman and some third person, possibly the assistant director, for the unexpected, and fatal, flaws in structure, lighting, sound and style.

Since Mr Chaplin has broken with his old convention in other ways, it is bewildering to find that he has not broken with a habit of unnecessary subtitles. I was prepared to accept these along with the saccharine, coy conception of the girl (which always does for his fantasy sweetheart). But when half the film has shiny labels of 1936, it's hard to notice lots of torn ones showing from 1915. Things like 'cured of a nervous breakdown but without a job he leaves the hospital to start life anew', where the caption comes first and the pantomime afterwards. All through there is this double statement for an incident that his pantomime could confidently cover. It sinks to unbelievable carelessness on captions like 'She stole a loaf of bread . . . !', 'No, she didn't . . . I did' . . . when the words are afterwards elaborately acted.

Again, the whole first section of the film destroys at one stroke the Chaplin stand against a restless camera. He swings and pans and dissolves as glibly as the rest of them. And from too close a range, the camera has the effect of making much of his pantomime seem muscle-bound. I am not pretending that Mr Chaplin is a unity any more than anybody else, any more than Dickens, say, with whom he has much in common; and it is possible to deplore their too easy pity of the workers, their Little Nells and little waifs, and yet to bow down and worship before a clear-eyed and irresistible invention. But let us have them as they come, and not even as Mr Graves might rewrite them, or Metro-Goldwyn-Mayer remake them. You may, by heaven, be MGM. Or you may, by the grace of heaven, be Charlie Chaplin. But you cannot be both. And I must point the issue by saying that *Modern Times* is like Chaplin the actor directed and produced by MGM.

This sentence, my positively final sigh, will hint, too, the fact that the success of this film is Chaplin the actor. For one thing, Mr Chaplin has kept his promise that he was about to extinguish Everybody's Little Ray of Sunshine. The tragic comedian is no more. This time, when a policeman pushes him about in the street he does not creep away, forlorn and spiritual. He turns and with a precise Latin viciousness indicates that he is on his way and will not be manhandled. The whole character has said goodbye to pathos, and that's very fine with me. He has gained, instead, an absurd perkiness, a mood that translates itself into gesture as a rhythm of alert petulance.

He sprinkles his food with dope which he thinks is salt and the cheerfulness, curiosity and increasing suspicion with which he yields to its effect is, in my mind, the best thing in the film. His ridiculous, athletically certain miming when he shouts 'Now we'll get a real home'; the parody of the suburban home; his determination to get back into jail . . . all these are blameless, and show his pantomime to be as swift, delicate, and inimitable as it has ever been and as it, presumably, always must be till the day he dies. Only in the rehearsing, the song, the fine gypsy impudence of the song itself, and once in the dope scene, does his pantomime leap away from a logical frame. But nowhere is there a moment of that absorbed insanity, that pure fantastic invention that came to him sometimes in a moment of grief and still recalls the 'Oceana Roll' in *The Gold Rush* – far and away the most beautiful comedy he has made and the only profound one, for it should be said with firmness and regret that *Modern Times* is never once on the plane of social satire.

After much thinking and rewriting, I see this piece sounds more grudging than it should. But though I had a personal reason for wanting and hoping this film to be a fine one, this criticism must stand. Yet under the streamlining of the production, there is the same incomparable figure, the neat, dancer's body, the minutely shifting patterns that make a nostril change delight to sarcasm, and a great gain in ribaldry and spryness. However saddened by the trappings, those strange visitors to our island could go home and truthfully write that this most famous man was last Tuesday, if not the funniest man, still the funniest clown alive.

¶ *Modern Times*. USA, 1936, Charles Chaplin Film Corporation; d. Charlie Chaplin. Charlie Chaplin, Paulette Goddard.

The song the European critics sang as they steamed in on 11 February was 'The Moon Shines Bright on Charlie Chaplin'. 'Mr Graves' is Robert Graves; his historical novels *I, Claudius* and *Claudius the God and His Wife Messalina* had just been published. Nervous of Chaplin's reaction, AC wrote to his *Listener* magazine contact, Miss Playle, two days before the review appeared in print: 'I've just seen the film again with an audience and feel I should like to delete a sentence or two where I think I've overstated my case. If nothing can be done, all right.'

Mr Wells Sees Us Through

The Cinema, BBC, 2 March 1936

To put a Frenchman and an American together in real life may mean a fight. But putting them together on English soil and having a Hungarian as a go-between seems to be a perfect set-up for a good British film. It worked pretty well with *The Ghost Goes West*. It has worked again with *Things to Come*, as visually exciting a film as ever came out of a British or any other studio. For this epic, the combatants merely changed corners while Mr Korda (Alexander, that is) again acted as promoter and referee. This time the American, William Cameron Menzies, is the director; the Frenchman, Georges Périnal, is the cameraman; and another Hungarian, Vincent Korda, came to from a bout of inspired nightmares and designed the sets. Mr H. G. Wells wrote the story and script, and we might have been able to forgive and forget if the piece were not already being tipped for the prize exhibit in a career of prophecy.

It travels the grim years between 1940 and 2036 in everything, it should be said, but its dialogue and psychology. Not since that woeful effort *The Dictator* has there been dialogue in the movies that would have sounded so commanding on the stage of Drury Lane some time, say, around the 1880s. However clean and tidy they made the world to live in, these Cabals and Passworthys were still talking in 1970 and 2030 like *If* and last winter's golf club dinner. The acting doesn't help at all, being performed by three actors who on the stage have grace and power and possibly even delicacy, but who here look and move like the latest additions to Madame Tussaud's. Perhaps the theme overawed them. Perhaps, but whenever there was some undertone of feeling to express, their faces did not show it, the camera had to crouch away and let them fling up an arm. Raymond Massey, Sir

Cedric Hardwicke and even Ralph Richardson should not misuse their powers in films until they can forget all about their golden voices and learn that the film microphone will take kindly to tiny inflections of humour (cf. W. C. Fields), pathos (cf. Zasu Pitts) and commentary (cf. Popeye); that the movie camera will not overlook infinite subtlety of facial play (*vide* Chaplin, Aline MacMahon, Jean Gabin, Victor McLaglen, Myrna Loy, Claudette Colbert, Otto Tressler, Charles Butterworth, Raimu, Hepburn, Lionel Atwill, Raymond Walburn et al.). But the microphone hates being preached at, and the camera hates being glared at or flirted with. In this film there is hardly a glimpse of a 1936 face or talent. They are all back in 1900 with Lewis Waller and Ada Rehan. All except Margaretta Scott, who looks the image of Theda Bara even down to the vamping costume.

To have had the acting and dialogue sound like this year would have helped a lot, but it wouldn't have made the thing profound or even satisfactory as prophecy. To look like Greta Garbo or talk like Groucho Marx may be a part of glory, but they are also a part of our present lively Inferno, whether you look on them as Dante and Virgil or just as inhabitants along with the rest of us. Armageddon will hardly respect the difference. And though he would be a great man indeed who showed in human faces and behaviour the development of human psychology over the next hundred years, I'm afraid that unless the thing's attempted, unless we hear people using language and see them using gesture differently from us, it's no good telling us that we are in 2036: it's just a fancy-dress ball, here and now, at the RIBA. Even as propaganda, and that would be the most charitable view of this film, *Things to Come* is well meant but not very shrewd. For it leaves out humour, thereby offering a strong debating point to stupid people, who may not know that man can still be funny, though wrong for centuries.

If you haven't seen *Things to Come* and have listened so far, you're probably disgruntled. And if you have seen it, angry. For when a film has bad acting, dialogue, psychology, what has it? Luckily, even when it has all these, it still needs the things by virtue of which it becomes a film and not a play in three acts with two intervals to drown its sorrows in. In a film showing the death of a nation and its rebirth in a new age of sight and sound, the only people who must have imagination are the scene designer, the director and the cameraman. And the achievement of *Things to Come* is no more and certainly no less than the ingenious hours spent around little white models by William Menzies, Vincent Korda and Georges Périnal. Without tossing a penny, I should say that Vincent Korda is the hero of the piece. For he has to start designing in 1970. When it comes to considering what sort of rooms we shall be living in in forty years (mine's in oak, just six feet by three), your guess is as good as mine. But it could hardly be as good as Vincent Korda's. By a few imaginative strokes on his drawing board he has made the piece a lovely thing to look at. At the same time, with the same stroke, he has been guilty of a rousing act of insubordination. For his drawing board and his models, come to life in the film, dispose of an argument that wastes a lot of words and all of Sir Cedric Hardwicke's part. It is the gayest mockery of the whole piece that Mr Korda's sets relegate Mr Wells's dialectic to the last and not the next century. According to Mr Wells, in another hundred years, after the intervening holocaust, the relation of artist and scientist will still be at the stage it has now got to in our country in the sixth form of schools; it's that charming superstition which the nineteenth century still leaves us groping through – the idea of a scientist as a man brewing smells and destruction in a test-tube, and the artist as a long-haired youth with the first claim on beauty. Mr Korda's imagination has left this piece of ancient pottery in the gutter, but it's a pity that it tinkles there in the intervals of Mr Bliss's music. Mr Wells as applied scientist probably gave a lot of help with the detail of the sets. But Mr Wells as sociologist should surely have called in Mr Lewis Mumford, who would have told him, what Mr Korda's settings visibly demonstrate, that the artist as beauty specialist will be a vulgar survival; and that if the progress of technics does nothing else it will destroy the necessity for a protest against elaborate gadgets designed to simplify needless activities (there will be no need of vacuum cleaners when carpets are a dirty anachronism); that it will, in Mr Mumford's phrase, 'devaluate caste and purify aesthetics'.

Mr Wells's conception is as severe and serious as any he has made. As serious as, for example, *The Time Machine*. But no newer. Not only in dialectic does Mr Wells's conception falter. But also in the detail of applied design. Of course, it's a thankless job being a prophet, for the more brilliant you are, the sooner somebody will take your hint and make your foresight look, in retrospect, like myopia. It must be heartbreaking for Mr Wells to be told that the costumes he predicted they'd be wearing in 2030 are to be the very thing in beachwear this summer. But there is a category of less inevitable error: the aeroplanes drone away from exhaust trouble just like the dear old *Hindenburg* of 1936 (remember?); the chairs are any modern chair done in glass; they have glass elevators, but the point is – they still have elevators. By abundance of such basic details, *Things to Come* shares with most Utopias the primary error of making today the premise, of pretending that new civilizations do not differ in kind but only in the degree of decoration, luxury, leisure and so on. I wouldn't have minded being asked to swallow a civilization in which the main idea of living was to stand on your head or worship domestic animals, anything so long as the idealism of Mayfair and Beverly Hills, 1936, was not going on as the regular thing in the next century. They might have spoken some new language – say Basic done in American with a sprinkling of Chinese, which is what they are as likely to talk as anything else, if they still have roofs to their mouths after that final air-raid. But anything rather than 'How frightful!' and 'My God, why must we murder each other!' But no. After the most accomplished, the most pestilential clean-up in history, the new civilization offers a trim-looking girl from Roedean, pretty but still straight from Roedean, asking Daddy's permission to go off with the good-looking juvenile, not for a weekend in Devon, to be sure, but I expect there's nothing against necking in a space-gun.

There is this to say, that if you can bear to think of the future as another hundred years of prosperity, without rebirth, revolution or misgiving, then M. Périnal and Mr Korda will make you think you've been there. When the lights go up and you look around everybody looks as dowdy and fussy as may be. And when you get outside the theatre, London is back in the Middle Ages.

They may say that they were only making entertainment, always a useful get-out for the movies when a pretentious undertaking turns out badly. But I hope for their sakes this wrangle has shown that almost for the first time in the movies a film of a sort has been made out of a social experiment. If this idea of the future rates less as a prophecy than as a materialist's dream of paradise, well, there will be time for others. Unless the coming peace overwhelms us before 1940. Perhaps, while there's still time, J. A. Hobson, Gerald Heard, Harold Laski and the Webbs in our country will now be invited to come into a world that sadly needs them, the world of the cinema. And let us hope that Mr Mumford will be brought from America to work on a more ambitious film with M. Périnal. Maybe that would be the best of all. If they can get Alexander Korda to act as referee, the first British masterpiece is practically assured.

¶ *Things to Come*. UK, 1936, London Films; d. William Cameron Menzies. Raymond Massey, Cedric Hardwicke, Ralph Richardson, Margaretta Scott.

Despite AC's engaging suggestion, British cinema never employed the talents of the science and technology historian Lewis Mumford, the historian-philosopher Heard, or economists Hobson, Laski and Sidney and Beatrice Webb. But Mumford, author of *Technics and Civilization* and *The Culture of Cities*, did provide the commentary for Pare Lorentz's American documentary *The City* (1939). Périnal continued to work on Alexander Korda productions until the mid-1950s.

Journalism on the Screen

The Cinema, BBC, 16 March 1936

The best film that has come our way this week, just about the best film that has come out of a British studio, is a short showing at the Carlton. It is called *Night Mail*, made by Basil Wright, produced – need I say – by John Grierson. It is not meant to illustrate a textbook on the railways of England. It is not a magazine article on 'How Do You Get Your Letters?', though under that title it might well be a documentary article in *Fortune*. Mr Grierson, I hope, is not in the least interested in softening the shock of knowledge when it is being given to people who have left school and who therefore feel that any information about the way the world works is an insult to what they fondly call their education. *Night Mail* is a fine piece of journalism, though I think that word hurts Mr Grierson more than it hurts me. It writes a documentary piece with a keen and literate eye for the incident or the process that is being described. It is an eye-witness account by a witness fortified with careful research. It sees the immediate fact as a part of continuous history. It does not assume that its audience carries in its head a complete knowledge of the previous history of the railways. It starts from the beginning ... it starts from a train leaving London and describes with the incisive eye of Wright's camera where the train stops, why, what it does, who are the human beings behind a daily process, a mere mechanical incident of His Majesty's mails.

Wright, the director, handles a camera with a lovelier dramatic movement than anybody in cinema. Its light values are therefore perfect. To anybody with an eye for patterns, to anybody who loves trains, to anybody who is excited by twilight, by human beings being sarcastic, by a filing system, by a cup of tea – this film is compulsory.

To anybody who loves to see the night fall over the English countryside it will be a joy, but never the sentimental joy they might want it to be. Grierson's train is there, sweeping through your tender musings, making the hills and valleys a grand background for a roaring train instead of a background to sentimental longing. Some of the commentary is sticky, especially at the beginning, but the verse supplied by W. H. Auden seems to me a complete success though difficult to follow against a high background. There are quibbles here and there. But *Night Mail* has one positive quality that is in everything Grierson touches. It never goes soft on you.

¶ *Night Mail*. UK, 1936, GPO Film Unit; d. Basil Wright, Harry Watt.

Magnificent Obsessions

The Cinema, BBC, 30 March 1936

There are good films, and there are bad films, and there are films that haunt . . . or impinge. This third group is outside the realm of judgement, or even of sense. They come, have their being, and go. But you haven't lost them. You wake up in the middle of the night and think of them. You see a man swallowing something in a café . . . nothing suspicious, just beefsteak or tea . . . and the motion of his Adam's apple reminds you of the agonies another hero suffered. Or a band in the park plays a tune and you are back wondering how Norma Shearer's getting along. Me, I now refuse to go down into a vault, even into the vault of the Bank of England, because twenty years or more ago I once saw a film called *Vendetta*, which opened with the burial of the hero, which meant – if only I had known anything about pictures in those days – that in order for the movie to go on at all he would somehow have to come back to life. Which he did. I have been, as far as vaults are concerned, a rag ever since.

You will gather by this time that I have been recently shaken by another such phantom. Its name is – I should have been warned – *Magnificent Obsession*. It tells how a great doctor dies because the lung machine that would save him is being used, it happens, on a good-looking ne'er-do-well. It settles down luxuriously – it knows it has two hours to run – to tell you how the young drunkard made impudent love to the doctor's widow, how he caused an accident which blinded her for life. How he then received a strange message from Ralph Morgan, how he resolved to become a great doctor himself. He goes off to Europe, and when his boat steams into New York six years later he has casually picked up the Nobel Prize for medicine, but has lost his widow. The story at this point – it being only

10.30 p.m. – takes a deep breath and tells how he went about finding her, how he operated and how – well, you may have guessed that this is no mystery story. And your final guess is bound to be right.

I don't know what sort of mark this film ought to have. The audience wept itself silly and stockbrokers staggered from the Regal breathing aloud that it was a beautiful film. I suspect that it is monstrous hooey. But I don't know. I know only that it is the all-talking, all-suffering masterpiece of the year. I know that the same feelings from people in real life would do everybody enormous credit; that the same problem in real life couldn't fail to move everybody but a hard-boiled surgeon and a beard from one of those squares near the British Museum. But on the screen it's a nightmare.

It is acted touchingly by everybody. I felt sorrier for little Charles Butterworth than for anybody else, because the other people's major crises pale before the sheer tragic pathos of Butterworth finding himself in a sewer. 'I think I've fallen in someone's grave.' 'No, you're in a sewer.' 'What again?' he says. Irene Dunne is poignant and noble and everything she should be. But as far as I'm concerned she's the Little Nell of the twentieth century. Robert Taylor, the playboy with a Nobel Prize, is ridiculously good-looking. He's Valentino, Gary Cooper and Fred MacMurray rolled into one. And I miss my guess if within two years he is not the idol of two continents. He may be Valentino to you, but he's Dracula to me. And he and Little Nell are going to give some of us many terrible nights.

¶ *Magnificent Obsession*. USA, 1936, Universal; d. John M. Stahl. Irene Dunne, Robert Taylor, Betty Furness, Charles Butterworth.

Thinking about the Boer War

The Cinema, BBC, 30 March 1936

There came on us last week, with rather less than the usual sounding of trumpets, a piece that will be increasingly respectable to look back on. I suspect, and hope, that when *Cavalcade* and *Sanders of the River* seem more and more swollen with dropsical pride, there will be *Rhodes of Africa* to chalk up for dignity. It is not merely the first British historical film that is decent and sensible to see and think about. It is the only one which moves at the slower tempo of our living and thinking, and makes of that slowness a positive quality and not a long-winded inability to keep up with the plot. We have previously tried to imitate the French literary detail, which we cannot act casually enough; or the American economy and dry speed. But these do not come naturally, and only add a fussiness and smart-aleckry we were trying to eliminate. *Rhodes of Africa* respects the psychology of its people accurately enough even to set a different tempo and a different mood for all the scenes with Kruger and his wife. Down at the Cape, Cecil Rhodes may be slipping quietly through doors, signing agreements, making committees enlarge their stock, raising an occasional fist and thumping it to declare that the country is going on and on and up and up. But Kruger sits motionless with the sun on the wall, surrounded by his wife, a piece of bread, a cup of coffee and an interior that might be any hack work by Vermeer or Delft. I have rarely seen the simple life represented so unapologetically on the screen. I can imagine Mr von Sternberg making Kruger's frugality epically, grandly simple, giving him a pipe shaped like a mermaid, a piece of bread ten inches thick, his coffee served in a great stone pitcher. But Mr Berthold Viertel lets him sit there, keeps the household intimate without ever becoming snuggling and folksy, and when

Kruger says, 'Momma, some coffee for Mr Rhodes,' the crashing masonry of *The Last Days of Pompeii* can show no greater change of heart or history. This film may not get better the more you see it. I don't know. But it certainly gets better the more you think about it. It manages to keep the balance pretty fairly between both sides. Not as fairly, perhaps, as Time or Providence will, but pretty evenly considering we were one of the heavyweights in the ring. The progress of the story – and that means the advancing of an argument, since this is a story of empire building – is done so gravely and modestly that the only drawback is – it makes you forget that the Boer War was just another attack of pirate measles our century must cure or die with.

¶ *Rhodes of Africa.* UK, 1936, Gaumont-British; d. Berthold Viertel. Walter Huston, Oscar Homolka, Basil Sydney, Peggy Ashcroft.

The Last Journey

The Cinema, BBC, 30 March 1936

A train driver crazed with suspicions about his wife's faithfulness refuses to stop his train at any of the suburban stations. That's all. The train characters are all the provincial leftovers from *Rome Express*, *Shanghai Express*, and all the other grand hotels on wheels. And they don't matter at all. What does matter is the careful building of the tension, the excellent editing – which may sound a very routine sort of compliment but is the only reason you feel the excitement you do feel. What matters even more is that you see a real train for thirty minutes dashing madly and unmistakably through English railway stations. It would be merely tired to call this excellent photography. It is a dozen suburbs of England caught in a moment of rest and pinned flutteringly to a screen. The same swift but simple problem has to be told with enough variety and urgency to keep you on the edge of your seat. And it is perfectly done. The train rockets through waiting porters, sweeps aside whole villages, and the detail is true enough to make this a modest but authentic regional film. We get very few of them in our country. Only Norman Walker of our directors, and once Maurice Elvey, seem to know that there is in every town in Britain a certain good film. *The Last Journey* is no more than a sentimental thriller. But its countryside is recognizable, its train is the one you took this morning, and the stations were not made in Elstree. It's a small beginning, but it is one.

¶ *The Last Journey*. UK, 1935, Twickenham Film Studios; d. Bernard Vorhaus. Hugh Williams, Godfrey Tearle, Judy Gunn, Julien Mitchell.
   AC passes over the irony that this 'authentic regional film' was directed by an American, the talented Bernard Vorhaus.

Lubitsch Times Two

The Cinema, BBC, 30 March 1936

Hands Across the Table is the first film to be supervised by Ernst Lubitsch, now that he has retired from directing his own films. There's hardly any point in telling you what it's about. It's one of those films that, thought about later, give you the nasty shock of realizing not merely that you've seen the story somewhere before, but that you see it every other time you go to the movies. So it's the direction, by Mitchell Leisen, that matters. And the acting of Fred MacMurray and a new Carole Lombard – madly, gaily, taking her place beside Claudette Colbert as one of the best kidders in the movies. It's very fine with me that Miss Lombard has stopped snubbing George Raft in her hard, disdainful way and is now delighted to count her pennies with Fred MacMurray and play practical jokes on the telephone exchange. She has grace and to spare, whatever she does. And she can throw off that flip, knowing dialogue better than most, not because she has a ready tongue but because she has a wicked eye. *Hands Across the Table* only once trips up, when it takes sentimentally a situation it has taken crazily and charmingly. Mr Lubitsch isn't all over this film, but it has his tautness, his spare and easy way of slipping from one sequence to the next without ever being missed. If you can't like *Hands Across the Table*, there is one whole chapter of the movies that you cannot appreciate. For this film follows on from *It Happened One Night*, *Strictly Confidential*, *The Thin Man*, *She Married Her Boss*: it's the kind of comedy, brisk and natural at the same time, which still remains the most dependable thing we get from American cinema.

Then on Friday there came another, charming film over which Mr Lubitsch had waved his magic wand. It has the unlikely title of *Desire*. If I tell you that Marlene Dietrich is its reigning goddess, some of you will switch off in the firm belief that here is the old fatal woman in another fatal film. You will be wrong. Whoever gave the film its title is just an old joker, that's all.

Mr Lubitsch earns our gratitude by sweeping Frank Borzage, the director, away into his magic box and taking complete charge of the film. There never was a Lubitsch film like this since *Trouble in Paradise*. It's good to see Mr Lubitsch has forgotten all about musicals, and plots that have to mean something to the box-office in terms of life and love. It's disturbing, though, to reflect that the material of his films is suspiciously like the material of Noël Coward. The passionate build-up to a trivial line . . . a warm embrace which is to end with the heroine asking the hero who makes his suits, or has he taken his orange juice for breakfast. But the happy difference is in this film – I hate to say 'in *Desire*' – it's being done by people who enjoy saying these lines, but don't think themselves particularly bright or modish for thinking them up. There's a scene at a breakfast table, with Marlene Dietrich and Gary Cooper – yes, the old rangy cowboy from Montana – deliriously in love. Mr Cooper looks anxiously across the table. Says he, with some feeling, 'Countess, may I ask you a very personal question?' The Dietrich, lovely and brave, all her defences down, swoons a willingness to tell all. 'Are you,' says Mr Cooper shyly, 'going to eat those eggs?' The point and humour of the thing is – it's done by a man who never meant to be funny, by a man with a genuine boyish charm, and not by an old smoothie from Bond Street.

There are dozens – literally – of scenes that end with the famous Lubitsch fade, that inimitable knowing drop of an eyelid. Mr Lubitsch must be more grateful than any man alive for the fade-out. It's always the moment when soft sentiment quietly fizzles out in contact with a witty line. Then there's that pretty metaphor when Cooper is being dangerously warned that he had better not meddle with Mr Lubitsch's suave crooks. 'What do you think America's attitude will be in case of war?' asks a rogue of an old lady at the table. 'Well, we'd like to mind our own business,' says Mr Cooper, 'but we get kind of dragged into things.' 'I think,' says the old lady, 'America should not meddle in European affairs.' 'After all,' says his crooked Highness with some point, 'America is a big country.' And Mr Cooper leans across the country and says magnificently, 'Six foot three!'

There are a few painful moments. But they count as nothing beside the whiff of spring that is Mr Lubitsch back in true form after three years' dark convalescence. And anybody who feels he would rather smell the whiff of spring for himself could not ask for a better substitute for it than long motor rides through the brilliant sun, the gracious trees, the smooth mountains of Southern California – which is here called Spain – to make you more certain of yourself when you exclaim aloud, as many people do, what a lovely country it must be.

¶ *Hands Across the Table*. USA, 1935, Paramount; d. Mitchell Leisen. Carole Lombard, Fred MacMurray, Ralph Bellamy.
Desire. USA, 1936, Paramount; d. Frank Borzage. Gary Cooper, Marlene Dietrich, John Halliday, William Frawley.

Requiem for the Amenities

The Cinema, BBC, 27 April 1936

You remember how in the old days, in the Stone Age of the movies, a boy used to come round just when William S. Hart had missed the last covered wagon, and used to pump perfume into the air. It was a nasty smell, but it was a pleasant sound.

This week a lot of people are going to be wishing that boy could be found to give us back our anaesthetics; or that the old pianist, who used to stagger five times through the *1812 Overture*, could restage his old performance, or go into the wrong piece, or do something to take our minds off the happenings on the screen. I hope this isn't a cynical view of the movies. There was a time when the amenities were half the fun, and it would have been as puritanical to judge the cinema by the films you saw as it is to judge a cricket game merely from what seems to be going on over the cucumber sandwiches in the tea room. But the cinema doesn't have amenities any more. You no longer go into a bare room and have a screen clatter down before your eyes, and have the lights click out one by one. In those days you really knew you were going to see something that hadn't the slightest connection with the way you lived outside the theatre. Nowadays, the trick is to make you believe that you haven't gone into a theatre at all.

If it's *Bengal Lancers* that's showing, it's a Bengal Lancer standing at the entrance telling you to pay your money to the siren with the veil and silk trousers. And Arab girls – at least they're wearing bedsheets – deposit you as safely as may be into your seat, while Oriental curtains (Arabia is in the Orient, isn't it?) silently part, and the picture itself sneaks stealthily on to the screen. The movie people know by this time how much we besotted film fans hate to try out a new experience ... how we would resist a gesture as radical, say, as having to turn over the pages of a book in order to read it. If the present trend goes on, they'll soon be sending us motor cars to fetch us to the theatre. I suppose the Hollywood millennium will have arrived when somehow they can link up their public world of dreams with your own private dreamland without any break at all, when screens and projectors will creep into your bedroom during the night, and you will waken into the arms of Greta Garbo, so to speak, painlessly from your pillow. I think I'm an average sensual man, but I can wait.

It was a fine thing that the North London Film Institute did last week. They put on a performance of old films, which I grant has been done before. But one of those films was called *The Cure*, and it was shown without the accompaniment of any soundtrack, any orchestra, commentary, without even a gramophone record. I went in while this was going on, and it was so quiet you could have heard Joan Crawford's eyelashes drop. The laughter – it was a Chaplin comedy of 1917, but there was laughter – was the most civilized sound I have heard in months. And in these bullying days it was a good sound. No big drums banged on the joke, no fiddles caressed a moment of tenderness. You missed the point or you saw it, and on your own account lifted your hat to it. It was a grave little ceremony, and I hope the North London Film Institute will give us more of them. If only as a change from clenching our knuckles and saying, surrounded by winning music and attendants in costume, 'I will not give in.'

Ah, Wilderness!

The Cinema, BBC, 27 April 1936

Ah, Wilderness!, about as charming a film as we've had this year, is the screen adaptation of Eugene O'Neill's play, set in the Connecticut of thirty years ago. We have to go a long way back to find a film directed by Clarence Brown which does not sooner or later go heady with prosperity. Anybody who recalls that opening tracking shot of *Anna Karenina* will look warily at any film that bears his signature. I still recall the nightmare which Mr Brown's camera took in as it receded from a portrait at the head of the dining table . . . turkeys and bowls of caviar, lobsters and grapes, pomegranates and goblets . . . in an aching, endless procession which gave you the impression that the cameraman had left the theatre long ago and was backing away somewhere towards Notting Hill Gate. Well, Mr Brown is still the same man, but the morning after. He was given the first literate script in months, possibly the best script he has ever had. And it must be O'Neill's script and the tender authenticity of his dialogue that give the film undeniable distinction. Yet in retrospect Brown is never mawkish, is more than ingenious in the graduation scene, is neat and economical with the big scene of the play, a dinner table conversation that might have grown woolly in the screen version. And the acting of, especially, Eric Linden and Lionel Barrymore saves Wallace Beery from the woeful emphasis he receives from being in the film at all – or even from the shock *we* receive at finding him within bellowing distance of Connecticut.

¶ *Ah, Wilderness!* USA, 1935, MGM; d. Clarence Brown. Wallace Beery, Lionel Barrymore, Aline MacMahon, Eric Linden, Mickey Rooney.

Maytime in Carlisle

The Cinema, BBC, 11 May 1936

There is a popular superstition that at the first sign of cherry blossoms we all rush off for our tennis racquets and the movie people go into bankruptcy. Dr Rowson's recently compiled figures show, on the contrary, that nearly as many people see movies in August as see them in November. May is, however, a low month, and I wish that this May could be lower still. Because anybody in the provinces in the next two weeks would be better off as a ball-boy on the local tennis court than in almost any movie house. There are an awful lot of movies released in the next fortnight and all you can say of most of them is, they are an awful lot. If you happen to live south of the River Thames there is still Mr O'Neill's tender and authentic piece about Connecticut thirty years ago. But I don't suppose that's any consolation to a man who lives in Aberdeen.

What then, if you are, say, a schoolmaster in Carlisle, are you going to do about a rainy evening in the coming two weeks, supposing that all the chemistry papers are marked and the dog is in? Well, *The Goose and the Gander* may be recommended to admirers of Kay Francis, George Brent and those interested in the lighter side of divorce. Those interested, on the other hand, in the lighter side of Josef von Sternberg may get a lot of unexpected pleasure from *Crime and Punishment*.

To indicate the kind of shock you are likely to feel, let me first remind you of Mr von Sternberg's characteristics. In *The Blue Angel*, he managed to clamp a grotesque mask on the face of a fine actor at the moment of his final pathos, and the gesture made that film into the cinema's most successful treatment of the old Punchinello theme. Since then Mr von Sternberg has meditated more and more painfully

1. Alistair Cooke, aged just 24, with his new 8mm camera in 1933, the year he was to film his new friends Charlie Chaplin and Paulette Goddard.

2. 'He will spend ten minutes trying to impress you with the grotesqueness of his heroine's surroundings.' Marlene Dietrich in Josef von Sternberg's *The Scarlet Empress*.

3. 'Tenderness is a prickly word, but it's nothing short of tenderness that has happened to the Garbo.' Greta Garbo with Freddie Bartholomew in *Anna Karenina*.

4. 'Hepburn's most difficult, best role.' Katharine Hepburn with Fred MacMurray in *Alice Adams* – 'the best of those embarrassing movies whose pathos is founded on the girl's family using the wrong fork'.

5. 'After Hollywood has tricked out its sirens with the last secret of sex-appeal, along comes a plain girl in a woollen sweater . . .' Geraldine Fitzgerald with J. Fisher White in *Turn of the Tide*.

6. 'My lords, ladies and gentlemen, I give you Robert Donat.' *The Count of Monte Cristo.*

7. 'Like the greatest of all Walt Disney's creations, who somehow escaped from an inkwell and is celebrating his freedom by dancing.' Fred Astaire with Ginger Rogers in *Swing Time*.

8. 'Under the streamlining of the production, there is the same incomparable figure, the neat, dancer's body, the minutely shifting patterns.' Charlie Chaplin in *Modern Times*.

9. 'The naked, whiskerless face of Ronald Colman . . . it's the first time we've seen it.' *A Tale of Two Cities.*

10. 'A school speech-day copy of the text, bound in morocco with a beautiful silk bow.' Leslie Howard and Norma Shearer in *Romeo and Juliet*.

on the grotesque, and by sticking mountain gnomes on the pendulums of clocks and carving dragons on to the backs of chairs has tried to make *What the Butler Saw* look like Ibsen. In his treatment of the story, Mr von Sternberg has been anxious to suggest what might be called the cosmic overtone: he wanted you to feel that his chosen incident wasn't merely happening to a soldier in Madrid with a night off, but was happening to the whole of life. His sentiments are admirable. The only trouble is, he's not Goethe or Shakespeare. His last and worst film, *The Devil Is a Woman*, was photographed wholly through the now famous Sternberg veil of tears; every sort of tricky hat, costume, screen, balloon, half-light, was used to make you believe that it wasn't a sixpenny novel you were reading after all.

To prolong the masquerade, somebody built a legend about Sternberg the Artist. This pictured him, through various stages of his career, as a garret-stricken genius, then a simple man who was touched by the beauty of seagulls at San Diego but could touch none of the more coarsened film producers for the money to put this vision on the screen. He was soon striding around in thought, having his picture taken in fancy bows, and when Marlene Dietrich arrived in Hollywood gave time and much care to seeing that she should embody for all time the Fatal Woman. To watch von Sternberg moving into action, cloak and all, to direct another epic must have been a terrible sight at the best of times. And you hardly can be blamed if you expect Dostoevsky to provide the most arty opus in the Sternberg canon.

But you will be wrong. Mr Sternberg must have been hurt or moved very hard since we last heard from him. And the shock of *Crime and Punishment* is no less than the shock of discovering beneath the Sternberg coloured – the Sternberg plain. And it's a likeable and occasionally perceptive director. The story of the brilliant student of criminology who leaves the university with no money and wants some seems a perfect set-up for Sternberg melodrama. But Peter Lorre is treated as just this particular student. Sternberg's attention to detail used to be that which could readily be imagined in a state of trance. But he has now abandoned this for a state of concentration. It's not remarkably better in quality, but it's less boring. In fact, I'm afraid that Sternberg plain is not more profound than the old one. But he has at least started again with a good enough melodrama, which sticks to the cinema's job of telling the detail of particular acts and facts without generalizing away passion, fidelity, repentance, the wages of sin or any other of the mumbo-jumbo that trailers promise you for the next presentation. If this isn't a new beginning for von Sternberg, at least it's a new sort of end.

¶ *The Goose and the Gander*. USA, 1935, Warner Bros.; d. Alfred E. Green. Kay Francis, George Brent, Genevieve Tobin.
Crime and Punishment. USA, 1935, Columbia; d. Josef von Sternberg. Peter Lorre, Edward Arnold, Marian Marsh.

The seagull film was *A Woman of the Sea* (1926), unreleased. Simon Rowson was a British film exhibitor and industry statistician.

The Missing Face

The Cinema, BBC, 11 May 1936

The best thing about *A Tale of Two Cities* is the naked, whiskerless face of Ronald Colman ... it's the first time we've seen it and it has fine eyes, a long humorous upper lip, and a tautness and intelligence you would never have suspected from the evidence of that moustache and those sideburns. There's not much else to praise. In the midst of preposterous aristocrats and absurd peasants, I found myself, when I saw the film, coming back to meditations about that face ... and other faces. It may have been because earlier in the day I had just seen again a Russian classic, *Potemkin*.

As I watched the heads being cut off that evening I couldn't help thinking that Hollywood has here given us a sadly truthful symbol of what may happen to our movies in the day of social rebirth. Of what in fact has already happened to the movies once in their history. Before the sharp knife falls on, heaven help us, Ronald Colman's neck, you don't see his face any more, you only hear a voice whispering intensely on the soundtrack those celebrated words from the Christmas almanacs about doing a better thing.

Until the Russians started to make movies most of us thought of a silver screen as just about the right size for two heads. Without much effort we learned to know the state of Ben Turpin's eyesight, we got to know the number of Mary Pickford's curls without even counting, our heart beat a little faster at the sight of Alma Taylor's nearly perfect mouth. The Russians must have known this was a bad thing. And because, I suppose, the face is the most bourgeois member of the body, they cut it off. We could no longer warm to a picture at the way the heroine winked. Because Russian heroines, if I remember rightly, don't have faces to wink with. I'm not saying this hasn't been a very fine thing. I would gladly sacrifice all the Wheelers and Woolseys and Laurels and Hardys in the world if Eisenstein wants to show me the flexing of somebody's bicep, the gleam of a Russian shoulder blade. But even a Russian ankle is no compensation for Myrna Loy, for her face, I mean, and the other evening I would gladly have swapped a dozen of MGM's tramping feet for a few more glimpses of Ronald Colman. Me, I like faces, and I've never been able to work out why it's fine and fancy for a novelist to describe the effect of a piece of dialogue on somebody's face and why it's vulgar for the movies to show it to you.

The latest news from Russia is that a halt is being called on the Soviet epic. They feel that we know by this time whereabouts they stand, and that the new regime can be better advertised for some time to come by light pieces showing what a joyous, rib-tickling affair life has become in the USSR. I wish I could believe that the Russians embarked on this new age in cinema with a merry heart and a twinkling eye. Or even that they are doing it from shrewd motives of policy. But I suspect that the Western world was tiring of all those limbs and bodies, acting though they were from the most noble ideals. And that the patrons of foreign cinemas, debauched as we are, got rather more pleasure and interest simply from watching the faces of the minor characters in the commercial, and probably quite grossly inspired, works of Hollywood and Elstree. Whatever your political opinions may be, it takes an awful lot of Russian sinew to make up for losing W. C. Fields's face. And though it seems to me he would be a madman who needed to think twice about the social honesty of the world of Hollywood or the world of Moscow, I hope the Russians' new move is done for purely business reasons. Then we can go back to our faces without feeling we've turned our back on a great experiment. We're still here, Russia, when you want us, but we want to know what your women look like and whether you have anything to offer in exchange for the Garbo's mouth, Lee Tracy's hands, and the cheekbones of Katharine Hepburn.

¶ *A Tale of Two Cities*. USA, 1935, MGM; d. Jack Conway. Ronald Colman, Elizabeth Allan, Edna May Oliver, Reginald Owen, Basil Rathbone.

In Praise of Shirley Temple

The Cinema, BBC, 8 June 1936

In London for the past fortnight there have been crowded houses at the theatre showing a star who earns more money for the box-office than any film star alive. I realized with some guilt that her name has never, so far as I can remember, been mentioned in these notes. For the simple, and equally guilty, reason that I had never seen her. When I sneaked off to see her the other day, in *The Littlest Rebel*, I expected to be embarrassed, and remained to cheer. The name is Shirley Temple. I went to see her not casually, but because I had just come across some facts which show her to be as a social phenomenon at least as important as Eisenstein, Hitler or the Dionne quintuplets.

She is just seven, has been in the business since 1932. Each succeeding picture she makes takes more and more money . . . she is never worth less, to the box-office, than a million dollars. Fifteen commercial firms are world sponsors for selling copies of her hats, shoes, coats, toys and books. She has been given endless civic honours in the United States, but it may be worth pondering that in our country, where we think twice about swearing loyalties, there are 165,000 children sworn to imitate her character and manners. All this may appal, disgust, amuse or dishearten you. Critics who have predicted for Lawrence of Arabia a positive effect on Western idealism, a group of disciples and possible canonization may think again and decide that for better or worse Shirley Temple will be the greater influence.

For perhaps the most disappointing item in the whole recital is that Shirley Temple is no spoiled precocious brat, nor even an ordinary funny child. Instead, she is something of a paragon of patience, unselfishness, horse sense and phenomenal talent. She has, like most children, a comic face which has no relation to beauty, but flirts in repose with the lighter side of ugliness. She is not coy or loud. She is merely a very good listener – a godsend to a film actor. She has a personal vivacity that makes Abraham Lincoln, in this film, seem a waxwork model of himself. And, what is even more depressing to listeners who had hoped for a cynical close to this commentary, she is absurdly sensible. I can see no way to climb up into a more lofty or amused attitude about this child. Her vast popularity may be founded in some stupid things, in much luscious thumping of many thousand hearts, but I suggest that it may too have some hard clues that no ridicule can wave away. The fact is that her alert health of spirit would assure any film company a star in a girl of any age. By some queer accident of birth, she has this gift twenty years too soon, and a lack of self-consciousness before a camera she could have at no other age.

¶ *The Littlest Rebel*. USA, 1935, Twentieth Century-Fox; d. David Butler. Shirley Temple, John Boles, Jack Holt, Bill Robinson.

AC's congenial response to Shirley Temple contrasted sharply with Graham Greene's attitude when reviewing *Wee Willie Winkie* a year later. The novelist's remarks about her supposed 'coquetry' led to a libel action mounted by Twentieth Century-Fox and a hefty fine of £3,500.

Fritz Lang + $8,000,000 = *Fury*

The Listener, 22 July 1936

When the exiled Fritz Lang arrived two years ago in Hollywood, it seemed unlikely that this morbid talent could take a permanent sun-tan. California is balm to the folksy virtues, and it was right that Will Rogers should be the sage of the Sunny State. lt was right, too, that when he died Irvin Cobb should take over those reassurances and keep alive the practical irony that the local dollar diplomacy encourages. But California is no place for de Maupassant. It will cure all sorts of things: a neurosis, precocity, the curious English snobbery against having a good body. But a million-dollar smile is no gain to literature. And the light of day that obliterated Feyder, Pommer, Freund and Pabst could be expected to drive Lang out of his psychological laboratory on to the cheerful thrills of a rollercoaster.

In those two years he must have put down his test-tube many times. But he went back, though the colony suspects black magic and said one time they couldn't pay for it. When Lang was finally assigned to this picture, a general gloom settled over the production. A production manager told him at the beginning, without any hope of convincing him, to remember the slogan 'Eight million dollars can't be wrong.' Lang pledged himself to this maxim, and has turned out a picture sociologically more profound, technically more competent, than any he made in the days when cardboard sets and a dozen extras were bound to be right.

The story so vividly resembles the San José lynching that Metro pointed the reminder by stating in an opening caption something to the effect that this was all going on in a mythical kingdom. Somehow, I kept thinking of the United States all the way through. Lang swears he thought of nothing but a story about a mob. 'Lynching happened to be the result,' he said. 'I've been through four revolutions and I've made an intimate study of how people act. They often start out in the best of spirits.' The studio officials, on the other hand, thought they were making a picture about a lynching. And they were scared. They must have winced while Norman Krasna was writing his fine script. And they warned odd people that hardly a foot of it would be likely to get shown. In the end, the picture was made. But Metro were unperturbed. They thought it mediocre, and considered running it as a second feature in a double-bill programme. *Wife vs. Secretary* they thought would take it nicely. Jean Harlow supported by Fritz Lang!

It is worth letting both parties stick to their stories. Somewhere between Lang's psychological absorption and Metro's disappointment over an unentertaining lynching, there slipped in the best film of this and maybe of any other coming year. What has happened in *Fury* is a crazy and blessed coincidence of two points of view, neither of which could alone make the movie half as good as it is. Lang wanted to see a mob behaving as accurately as he could make it. Metro sensibly knows that the movies are a business and not a crusade. So they together spawn a film of fundamental social significance, a social document that if it had been seen on paper first no censor would allow. And $8 million begins to tell nothing less than the truth.

It's superficial (and I think dead wrong) to think of Hollywood as a cynical check on brave artistic impulses. Hollywood puts out less nonsense than most art theatres. And in its ordinary product shows a sense of life that would galvanize any repertory theatre movement. But these are incidental artistic ideas. Hollywood's first notion is to sell a product. And *Fury* has made it important to see that that standard can have remarkable integrity. Whatever will sell is allowed. Our own industry is not so clear-minded. If this film had been about South Wales – about, say, a Chinese riot in Cardiff – I doubt if it would ever have seen the screen.

So *Fury* becomes, both as propaganda and entertainment, no dialectical protest against the immorality of lynching. Where *Fury* passes superbly beyond the apt melodrama of *Barbary Coast* and *Frisco Kid* and even *The Birth of a Nation* is in exhibiting (through Fritz Lang's direction) and diagnosing (through Krasna's dogging script) the kind of emotion that unites nice middle-class people in obscene hysteria. It fails to show the *sequence* of that emotion. And the real dénouement, the kinds of reaction that the lynchers feel between the fire and when they appear in court – this is not there. But *Fury* is a tremendous beginning. The end for the cinema will be in a Dostoevsky, who knows the tragedy of these emotions. Or in a fascism, which merely likes to feel them.

¶ *Fury*. USA, 1936, MGM; d. Fritz Lang. Spencer Tracy, Sylvia Sydney, Walter Abel, Bruce Cabot.

   On 26 November 1933 in San José, California, a mob dragged from jail, tortured and hanged two men on a murder charge, awaiting trial. The incident directly inspired Norman Krasna's script.

Hollywood through the Customs

The Listener, 12 August 1936

The banning of *The Green Pastures* in this country was bound to be automatic: the Lord Chamberlain, a legally constituted censor of plays, does not permit the representation of God. And the British Board of Film Censors, an arbitrary 'body' appointed by the trade, has apparently appropriated this simple and ruthless technicality for its own convenience. At least, that is what we must assume, until the Board will favour us with one educated reason why a noble and charming play should be summarily banned the moment it is accurately transferred – under the beloved supervision of its author – to the screen.

Presumably the most offensive note of the play was what simpler people took to be its moral peak – that moment when the archangel Gabriel lowers his trumpet and thunders, 'Gangway for the Lord God Jehovah!' And that is what, with apologies to the Lord Chamberlain, happens. Richard B. Harrison, who, after forty years' obscure elocution teaching, started his stage career at sixty-five with that tremendous entrance – he, the great original, is dead. And in the film version De Lawd is played by the negro Rex Ingram well enough to satisfy Marc Connelly, the author. But the fact that he plays the part at all is what allows this tolerated Board to deny to British filmgoers a charming religious idyll. Still, if it's any compensation, you'll soon be able to see Jean Harlow in *Suzy*.

It is not, however, with this particular absurdity that this talk is concerned so much as with the blunder that made it possible. The amnesia of some official in the foreign department of Warner Brothers recalls a much neglected chapter of cinema censorship. Most critical discussion of the topic focuses on the outlines of a workable code, on sexual ethics, on the position of the artist in society, and, in its more searching moments, tries to bring into some visible focus all the blurred images of the censor himself, an intangible Pooh-Bah who has been at various times, and may be again at any minute, the Home Office, the Board of Trade, the Roman Catholic Church, the Admiralty, the Sunderland Watch Committee, the county council, the local fire brigade, the Lord Chamberlain, the House of Commons, the shopkeepers of Beckenham, Sir Austen Chamberlain, the public conscience of Huddersfield and the Chief Constable of Cardiff. But Hollywood, most of whose virtues shine from that eye steadily turned on the box-office, has long learned that of the many ways of losing a fortune there is none sillier than to make and deliver a movie and then have it banned by a foreign country. And the record that disturbs Hollywood is not the memory of *The Sign of the Cross* or *Rain*, but the memory of losses on *Gabriel Over the White House* and *The President Vanishes*, both banned abroad on account of their fiery politics. Hollywood's dictator is no longer the tired businessman; it is every country's Foreign Office.

A typical Hollywood studio does an annual business in feature pictures alone of £10 million throughout the world. Half of this comes from abroad – first, about £3.5 million from the British Empire; then, in order, Central Europe, France and Italy. Hollywood had merely to introduce into the harmless *Dinky* an amusing Italian who couldn't understand a baseball game, and several thousand dollars were automatically thrown away, for the film was banned in Italy. Paramount took timely warning and deleted from *Give Us This Night* an Italian policeman who was knocked on the nose. But it is impossible to know, at any moment, what some foreign secretary may be thinking in a private theatre, and Hollywood has paid dearly for many a scarcely perceptible slip. Spain succeeded in having every print of *The Devil Is a Woman* destroyed, not on the excellent grounds that it was an appalling film, but because one scene showed an officer of the guard drinking with a commoner. A Greek society in Chicago appealed to its government against *Riffraff*, whose villain was seemingly a Greek. *The Thin Man*, an enviable money-maker in Western Europe, ran three days in Baghdad until its audience could no longer stand what to Oriental eyes was the outrageous detail of a dog sniffing for a corpse. And you may have thought you were seeing *The Informer* last year, but what you were seeing was *The Informer* less 129 deletions, which the United Kingdom insisted on.

Nowadays, Hollywood's scouts go out prospecting before they claim their revenue. Most studios have drawn up a list of international taboos. Experts know each nation's tenderest corn and have trained themselves to feel the wince with every change in the political weather. They are not likely to make another *Forty Days of Musa Dagh* after Turkey has once taken insult. Britain's stipulations for newsreels (made after disastrous deletions from an issue of *The March of Time*) are refreshingly precise. 'All references to Sir Basil Zaharoff, British firms, the International Rail Workers' Association and remarks by Mr Nye must be deleted. Also scenes of a gun made by a British firm and scenes of a cemetery.' Taking no risk of misinterpretation abroad, a government may insist not only that a film must be banned at home but that it must not be shown in America. MGM paid £50,000 for the rights of *It Can't Happen Here* and then began to count the countries that would almost certainly ban the finished film. They started with Germany and Italy, threw in England, gloomily added Japan, sighed at the thought of France, and finally abandoned the project, convinced that the film was certain to be barred from any country where 'it' could happen, which currently takes in most of our known geography.

Meanwhile, the latest antic of our own dear censor restores the balance of absurdity. A film called *The Devil Is a Sissy* will, on pain of banning, have its title changed, and the censor has demanded that the word 'sissy' shall be deleted throughout the soundtrack. 'Sissy' is a harmless American word, a popular diminutive for the now outworn phrase 'a weak sister'. It means a weakling, and would quite normally be used by a small girl of five to her younger brother. But the censor's mind has been busy with this word, and apparently reads into it a meaning which America wots not of. Hollywood indeed is the scapegoat of a cruel world when it has to suffer the displeasure that foreigners feel while misunderstanding its native tongue.

¶ *The Green Pastures*. USA, 1936, Warner Bros.; d. Marc Connelly, William Keighley. Rex Ingram, Oscar Polk, Eddie Anderson.

Following its English publication in 1934, MGM planned and aborted a film of Franz Werfel's novel *The Forty Days of Musa Dagh*, concerning the Armenian genocide in Turkey in 1915; the novel had already stirred Turkey's ire. *It Can't Happen Here*, based on Sinclair Lewis's cautionary novel about totalitarianism in America, was abandoned in February 1936.

Basil Zaharoff, a veteran arms dealer, had been filmed surreptitiously for an inflammatory item on munitions in the third issue of the *March of Time* newsreel (April 1935).

Technicolor Strikes Again

'Films of the Quarter', *Sight and Sound*,
Summer 1936

The Trail of the Lonesome Pine came on us like a seaside holiday, lots of lobster-like suntan and a spate of highly-coloured postcards. It was cunningly presented, the distributing company giving the clever impression that the thing was like the coronation and overwhelming to handle, but as far as I'm concerned it's far below the monochromes of the quarter. Sylvia Sidney may be feeling awfully well these days, but she's no more than in the pink of condition. I've seen her in Hyde Park, and I know. And I couldn't wish Fred Stone anything less than an infinite life. But he's sixty-five and even the San Bernardino Mountains posing as the Appalachians can't tone a man up like that. In spite of the spectrum, it was just another hillbilly, and deadly dull.

¶ *The Trail of the Lonesome Pine*. USA, 1936, Walter Wanger; d. Henry Hathaway. Sylvia Sidney, Henry Fonda, Fred MacMurray, Fred Stone, Beulah Bondi.

How to Understand the Marx Brothers

The Cinema, BBC, 25 August 1936

There is a conspiracy in Bloomsbury to make out that only a beard and a consumptive complexion will help you to understand the exquisite subtlety of the Marx Brothers. Well, I hold that the Marx Brothers are as subtle as my bicycle, but they move quicker. And anyway, as Groucho might say, I haven't got a bicycle. Many excellent and humorous people in this land have been put off these great comedians by the absurd highbrow tip-off that the Marx Brothers are unique, and that their humour is a strange and rare invention of their own and of the Surrealist ocean diver, Salvador Dalí. But Groucho's middle name is Bronx, not Dalí. And the Marx Brothers are no more, and certainly no less, than 3,000 American comedians brought to the boil and reduced to three.

Every American burlesque house sports a wretched bawdy fellow who is a potential Groucho; every vaudeville act a lunatic as deft and silent as Harpo; every immigrant quarter a hesitating Italian as charming and sly as Chico. I grant that nobody can keep a cigar straighter than Groucho. I'll also concede that Groucho's twisted a nation's Jewish humour into an endearing form of hypocrisy . . . or rather into a hypocritical contempt for hypocrisy. But these three madmen have nothing but common sense behind their eyes and foreheads. Now we always think of common sense as moving like W. G. Grace going into bat. The transatlantic habit is to think of its normal action being that of lightning, or a baseball.

If you can learn to watch the flight of it, there is nothing in *A Night at the Opera* that should baffle you at all. And for people who dislike opera, who dislike the whole convention of a murder being interrupted to allow a tenor to throw meditative notes off his chest – for these people the Marx Brothers' single and successful effort to smash up a performance at the Metropolitan is a godsend.

¶ *A Night at the Opera*. USA, 1935, MGM; d. Sam Wood. The Marx Brothers, Kitty Carlisle, Allan Jones.

On 1 July, enclosed in a deep-sea diving suit, the painter Dalí had attempted to deliver a lecture at the International Surrealist Exhibition in London. Near-suffocation and an emergency rescue by a poet with a spanner followed.

High Lights of Broadway

The Cinema, BBC, 11 October 1936

If I turn slightly to the left and look out of the window and down about seventy storeys or more, I can see laid out below me the orderly skeleton of this fish that the sea washed up – I mean Manhattan Island. And if you let your eye follow the illuminated bones of this fish, you will come on a patch of light rather brighter than the rest, that looks like a section of a lung under X-ray treatment; and this is Broadway. At the moment I can see a streak of red and yellow, saying *Dodsworth*; a white line panting out the news that *The General Died at Dawn*; there is another splatter of light announcing *Ramona* in Technicolor; there is *Nine Days a Queen*, Robert Stevenson's movie, which we called *Tudor Rose* – a movie as popular as all English costume films seem to be over here; and then there is *Swing Time*, the new Mickey Astaire and Minnie Rogers film; and separating the *Great Ziegfeld* from the *Girls' Dormitory* is a Catherine wheel that spells three words – *Romeo and Juliet*.

All this is very impressive at this distance, but as Tallulah Bankhead said of a very elaborate production of a very thin play, 'There's less in this than meets the eye'; for Broadway is only the shop window of the island's entertainment. Inside the shop there are some special lines that have to be brought from under the counter. It's as well that I should remind myself that the names I have just quoted are the names of the newest films, but if I had been asked what there was to see in New York in the way of movies, the first two recommendations that would have come to mind are Max Linder and a Chinese talkie.

On 42nd Street there is a Flea Circus, where for a nickel you can reclaim your youth; you can see John Bunny and Flora Finch and Max Linder performing their ancient antics through downpours of that pre-war rain. Nearer to the patch of lung we are working on, there are two Italian films; uptown a Spanish Music Hall with Spanish talkies; next door to a Yiddish theatre, a new and brilliant French comedy, *Carnival in Flanders*. Way downtown you might meet Mr Pond Wing, who gets films rushed straight from Hong Kong that have no English titles, so the censor has to see them with Mr Wing shouting himself hoarse translating in case there is a line an American might object to if only he understood. And then along the Bowery is another Chinese theatre. Possibly the most memorable experience of the week was the awful crisis in which the young heroine was rescued from the wheels of an oncoming train. That of course has happened before, but in this film the whole thing was very realistic, very harrowing, and the few pallid whites in the audience were quite unprepared for the rollicking guffaws that went up from the rest of the audience. But the fun I got out of a Chinese film called *Crazy Detectives* is an experience not likely to be repeated in London.

Which brings me back uptown to the Catherine wheel and *Romeo and Juliet*. I hope as I talk about Hollywood's latest Shakespearean effort that, whatever sounds are managing to swim into your loud-speaker, you don't detect a sneer. It became almost the automatic duty of every English film critic when *A Midsummer Night's Dream* was produced to damn the film in advance. I never did see why it should be so funny that Hollywood tackled Shakespeare. I've seen some funny productions of Shakespeare myself. The funniest was one of *As You Like It* by Beerbohm Tree, where one of the real sheep fell into a trombone. Compared with that, the present *Romeo and Juliet* is a miracle of taste and understatement; in fact it's so tasteful and understated that it almost manages to say nothing at all.

Mr Oliver Messel's work with Adrian on the costumes and settings is as careful and authentic as any Renaissance painter could wish posterity to thank him for. But that is not the only exquisite thing in this film. There is the dance in the Capulets' home, where Agnes DeMille has done a beautiful job. And there has gone into the actual performance, especially from Norma Shearer, much easy and beautiful speaking.

I was aware of these merits at the time, and when it was over picked up my hat as reverently as anybody else. But I could have jotted down notes in a diary without doing any of the actors or the director a disservice. I could have gone outside for a smoke and done nobody any harm, for when I came back the film would be biding its time, quietly building up to a crisis that never comes. Maybe that smoking restriction in American theatres has more to do with my feeling than I know. That still and crystal-clear atmosphere that you find in any American cinema does add to the impression of coldness. Here I felt I was assisting at a nice orderly funeral. Possibly, if you saw *Romeo and Juliet* in the ribald, friendly smoky fog of the Empire in Leicester Square, you would find the movie so dangerously warm-blooded that you'd feel that all John Barrymore's part should be cut out.

Running through the credit titles afterwards, I wondered who could be to blame. Not the author I think, whose original script I saw, and it is a good job. But all these people have done nobly by the film – the adapters, the musical arranger, the literary adviser. The music especially is charming when it doesn't offer you a formula of pathos for the actual pathos you might be getting from the lines themselves. We have to go back and look, I am afraid, at the first name – that of Mr George Cukor, the director.

Mr Cukor has directed some pretty irreproachable classics – I mean that they were classics before Mr Cukor got busy. He has been – 'responsible' I think is the word – for *Little Women*, that frosty Christmas card, and for *David Copperfield*; and there is no question 'reverent' is the word for Cukor. But in this delicate handling of great books, all the character and life goes out of them. Dickens, and now Shakespeare, are both trimmed of the exquisite, the intense, raw and often disgusting. *Romeo and Juliet* is a school speech-day copy of the text, bound in morocco with a beautiful silk bow and twenty charming woodcuts by the Messrs Adrian and Messel.

It is a terrible thing when a film critic longs for the stage performance of an adapted play. I wanted somebody to pull the camera back and let us see in the shape and postures of their bodies the tender agony of first love. Instead, you have close-ups of two faces speaking nice lines simply and carefully, and it so happens that neither Miss Shearer nor Mr Howard are at their best in close-up. Mr Howard's strangely weak, barely open mouth gives him the moment he looks ecstatic an almost terrifying appearance, as if he were ready to fall down in a fit, or whip out a clumsy knife; and Miss Shearer's hands, which are not her best feature, get constantly between the audience and her face. So *Romeo and Juliet* is another album of Mr Cukor's tasteful collection of family postcards. They are good postcards, carefully composed and affecting to look at for a little while; but he can never flick them fast or trickily enough to turn them into a moving picture.

¶ *Romeo and Juliet*. USA, 1936, MGM; d. George Cukor. Norma Shearer, Leslie Howard, John Barrymore, Basil Rathbone.

AC's talk was recorded from New York. 'Naturally no advance script,' a nervous BBC man cabled London beforehand. 'Has our friend Alistair ever been known to produce a script seven hours in advance, let alone seven days?'

Do We Want Fine Speaking?

The Cinema, BBC, 8 November 1936

One of the saddest conventions of our journalism is that of inviting a great chemist to say for publication what he thinks about Hitler, or of seizing a round-the-world aviator, the moment he catches his breath at Croydon, and asking him if he really thinks Proust was a snob. This complaint comes along at the height of the silly season for prophecy. A spruce, and I am sure a very competent, businessman (textiles) has just been consulted for his ideas about the aesthetics of colour film. And an admittedly great dramatist, who was yet learning to write dialogue when Irving was croaking soliloquies to the gas flares, has been telling us how such apprentices as William Powell and Claudette Colbert must learn to speak if they would succeed on the screen. 'We have not thought enough about these things,' he says, and I can only think he refers to himself. 'In spite of the popularity of the film, nobody to whom you talk ever talks about the voices or about wanting better voices, or understands anything about phonetics.' (Don't they indeed? Doesn't Mr Shaw own a wireless set?)

But surely 'wanting better voices' is the business of elocution schools and academies of dramatic art. It can hardly have much to do with phonetics, which is a science, and concerned with explaining sounds and voices as they are. As a movie critic, temperamentally appalled at the mincing and prating of the average stage actor, I have tried for a year or two, while the movies are on trial, to hold a watching brief for phonetics in the middle of a bombardment of fine diction from the prosecuting counsel. I can see that stage actors have to learn somehow to throw their voices high enough and clearly enough to be heard by most of the audiences. So I suppose there is an elementary excuse for schools of elocution in the theatre. But it rarely stops there.

Most actors transfer these tremendous sounds to their private lives, and when you ask them something like have they got a match or do they think it'll rain, they start to chime like Christmas morning. This trait doesn't often get talked about by actors themselves but only by their lay friends, who wonder what's come over them since they left school. I don't mind sitting through a clatter of fine consonants and what is called 'a distinguished performance' provided I can go home after the show without having to meet the man who gave it. But if it spreads to the movies, then it will be time for a Royal Commission.

I like to think that Fredric March and William Powell, if they walked in now, would be as tidy and unfussy and humorous as they are on the screen. The nicest thing about screen speaking is that, even if the plot is awful and the social conscience nowhere at all, nine film actors out of ten seem like pretty nice people to meet. They sound like people you might meet on the bus, or in a library, at a football match, or over a drink. But again, our great dramatist has the whole answer pat: 'We must remember that what you call "natural" speech is no use at all either on the stage or the screen . . . If anybody imagines that the dialogue in my plays is natural, they are making a fearful mistake. I write exactly like Shakespeare, and I find if only people will get the rhythm and melody of my speeches, I do not trouble myself as to whether they understand them, so to speak; once they get the rise and fall of them they are all right.' Naturally he doesn't trouble himself, he's drawing the royalties, while we are only the audience.

Happily the whole issue is blown up and pricked into thin air by the only general release of the month which is worth calling compulsory. It is W. C. Fields in *Poppy*. There's no plot to the whole thing, no rise and fall, no rhythm or melody, no anything but Fields. He wanders through small shops and circuses, public bars, children, sideshows, straw hats and nagging women with a bemused aloofness that makes him in this life but not of it. He's Bacchus dropped from the clouds and made to work in the corner grocer's. He has every decent human motive and would almost choose to act out an honest life, but around him he sees small-timers cheating each other all the way. That wouldn't distress him either if there was any style to their tricks. But people are so mean and clumsy he feels obliged to give them a lesson or two, an accomplished robbery here, a short bargain there, done with enough flourish to give the human game some dignity.

It was cruel that Mr Shaw, who writes exactly like Shakespeare, should be asking for 'better voices' on the week that Fields came along. For he stands as a convenient symbol of the war between stage and screen, between 'fine speaking' and ordinary day-to-day thinking aloud. He plays with two voices – a smooth, pompous, trained voice, and a mumbling bemused one. He uses the first, the overripe voice, for all his artifice, the public occasions when he is trying to swindle somebody or claim a family tree. But he is always caught out by the second voice. He may with a fine flourish of hand and elbow say: 'I have here, gentlemen, a very fine timepiece that cost $500, yes, sir, $500,' but you can hear him saying under his breath: 'You'll never get away with it.' It's Everyman's misgivings, second thoughts, fits, delayed humility. It's the common language of cockneys, French taxi-drivers, Texas cattlemen and all simple men permanently impressed by the irony of human dignity. It's a precious language that belongs more to the movies than to any other form of deception – the phonetic equivalent of a sense of fact. No, I will sit through the movies so long as the natural voice is accepted as the standard. When Gary Cooper gets busy with his diction, I shall take to a tricycle.

¶ *Poppy*. USA, 1936, Paramount; d. A. Edward Sutherland. W. C. Fields, Rochelle Hudson, Richard Cromwell.

AC was currently serving on the BBC's Advisory Committee on Spoken English; his first meeting, a year before, had adjudicated on the pronunciation of 'scone', 'hegemony' and 'tricolour', among other troublesome words. George Bernard Shaw was its chairman; his comments on talkie speech had been published in the November issue of *World Film News*.

Help! Murder!

The Cinema, BBC, 6 December 1936

Miss Dorothy Sayers, speaking at the recent Book Exhibition, began her lecture: 'If you want to commit a really good murder . . .' I've since forgotten the recipe, and I suppose a psychologist would say that to remember only so much shows a Puritan conscience which registers a shock before it has time to register an impression. Well, I think in the matter of what Hollywood calls 'horrific' films I am as squeamish as anybody, and I know that there are excellent objections to showing any films which genuinely excite an audience over a murder. The usual objection of parents is that they are a monstrous thing to show to children, who in point of fact know more keenly about the instinct to murder than us fumbling adults. We, when we are insulted in public, begin to wonder vaguely about solicitors. We, when we hear the voice of our enemy, look around for our hats and say we think we ought to be getting home. But children want to let fly with all their limbs and it's only when they have been educated – that is, only when they have had the teeth of their instincts pulled – that they can go and watch, for instance, Lionel Barrymore as a wicked old man planning a neat murder and think what a nice old gentleman he is. Children should be kept away from murder films all right – not because they might get like that themselves, but because they are already there, they know all about these violent impulses and it's no use egging them on to lose their temper. They are bad enough as it is. So I for one will applaud any parents who keep their child away from a couple of excellent general releases about killing. Even if, when the child gets to school, the schoolmaster breaks down all the good work by setting for homework De Quincey's essay 'On Murder Considered as One of the Fine Arts'.

I introduce *The Devil-Doll* and *Murder in the Big House* [US: *Jailbreak*] in this general way because a lot of friendly people – mostly parents, I imagine – have asked me to campaign against the 'horrific' film. And Mr Disney has recently given some of us a nasty turn with his new obsession with pain. Well, I should like, if I were a moralist, to raise what voice I could against such films. But as long as I'm a film critic I can't honestly swing it. The only murder films to campaign against are murder films which make murder dull. Entertainment is, unfortunately perhaps, a fairly amoral word. And entertainment in the cinema covers many sins that would be awful if you did them or I did them. *I'm* sorry, too, that Mr Disney should be so eager to send little wolves roaring through somebody's roof with their tails burning, and putting popcorn into anybody's trousers is a mean trick. But it's a very funny one. In the same way, I don't approve of the medical trick, whenever it happens, of turning human beings into little working models about ten inches high, who are then used to do stealthy murders by using tiny daggers on sleeping grown-ups. But *The Devil-Doll* happens to be directed by Tod Browning, who has given a lot of energy to the question of what thrills a lot of people all at once. And *The Devil-Doll* is consistently entertaining. A man wrongly sent to gaol comes out to invent this process of reducing his enemies to the size of dolls. Since Lionel Barrymore is the wronged man the whole proceedings seem very benevolent. And since to do his tricks in peace he puts a skirt and shawl on and dresses up as an honest woman, the movies offer you a pleasure you could hardly ask in a lifetime – Lionel Barrymore squeaking around Paris as a dear old lady. And, by some miracle, nobody in Paris recognizes him.

Murder in the Big House was made, I suppose, as a routine thriller. But the care that goes into the filming of such routines is still a standard which any studio might be proud of. The story is the old racketeer gone straight, jailed again, and being joined by his most dangerous rival. Ever since *The Whole Town's Talking*, which this film at times painfully copies, murder movies seem to think it's more daring to do the killing inside the prison. And the dialogue is the old gangster patter, the 'so what? – get going' tough guy talk, no better and no worse than the average. But *Murder in the Big House* is the kind of supporting film you somehow have to see through even if you slept during the big film. Because it moves in step with the story, however trivial. It goes leaping ahead with anybody's anxiety for anybody else. If this were in Russian and called something like *Maggots of Humanity* or *Four Ways That Shook the Prison Bars*, there'd be a big audience for it and a sizeable press, and there'd be a lot of whispered admiration for its montage. Well, it's called *Murder at the Big House*, is a hackneyed story with dull dialogue, and is made by somebody in Hollywood with a pair of scissors and a good blunt gift of saying so long and no longer to any given incident. And so when it's not talking, it moves with the stride of a whippet, and is good to watch.

¶ *The Devil-Doll*. USA, 1936, MGM; d. Tod Browning. Lionel Barrymore, Maureen O'Sullivan, Frank Lawton.
Murder in the Big House (US: *Jailbreak*). USA, 1936, Warner Bros.; d. Nick Grinde. Barton MacLane, June Travis, Craig Reynolds.

Mr Deeds Goes to Town

The Cinema, BBC, Winter 1936

It has become almost a reflex with this critic when the word Capra is mentioned to drop the job in hand, rush for a pen and scribble the phrase 'engrossing affection for small American types'. Well, after *Mr Deeds*, I'm not so sure. It has nothing as affectionate or authentic as the eve of the Derby in *Strictly Confidential*, or the Southampton wedding in *It Happened One Night*. And the judge in this new picture, and the two old ladies from Maine and any amount of other characters are all grand ideas, but they are not like Happy and Louis the Lug, and the feedman and Raymond Walburn's colonel, and the man who wanted to swap a cane for a hot dog ('What d'yer want for a hamburger, a telegraph pole?'). They are more like Capra characters than Americans. Whereas those others were both.

As an idea-movie it's irresistible, and apparently means more to more people than his previous Tarkington-cum-Clarence Budington Kelland comedies. This is just Kelland injected with the Capra drive. Capra's is a great talent all right, but I have the uneasy feeling he's on his way out. He's starting to make movies about themes instead of about people – *Mr Deeds* is tremendous because the idea is taken charge of wholly by one person and one glorious part, Mr Deeds himself. But the dramatization tends to get tense by night and inside rooms, and to mist up when it gets outside in the street. In the earlier films, the best scenes were cheerful sequences in an unambiguous sun – going to see Gallant Lady arrive (*Strictly Confidential*), the crazy drive with the rascal baritone (*It Happened One Night*). Capra has been used to seeing Americans briskly and comically by the dawn's early light. Perhaps only when he has finished his next film (which gloomy rumour has it is to be a literary morsel of James Hilton) will he know which is his lost horizon.

¶ *Mr Deeds Goes to Town*. USA, 1936, Columbia; d. Frank Capra. Gary Cooper, Jean Arthur, George Bancroft, Lionel Stander.

Capra's *Lost Horizon*, glisteningly solemn, duly arrived in 1937. Kelland and Booth Tarkington both specialized in affectionate, well-observed tales of American life; *Mr Deeds* was based on a Kelland story, 'Opera Hat'.

A Gift from the Gods

Spectator, 8 January 1937

I found myself the other night at a musical comedy (I mean with real people on a real stage and curtains going up and down and everything). The lights went down, out came the purple spot, the conductor signalled to the man with the triangle, and the leading lady – a feat of preservation but no hoofer – started to dance. She has, I was told, a considerable West End reputation, but though her legs moved freely enough her trunk never seemed to belong with them, she looked untrained, her head was a marvel of bad pointing, and her arms were just comic relief. She seemed in fact to be one with the majority of English musical comedy stars in insisting on the essential refinement of thistledown. She can't dance, so watch her be a snowflake. When she had finished, my companion, a dancer, left the theatre quietly in a hearse while a large audience flicked the dewy tears away and applauded loudly, no more and no less roundly than they will next week, next month, at Eleanor Powell, who has a figure, exquisite balance (remarkable in a tap dancer), a pair of heels unique in Christendom, and the retrospective record of thousands of patient working hours, at least one sweating year spent at the magical black feet of 'Bojangles' Robinson, the master himself. She has also a grin pinned from ear to ear which dismally insists she's just a nice, fresh girl in there trying to please. But that's neither here nor there, it's the heel you're watching, and failing to follow with hearing that is, alas, no more than human.

And where does it get her, this training, this astonishing if monotonous talent? Who really feels the thrill of the thing and can offer the sincerest applause? The film audience? They'll be reacting next week with similar gasps to the Three Pippins performing in pantomime or somewhere along the Edgware Road. The film critics? There's not one of them even knows the difference between softshoe and tap. So it must be the half-trained regiments of vaudeville itself that packed the Empire this week and took a lovely revenge they have had coming to them ever since they knew they were too low to appreciate the brooding epics of Flugenspiel, the superb montage reserved for patrons of the Academy and Studio One. It's sad to think how conscientiously the critics, the Cambridge School for instance, with their alpha minuses, distribute the 'levels' of appreciation, assigning *Born to Dance* to somewhere pretty low, whereas the *Alcestis* is admittedly high, but no higher than even you may aspire by the grace of education. And then you go into the Empire, and here is the East End and an odd darkie knowing what it's all about, and the film critics nowhere at all. Thus does life get its own back on I. A. Richards. So God, having created Aristotle, creates for spite – a darkie.

And what is left for the film critic to understand? Well, there is Buddy Ebsen, nearer our ken because his gift is expressed not only in dance but in the human terms we know something about; his grotesque gravity turns to kidding not only in his steps but in the curling of a lip, in the slow spreading of a gawky thumb. There is Raymond Walburn, alertly absent-minded. There is James Stewart, trying to be ingenuous and charming like Gary Cooper but many tricks and years behind. There are several Cole Porter lyrics, a couple of good tunes and more than a hint of his genuine musical wit. There's Reginald Gardiner conducting an invisible orchestra, by the precision and mock ecstasy of his gesture recalling another clown's name, and that the greatest. There is a sequence when the US Navy dives overboard in a body, funny in itself but suggesting suddenly what a movie *Zuleika Dobson* would make, the mass suicide the high spot, the beads of perspiration on the Roman emperors' statues as funny and more credible than the book. There is Frances Langford – but there again we are back where we started. For though she's just another crooner to us critics, it's the swing fans this time who will know her voice is a rare one and her jazz phrasing a gift from those wise and cynical gods.

¶ *Born to Dance*. USA, 1936, MGM; d. Roy Del Ruth. Eleanor Powell, James Stewart, Virginia Bruce, Una Merkel, Sid Silvers.

Max Beerbohm's satirical novel *Zuleika Dobson, or An Oxford Love Story* (1911) still hasn't made it in cinema. Neither has the fictitious Flugenspiel. The Cambridge literary guru I. A. Richards brushed against cinema when he made educational shorts in the 1940s promoting the simplified vocabulary of Basic English.

Technicolor versus Monochrome

Spectator, 15 January 1937

It is *Ramona* in Technicolor which is meant to attract passers-by into the Tivoli this week, but it's *15 Maiden Lane*, a simple monochrome, that should keep them there. *15 Maiden Lane* is about a particular New York jewel robbery. *Ramona* is the California heroine of the 1880s generalized into a tinkling symbol of Womanhood.

So far it has been impossible to copy in the movies the quality that makes the Hulls and the Hichenses and the Stratton-Porters – the mental unity, the single-mindedness denied to any author higher than the fourth-rate, to possess which all better writers would gladly sell their 'discriminating' public and their old grey flannels. We sensitive hacks stammer at a subtlety, express pity in many a pondered adjective, but the most we achieve, by way of circulation, is the swapping of curious anecdotes, the exchange of private snifflings, while the tears of a Hichens drench the lending libraries of the world. Black-and-white film is too kind to character, to the undramatic details of an etching. However brilliantly they light the Sheik and Freckles, the shadows that set them off are nothing short of black, they are dark, confused, and may hide real people, small men in drab clothes as well as cloaks and daggers. But in colour even the shadows are a succulent and penetrable blue. Any single still, however tragic its title, could be made into a postcard and mailed confidently to old men and maiden aunts, for the tone of the suffering is as comfortable as the groups of G. F. Watts. Just as you notice with him that a stricken angel is as nicely posed as the next unlucky spirit, so in *Ramona*, when Don Filipo is dying – I think it was Don Filipo – the two visible walls of his rooms are differently lit, though equally pleasing. And it's clear there's no sense in worrying for his health, he's pretty certain to pull through when even the director is *that* interested in the decor. *Ramona* is unlucky, too, in its locale, that is if it was meaning to move and depress us. Since Southern California is itself not unlike a colour film, it is here able without any strain to reflect the rich cloudless complacency of the novel. In monochrome it would have been cheerful enough. But colour adds to it the last platitude, the encircling halo that bestselling epics are always straining for.

Poor *15 Maiden Lane* by comparison is merely competent, smooth as a billiard ball, amusing, and ninety times more exciting and intelligent. It has nothing at all to say about Devotion, Self-Sacrifice, Man's Inhumanity to Honest Injuns – it's just there to explain as neatly as a supporting film dare how a jewel robbery was solved and how the 'fences', or receivers of stolen goods to you, were tricked and exposed. *Ramona* is all about mixed blood and that old knotty cosmic problem of the difference – remember? – between 'love' and 'being *in* love'. Whereas Claire Trevor asking Lloyd Nolan, in the last three feet of film, to take her out to luncheon is the nearest *15 Maiden Lane* comes to a carnal statement. Not that it's a mere hygienic thriller, with the characters as human as chessmen. Claire Trevor, a hard and humorous talent, never forgets that she is meant as the sustaining overtone of Sex, making even Cesar Romero lose his well-oiled head, throwing tough guys and gangsters' henchmen off their job with the bewildering variety of her Bonwit Teller clothes, the clean groomed limbs of her. But that's the only note that spells box-office for this sharp, delightful little picture, which two years ago might have called itself *The Thin Man*, and nobody would have known much difference.

¶ *Ramona*. USA, 1936, Twentieth Century-Fox; d. Henry King. Loretta Young, Don Ameche, Kent Taylor.

The Technicolor *Ramona* was the fourth American film based on Helen Hunt Jackson's novel (1884) concerning an aristocratic Spanish girl and an Indian, deeply in love. The novel was plundered by the movies as avidly as E. M. Hull's *The Sheik*, *Freckles* and the novels of Gene Stratton-Porter and Robert Hichens. The Victorian artist

G. F. Watts was famous for painting and sculpting allegorical figures. No mention, note, of Loretta Young, AC's old heart-throb.

15 Maiden Lane. USA, 1936, Twentieth Century-Fox; d. Allan Dwan. Claire Trevor, Cesar Romero, Douglas Fowley, Lloyd Nolan.

We Who Are About to Die

The Cinema, BBC, 17 January 1937

Hollywood knows that fun and games in a million American families is not terribly dramatic, that generous hospitality from all people rich and poor may be a characteristic of Americans, but it's not going to make a profit on celluloid. So this week it returns to the excitement of showing life in a state prison, and the foolish miscarriage of justice against a young aircraft worker, honestly and beautifully played by John Beal. The film is called *We Who Are About to Die*, and is modelled almost move for move on the earlier film *Injustice*. Its tension is for once something keener than Hollywood tension. Of course the precious evidence arrives about two minutes before John Beal is going to be hanged. But even when you know it's going to come out all right, there's a whole stretch of film in the prison itself, showing the men waiting, hearing the testing of the gallows, singing, stopping each other singing, trying to read, all eyes watching an Englishman near his end order an epicure's meal. There's an incident with a Chinese, who croons with gratitude when the parson promises him his bones will be sent to lie with his ancestors, and the Chinaman walks out of his cell, absorbed and looking all the time at a small statue he carries. The other men, toughs and weaklings, are looking on, gasping, sniffing, and Beal has the terrific line, turning bitterly from the bars into his cell: 'Death's no fright to a Chinaman when he knows he's going to join a family reunion.'

It's moments like that which give us hope whenever we think the films are slipping. The movies may not yet be able to project an individual philosophy or provide cultivated young men with a medium for their distinguished little thoughts, but in the middle of the waste, and the artificiality, and the sentimental conventions of the cinema, it's John Beal making that remark, it's the urchin in *Fury* climbing a lamp-post at a terrible moment and squeaking above the crowd 'I'm Popeye the sailor man', it's lines and moments like those that let us see, keener and quicker than any novel, the very spit and image of life itself.

¶ *We Who Are About to Die*. USA, 1937, RKO; d. Christy Cabanne. Preston Foster, Ann Dvorak, John Beal.

The Night I saw *Ernte*

Spectator, 29 January 1937

It's always supposed to indicate a keener sensibility to be sniffy about the beauty conventions of one's own day and age. When Dr Johnson was asked what he thought about the London beauties of the time and their habit of making up their faces, he replied: 'I don't like to see an Englishwoman sailing under French colours.' Me, I've tried to keep up with the movement, and I get along all right just so long as they keep Carole Lombard in long-shot. But the moment she's in close-up, I can't swing it. One glimpse of the impudent nostrils, the swelling bosom, and I'm a stricken man. This may be 'conventional beauty' to the intelligentsia, but I never yet minded being in a house with a beauty, however conventional. Yet this fault has its compensations. I can look on, for instance, with comparative calm, at practically any Central European with frizzy hair, thighs like market day and a silk ribbon tied in a bow round the middle of her evening gown. My appetite may be low and panting, being content merely to watch Myrna Loy and Ginger Rogers moving about up there, but I feel no restless urge, like more intelligent critics, for a Viennese actress with a 35" waist and eyebrows that meet in the middle. Anybody with my gross standards cannot hope, therefore, to judge Paula Wessely [in *Ernte*]. Of course, she's a good actress, she's sincere and calculates her naïvety very cleverly, and is downright and plucky through her peasant tears. On paper, she's fine. But she's not acting on paper. She's acting in a dark room on a dark night with a lot of people sneezing and at least one film critic risking flu on her behalf. And sincerity is not enough. Neither is clever acting, and cute horse-play, and stirring feudal devotion to the *Rittmeister*, and brave tears. Any other time she'd be given marks for all these things. But they were nothing short of a stab in the back, the night she gave me influenza.

Manhattan Madness [US: *Adventure in Manhattan*] is kinder to the rheum, and its conventions are less nostalgic. It doesn't madden a blear-eyed audience with shots of swaying corn and a spring that will never, never come. On the contrary, it's a crisp, incredible newspaper story in the credible fairyland which Hollywood so cunningly represents as Manhattan. But for all it's only a convention, along with the balloons and the gaiety in Viennese films, the policemen and cockney moustaches in Hitchcock films, it's more plausible than most and has a life of its own. Joel McCrea works in a newspaper office that looks like one, his Press Club might be a press club, he takes recognizable taxis and blows steaming coffee, sitting up at two in the morning on a stool at quick-lunch bars with Jean Arthur, who's as husky and friendly as any New Yorker we know. Though the story is nothing, and the pace seemed slow the night I was there because the soundtrack was being played too low, it was this Hollywood convention that made the evening, the visual convention of a New York that is nearer the New York of Ed Sullivan than *Ernte* is anywhere near Vienna or Hungary, than *Love from a Stranger* is near the Bayswater it supposedly starts out from. It's the background of *Manhattan Madness* that cheers and stimulates, whereas it's the background of *Love from a Stranger* that for more than half the film gets in the way of a first-rate melodrama. Trafalgar Films, Ltd, do their part to scotch these nasty rumours about the local film industry by introducing us to Ann Harding as an object of pity, a poor working girl living in a flat that would cost, at a modest guess, about 600 a year. Our hopes pick up when she wins a sweepstake and when Basil Rathbone, his cultivated brow pained at the mention of 'guide-books', offers to show her a strange, lovely Europe, personal 'out-of-the-way' places. Mr Rathbone's untrodden ways take in the Champs Élysées, the Folies Bergère, Rome, Cannes, a suite at the Dorchester and – believe it or not – a 'place' in Kent. It's only when Miss Harding is finally locked in that cottage in Kent, with no hope of escaping to Stratford-on-Avon, the Taj Mahal or Lake Killarney, that the movie can settle into a single episode of beautifully developed and well-written masochism.

¶ *Ernte (Harvest)*. Austria, 1936, Vienna Film; d. Géza von Bolváry. Gina Falckenberg, Attila Hörbiger, Paula Wessely.

Manhattan Madness (US: *Adventure in Manhattan*). USA, 1936, Columbia; d. Edward Ludwig. Jean Arthur, Joel McCrea, Reginald Owen.

Love from a Stranger. UK, 1936, Trafalgar Films; d. Rowland V. Lee. Ann Harding, Basil Rathbone, Binnie Hale.

High Trumpets for Mr DeMille

The Cinema, BBC, 28 February 1937

I have racked my brain, such as it is, for an opening sentence that would sound splendid enough to introduce the subject of Mr Cecil B. DeMille. To pay tribute to Mr DeMille is about as presumptuous as it would be to write a testimonial for Garbo, or President Roosevelt. Mr DeMille is an expert himself in the art of paying tribute to Mr DeMille. And no film of his starts until high trumpets have shattered the silence and scrolls of reverent parchment have unfolded on the screen the names of Mr DeMille's grateful, humble helpers. There is then usually a rattle of drums, a sweep of fiddles, and to the strains of martial music the magic name writes itself across the screen in letters of Tudor Gothic. After this mighty introduction, it has always seemed a shame that the film which followed was never more than what a Hollywood producer once described as 'terrific, tremenjous, colossal – even mediocre'. Mr DeMille has spent a lifetime making films that were epic and colossal, and now he has made a film that is just extremely good.

Since Mr DeMille is nothing if not biblical I hope he appreciates the biblical irony in the fact that he has roamed the ancient world for stories worthy enough, has handled the Caesars, the pharaohs, Cleopatra and the twelve apostles – and all the time his wealth has lain buried under his doorstep. Or at least on the western border of South Dakota.

The Plainsman tells a story that is neither truth nor fiction. The facts are all authentic. They have been combined in a new order to make a swift and pathetic story. The people who here become heroes and heroines were hardly that, though they were courageous men and women with a miraculous flair for handling whips and revolvers.

Annie Oakley, who doesn't appear in *The Plainsman*, was a hardy girl who could shoot in twenty-seven seconds twenty-five shots at a playing card, placed at a distance of twenty-five yards. When she had finished, the card had its ace neatly shot away – rather neater than I could manage with scissors (nail scissors) – and the rest of the card was untouched. *The Plainsman* doesn't attempt to recreate a feat like that, but it does make believable and exhilarating the kind of life and town where that sort of gift was a necessity. When a man downs his drink quickly and makes for the saloon's swinging door, there's a sudden whistle in the air and a ten-foot whip has coiled itself round his ankle and drags him slowly back to the counter to pay. This is the sort of detail that you'd lay an even bet that Mr DeMille would muff. No, you're wrong . . . the camera is first watching the man tossing off his whisky, then it turns round on him and follows him to the door, then it sidles down to his ankles. You hear the ominous whistle of the whip. Then the camera is slowly climbing the whip, going along to the hand that holds it, and moves and comes to rest, almost with a chuckle, on the face of Calamity Jane, the girl behind the bar.

There are scores of other incidents which would be too emphatic if they made their point in dialogue, but which when left to the camera have a grave and exciting simplicity. Looking back on *The Plainsman*, much of its success, its clear swift impact, is due to the same merit that made *Mr Deeds* not only an American comedy, but a universal comedy as well. Call it the comedy of human needs. Things like being short of money through changing suits, like being asked to spend an evening with somebody and you gather after a couple of hours that the invitation wasn't meant to include dinner. *Mr Deeds*, a world-wide success, glorified horse sense and canniness at the expense of subtlety, business acumen, and saw the conflict as dramatic as well as humorous. *The Plainsman* has exactly this quality, this mixture.

The film, I understand, is an equal success with simple and with sophisticated audiences. Which should be proof enough that in movies the plot means nothing at all, it's the mere skeleton. *The Plainsman* is not only dramatic in its humour. It has the inevitable excitements of frontier life, or, let us say, of the romantic view of frontier life . . . of stagecoaches and buffalo herds, and old friends being found mysteriously silent leaning up against trees, with an arrow in their back. All this obvious drama is magnificent, and Mr DeMille's production staff has done a grand job in recreating these small frontier towns. It's usually Viennese films we praise for the subtle 'rightness' of their atmosphere – 'Ah, now, Central European,' we say when we see a tea-party in a Viennese flat. Well, *The Plainsman* is about three cities and some of the plains of South Dakota, and the atmosphere is no less than the very sound and smell of Hays City and Custer and Deadwood as they were, and are, and for ever, let us hope, will be.

¶ *The Plainsman*. USA, 1936, Paramount; d. Cecil B. DeMille. Gary Cooper, Jean Arthur, Charles Bickford.

Will the Real Katharine Hepburn Please Stand Up?

The Cinema, BBC, 28 March 1937

It seemed when Katharine Hepburn first appeared in *Morning Glory* that she had an almost painful surplus of charm: she could have given you and me a handful of it and still have left us dull. But the title of that film should have been a warning. For it was very nearly her swan song. She is still having to wait for her producers to do right by her, and I hope she goes on waiting. I suppose when you've been launched as a star, nothing short of high tragedy will do for you. Your emotions have to be in scale, and if I know anything about studio methods, those emotions are probably plotted on a graph and rise and fall in proportion to the dollars spent on any given scene. But it seems a pity that so sharp and sensitive a person as Katharine Hepburn should have to bear the brunt of being a star. She's probably itching to show us how charming she can be when she sneezes or blows her nose, but 'Come come' – she hears the voice of the studio executives calling to her – 'come, you may be Katie to your pals, but you're La Hepburn to us.' And so she must not feel sad and sniffle in a corner. She must wear a long gown and throw her head back at an angle of ninety degrees and let us see tears that come from depths Shakespeare never knew.

I'm not complaining about Katharine Hepburn. But only once in four years, in *Alice Adams*, has she been acting a sort of girl she might reasonably be. I wish she could be given a rest from Great Loves and take, instead, a walk with the young man next door. I wish she didn't have to say lines like: 'It's no use, my darling: wherever we go, whatever we may become, it'll never be the same again, never.' And let us hear this gangling college girl say, what she must have said a score of times when she was at Bryn Mawr: 'Sure I like you, but I still think there's time for another hot dog.' I'm not offering this as a universal recipe. Janet Gaynor, for instance, might well be given a rest, after all these years, from dabbing *her* nose. She's been in love with so many teentsy-weentsy boys next door that it would be nice to see her rise sometime to, well, a bank manager, say. But on the whole, Katharine Hepburn's is the more dangerous case. And it's the more typical of the way the studios think.

Long long ago I remember a movie in which Joan Crawford stood against a railway siding, a lumpish, straightforward girl in a smock, waiting for her boy to leave his job – he was a stoker, I think, and ten to one he was Clark Gable. It's the only image of Joan Crawford I can remember straight off, a long shot of a railway line, and a signal down, and her blunt features blinking in the sun. But much has happened since that train came in. When you see *The Last of Mrs Cheyney* you will be given the hint that from now on Joan Crawford and Lady Macbeth are to be considered sisters under the skin, only Miss Crawford dresses better and moves in rather better circles. It's a sad end for a girl in a smock, but it's no sadder than Katharine Hepburn as Mary of Scotland, or this week, as a woman rebelling. There is one consolation, however, for Hepburn addicts. You don't have to have taken drawing lessons to see that Katharine Hepburn has a lovely skull and that's one thing that the studio can't change. It's on view all the time in *A Woman Rebels*.

¶ *A Woman Rebels*. USA, 1936, RKO; d. Mark Sandrich. Katharine Hepburn, Herbert Marshall, Elizabeth Allan.

¶ Within six months of leaving England in April 1937, AC secured a regular slot on the New York City radio station WEAF with *A Critic on Broadway* (September 1937 to April 1938), a mix of film and theatre reviews conveyed in a slightly diluted version of his BBC manner. At the same time he broadcasted back to Britain in *Mainly about Manhattan*, for the BBC. 'He doesn't gossip,' wrote the *Variety* radio critic, reviewing him on 22 December 1937, 'but incisively dissects films with a regard that is genuinely warm. What he has to say is of interest to the thinking filmgoer who shops for values ... With a pair of highly plausible pipes for such a job, spieler will attract a class listening audience.' Surviving scripts reveal his speedy adoption of American spellings.

*   *   *

The Hurricane

A Critic on Broadway, WEAF, 17 November 1937

This week a hurricane hit Broadway, and when it was all over – the movie, I mean, called *The Hurricane* – the most cynical sots in town came out and looked up at the Wrigley's sign with the pure eyes of a child, wondering that Broadway still stands. *The Hurricane* cost an awful lot of money to produce and so, in its Broadway reincarnation, is introduced twice a day only, with elaborate dignity and a special overture. It has lots of things which might be fun in private life, but don't add much to this movie – it has, for instance, love, self-sacrifice, dungeons, Dorothy Lamour, expectant mothers, native dances, girls, bronzed chests and some first-rate mug-pulling by Raymond Massey. But all this is so much chaff before the wind gets under way. In the governor's palace, on this South Sea isle, the French doctor is saying something witty to Mary Astor. And a wind sighs through its teeth, a door bangs, the pages of a book lying near the window climb up and flap back again. And it is time to hold on to your seat. There has been no sound, sheer ear-splitting detonation, in a movie theatre, since your local movie house did *Ben-Hur* with the local drummer clanging chains. The trees bend, railings tie themselves in knots, the roof goes, the sea crashes all over the island, rips up ancient trees, sends the Old Mission to earth like a deck of cards. And it's so loud you can't shout a word to your neighbour. There's only one thing you can hear above the storm. It is, guess what – the cry of a newborn babe! And when it's over, all that's left is a desert island and the feature players. The poor wretched extras have no way with hurricanes and they die in hundreds. *The Hurricane* is one of those movies that do not call for criticism. The story is fantastic and funny. The acting is hardly to be seen. I don't know whether it's a great movie, but like the measles or your first long pants it's certainly a great experience.

¶ *The Hurricane*. USA, 1937, Samuel Goldwyn; d. John Ford. Dorothy Lamour, Jon Hall, Mary Astor, C. Aubrey Smith, Raymond Massey, Thomas Mitchell.

A Damsel in Distress

A Critic on Broadway, WEAF, 1 December 1937

Looking at his new movie *A Damsel in Distress*, it's unbelievable that a few years ago the Hollywood moguls looked him over with their shrewd specialized eye and said Fred Astaire lacked personality. It doesn't matter much whether the script of this new film is wittier than the old (which it is), or whether the story is more plausible (which it isn't) – Fred Astaire needs a camera and some music and a lot of ground, and just to doze and look at he remains a thing of beauty and a boy for ever. The stage could never do for him what this movie has done. For it lets him, for five minutes at a time, wander over somebody's garden, a river bank, an amusement park, improvising a run here, a step there, tapping out ghostlike rhythms on stray benches, trees, moving stairways.

A Damsel in Distress does not have better music than, say, *Top Hat*. But I think it has more appropriate music for the Astaire genius – Gershwin was always his best music master. And though as a whole *Top Hat* is still the best of the bunch, if it's Astaire himself you're looking at this is easily his best work to date. The clown grace that William Powell is just catching on to, that Donald Duck has by permission of a drawing board, that Chaplin has all the time – this is and always will be the supreme gift of Fred Astaire. It's almost indecent to think of him growing old, for then it will be evident that he is made, like the rest of us, of flesh and bone. At the moment, and more than ever in *A Damsel in Distress*, he is in this world but not of it. He's like the greatest of all Walt Disney's creations, who somehow escaped from an inkwell and is celebrating his freedom by dancing, this time, all over the English countryside.

¶ *A Damsel in Distress*. USA, 1937, RKO; d. Mark Sandrich. Fred Astaire, George Burns, Gracie Allen, Joan Fontaine.

Knocking a Man Upstairs

A Critic on Broadway, WEAF, 22 December 1937

True Confession is yet another in the cycle of goofy movies where the comedy makes no sense and it isn't meant to. It's another wreath laid on the grave of *My Man Godfrey*. It'll be, on the whole, a happy day when somebody makes an old, slow-paced, quiet comedy which doesn't try to drag horse-laughs from the credit titles. Fred Mac-Murray has a fine talent, but in this picture it hides behind his moustache. John Barrymore used to have moments of meditation, but here he looks as if he's trying to chew off the soundtrack which runs, as you know, alongside the celluloid strip that frames the picture. And Carole Lombard knows about the higher realms of comedy, if only the director wouldn't make her stay there all the time.

But Popeye's another story. This Ali Baba film is one of the first of Fleischer's colour cartoons. And it's very funny. I don't know how you would describe the particular quality which belongs to Popeye and to none of Disney's feeble imitators. Disney is the great popular genius of the movies. More than any novelist of our day he is the Dickens of the twentieth century. He has invented more independent characters than all the other studios put together. Once he gets an idea, he works it out in full and brilliantly drawn detail. Fleischer, or the Fleischer collective which draws the Popeye films, has none of these gifts. But Disney is also, like Dickens, a good sentimentalist. And Fleischer is not. There's a hard, unyielding streak in him which makes Popeye a good tonic any time you're feeling a little too self-satisfied. It's typical of Popeye that he rejects pretty girls for the almost hideous Olive Oyl. He has a rich, cruel Celtic strain, a pioneer grimness. I think if Mark Twain were alive, Popeye is the only character he would have envied and put into *Life on the Mississippi*. Nobody can draw a man or a mouse falling downstairs better than Disney. But it took Popeye to think of knocking a man *up*stairs.

¶ *True Confession*. USA, 1937, Paramount; d. Wesley Ruggles. Carole Lombard, Fred MacMurray, John Barrymore.
Popeye the Sailor Meets Ali Baba's Forty Thieves. USA, 1937, Paramount; d. Dave Fleischer.

The Longest Trailer Ever Made

A Critic on Broadway, WEAF, 5 January 1938

Wells Fargo starts in the 1840s and ends in the late 1860s. Joel McCrea is represented as an ambitious young gawk named MacKay, who as far as I can gather practically settled this country and ran it single-handed. You will find no mention of his name in the authoritative histories, in Adams, or Morison, not in Brogan's book or Woodward, or even in Mark Sullivan. But now Paramount and Frank Lloyd have given the devil his due.

It should be made explicit for the record, then, that Joel McCrea started the mail service between New York and Buffalo; then he ran, rode, walked, swam, and I guess drank his way across the Mississippi in full flood, and extended the service down to St Louis. Why St Louis? Well, Frances Dee lived there, and since she's the heroine they had to get married sooner or later. In order to marry you have to *see* your girl now and then, don't you? That's how the overland route was established. They marry, but not for long: it's getting to be around 1849, and McCrea has the Gold Rush to take care of. Then what's going to happen to the Pony Express if Frances Dee and husband settle down? Just when Frances Dee is going to have a baby, along comes that tarnation Civil War. So McCrea has to get busy, go and see the president (a man called Lincoln, I think), get gold across the plains, even though his venerable mother-in-law from the Old South has given directions how to catch him with it. Well, he comes through, and at the end of the picture Joel McCrea is a silver-haired Santa Claus. Luckily, the movie doesn't go on until 1871, or McCrea would have to go to Chicago, to be Mrs O'Leary's head milker, also to organize the fire brigade.

Kidding aside, Mr Lloyd has let his heart run away with his head.

He has made the old Hollywood mistake: it's the idea that if you want to show an exciting battle, you can play for safety by having five battles just in case two misfire. You just about get launched in one episode before the picture dissolves into a date, 1850 or 1861. Mr Lloyd might say with the seventeenth-century poet, 'always at my back I hear Time's chariot'. The result is that *Wells Fargo* isn't so much epic as epileptic. There is plot enough for twelve careful, dramatic recreations of some episode of American history. But though Frank Lloyd has a good sense of excitement he has, so far as I can discover, no sense of drama. What he's presenting, it soon becomes clear, is a panorama of the love of Frances Dee for Joel McCrea, and it's American history, darn it, which gets in the way of their embraces, just as Gertrude Stein recently announced that the Spanish Civil War had obtruded into her private life. *Wells Fargo* has its moments: a swift clatter through eucalyptus and pepper trees, the ride up to a changing post in New Mexico which is just a mess of corpses and a gaunt stick of wood against the baked sky. It's too bad these are the only moments. I'd like to say *Wells Fargo* is a terrific, breathless, shining picture. But it's not, it's a long and restless trailer for a movie that was never made. It's the longest teaser in motion picture history.

¶ *Wells Fargo*. USA, 1937, Paramount; d. Frank Lloyd. Joel McCrea, Bob Burns, Frances Dee.

The 1871 Chicago fire, the climax of Fox's forthcoming *In Old Chicago*, was supposedly started by a lantern kicked by Mrs O'Leary's cow.

The 'trailer' comment caused serious trouble. Arguing that audiences might actually believe the film was never made, Paramount threatened to sue WEAF's parent company NBC for millions of dollars. After heavy lobbying from NBC's vice-president, John F. Royal, the matter was settled amicably. NBC, *Variety* reported, 'promised close watch-dogging on the commentator's copy'.

Ballyhoo in Old Chicago

A Critic on Broadway, WEAF, 15 January 1938

Outside at the Astor Theatre in Times Square last Thursday evening, there was a sprawling crowd. It was the first night of last week's epic, *In Old Chicago*. The milling mob was not noticeably trying to get in the theatre. It was in the tricky process of trying to stay outside. But the inward surge of celebrities, actors, distributors, ad men, press men and yes men had the compulsion of a vacuum cleaner, sucking into its wake all the stray gazers, the mere dust of humanity wandering there on the sidewalk. At least one bystander got whisked into the stream of incoming goldfish, and when he found himself inside the theatre started panting for breath, perhaps even for water. He disengaged himself from the inner petals of a lady's orchids and stood at the back, hot about the neck, hat clutched in his hand. When he caught his breath, he said, very loud, 'Where am I?' Some nearby wit – all right, half-wit – said, 'In Old Chicago.' The stranger's eyes goggled, he stood wobbling for an instant, then he yelled 'Mother!' and fought his way through the lobby back to New York City again.

Out there, the mob – a few hundred, maybe even a thousand, souls – were like the dust the cleaner left behind, spinning a little, gradually getting back to its feet, waiting for the moment when they could decide whether to go uptown or downtown. Inside the theatre, the air was hot and choky. Mr Darryl Zanuck stood neat and excited at the back of the orchestra, looking at his watch from well inside a huddle, calling out numbers, and saying, 'Let's go, boys!' There was a moment's hushed pause. Miss Alice Faye swept down the aisle, took her seat, there was a broken wave of clapping, the lights went down, and the theatre was filled with Twentieth Century-Fox's stirring signature tune.

What followed – believe it or not – was a movie. Just a movie. Not a very remarkable one, sometimes endearing, sometimes nauseating, a movie which ended on the very note it started on – hollowness and false emotion. But this time the lights and the crowds were on the screen, not on the Broadway sidewalk. It was the end of the Chicago fire, and for fifteen minutes we had watched the studio production department embarked on its annual field-day. Buildings crashed, the villain trying to climb a wall clutched vainly at a loose brick and fell down into a stampeding herd of cattle, there to be well and truly skewered. Flames burst from every street and cranny. The rescued hundred sloshed in the mud of Lake Michigan. At the very end the camera picked out our hero, Tyrone Power, sloshing too – shouting, smiling, for he had picked out one small boat and on it, standing there like the Statue of Liberty, the person he loved best in the world, his mother. Huddled on the sidelines sits the uncomplaining figure of his sweetheart and wife, and as the film fades she is lucky enough to be given the full radiance of Tyrone Power's kindly smile. Mrs O'Leary, meanwhile, stands sharply outlined against a city in embers and starts to speak slowly, with the spooky inflections of an evangelist, expressing a few pious hopes that from the ashes of the old there will arise – guess what, the new. At this point you pick up your hat and tiptoe out into the comparative understatement of Broadway's neon signs.

For the second week in succession we have seen potentially fine material jazzed, peppered with tinsel, made to submit to the Twentieth Century mania for build-up. I do not believe that Mrs O'Leary made such a speech either on that barge or from the family pulpit of the old armchair. I didn't get to the Chicago fire, but I feel pretty sure that as a general rule people living a moment of history do not make forward-looking speeches in unrhymed blank verse, for they rarely know they are living a moment of history. A revolution has a build-up, so does a battle, but history refuses to be coaxed into drama, and the most poignant moments of those revolutions, those battles, come and go like a change in the wind. Hollywood will begin to make good historical films when it takes the build-up out of history. And those films will be worth seeing when, for decency's sake, it takes the build-up out of premieres.

¶ *In Old Chicago*. USA, 1938, Twentieth Century-Fox; d. Henry King. Tyrone Power, Alice Faye, Don Ameche, Alice Brady.

New York City hosted the film's world premiere on 6 January 1938.

Grumpy Reports on *Snow White*

A Critic on Broadway, WEAF, 22 January 1938

At the Music Hall is presented to daily thousands the first full-length Disney feature, in colour, called *Snow White and the Seven Dwarfs*. The movie has a lot of charm, a humorously grave re-telling of the old Grimm legend faithful almost to the end. It's a detail, but it's the slip twixt Disney and truth. Snow White in Grimm finds that the fatal apple which brings on her coma will not stay put in her stomach, so she pukes to get rid of it and bring the whimsy to an end. This is too harsh and unladylike a detail for our modern spirit. Maybe, as George Moore moaned fifty years ago, the spirit of 'villa-dom' has settled on us, and we must have even fairy stories refined out of character. But then, to Grimm, Snow White was Snow White. To us she can't help being some sort of Garbo; to Walt Disney she's an investment in stardom, and it certainly wouldn't help to see her in next month's fan magazine bringing up unpalatable food all over the Brown Derby.

Snow White has received ecstatic notices, from which you would gather that it has all the saintliness and permanence of Santa Claus sitting on the Rock of Ages. Mr Westbrook Pegler squeaks through his tears that there has been nothing like it since the Armistice. I think it can be fairly said that those who have preferred the Disney of Christmas fantasies, of fairy princesses and dewdrops, will here find their fondest dreams come true. Whereas those who honour Disney for the muscular and naked humour of Mickey Mouse, Donald Duck, Maxie Hare and the grasshopper with the Western drawl – these people should pray that millions will crowd to see *Snow White* so that we shall be assured of more character inventions freed from the eiderdown of whimsy with which Mr Disney has tried to satisfy both publics. We have little cause for complaint from Disney. It's only a month since we had that masterpiece, *Modern Inventions*, a lesson in the anatomy of the tough guy and a permanent representation of the American sophomore from our great and good friend Mr Donald Duck. Disney has done no harm, but I hope he feels sick when anyone mentions Snow White.

¶ *Snow White and the Seven Dwarfs*. USA, 1937, Walt Disney; supervising d. David Hand.

Ordinary Hat versus Lobsters

A Critic on Broadway, WEAF, 19 February 1938

Just ten years ago this week, I heard a motion picture producer stand up before an audience of earnest undergraduates and tell them without so much as dropping an eyelid that in ten years 'you will rarely, if ever, see a silent movie'. The audience gaped, snickered, looked at each other to gain confidence, and then made the room shake with a thundering guffaw. Prophecy in any of the arts is always a scary business, and prophecy about motion pictures has been wrong, on average, about ten times in ten. But when those college boys heard that sentence their usual gullibility melted away. Movies had always been silent. Unfortunately one day in 1927, Al Jolson went down on a bended knee and sang 'Mammy' – and in spite of that cosmic gesture there never was any question that the talkies had come to stay.

We are now generally agreed that if many good and a handful of great movies happened to be silent, the best movies have been talkies. And anybody who today goes around bucking sound puts himself down as a constitutional Tory – and constitutional Tories have not in the world's history been in the habit of producing living art. I think it's worth bringing up this ancient controversy just to make clear where and how we stand on colour film. It can be said right now, without very bold foresight, that in another ten years we will rarely if ever see a film in black and white. Faced with that prospect, I know people who'd walk out of the first available movie theatre in protest, and I think they'd be right – today. But tomorrow they'll be wrong. Sooner or later, even Hollywood will catch on to the fact that the best way to use colour is not to use it all the time.

When colour film came in, every amateur movie-maker in the country dashed off to the nearest bed of tulips and started choking a camera with more sheer daubery than any eye or garden could hold. It's surely a human thing once you get a toy railway for Christmas to run your train from the crack of dawn, through the living room, the bathroom, the kitchen and if possible right through the Christmas dinner. We're still in that phase with the colour film. If Hollywood assigns its ranking star to a colour film, you can bet your boots it's going to be a film about California, or Holland during tulip week or a life of Joseph inside his coat of more colours than he ever saw. Colour film is still too crude to capture the colour of the scenic marvels Hollywood just now is trying to take in – the blinding subtleties of the Arizona desert at sunset, the Sacramento Valley. Maybe they know how bad it is and are scared stiff of showing just streets and people, since the streets come out like summer resort ads and the people come out like lobsters. But like it or not, that's going to be the test. When they can make a gangster film in colour, then they've got something. When they can take an ordinary hat and make it look like itself, colour will be with us for life.

I wish I could report that Hollywood is trying something new in every colour film it makes, and that we'll soon be on our way. But it isn't. We are where we were in 1929, when every bedroom, bus, and train had to squeeze in a piano because – well, hadn't we got sound and wasn't it a wonderful invention? There's a fortune waiting for the first movie producer who will leave the fantasy use of colour to Walt Disney and get down to a film where people will look neither feverish nor far gone with gangrene, but will look like you and me, somewhere in between, suffering from average good health with an overtone of indigestion.

¶ On 25 January, three weeks before this broadcast, AC informed his extension course students at MoMA about his personal taste in colours: pastel grey was top, with pastel green, solid blacks and red the runners-up. To further his point about the quirks of visual perception, he also pointed out his astigmatism and dislike of vertical lines: the natural consequence of being a 'tall, thin person'. Hence his fondness for holidays in the plains of the American Southwest. And his preference for apartments: where his wife liked high-ceilinged rooms, he would feel more restful, he said, in a room four feet high.

Starring Anthony Eden

A Critic on Broadway, WEAF, 26 March 1938

The best movie I have seen this week was the item about the League of Nations in the current *March of Time*. This item is so swift and clear that I'm worried about it. As a piece of entertainment it's first-rate. But as an argument it's almost too persuasive. This short movie dramatizes no actual situation; it dramatizes a point of view about the League of Nations. An equally clever director could take other, equally valid facts and suggest a very different moral. He could take, for example, Ferdinand Kuhn's piece in last Sunday's *New York Times*, listing all the parts of the globe that Great Britain must fight for on her account, quite aside from anything she might want to fight for by reason of a traditional friendship or a momentary impulse of quixoticism.

The *March of Time* version tells of the Wilson inspiration, of the high hopes that founded a federation of Europe, of the flouting of that league, the slow seeping away of principle and indignation. In this story are placed two heroes. President Wilson appears at the beginning and the end as a sort of protective deity. The real hero is Britain's Anthony Eden. I never saw a man made by one movie into so glamorous a Galahad. I have the impression Anthony Eden could sign his own ticket in Hollywood, though they could hardly find him a more striking role than the one he plays in *The March of Time*. It's a fine, outraged, scornful piece of movie-making. And it appeals to all that is most noble, but at the same time most vague, in our wishes for world peace. It mixes the Joan Crawford nobility with the gangster movies' agile camera, with the urgency of ominous trains, men making speeches, crowds cheering, booing, small figures making dangerous decisions with a nod and a pencil on paper.

The movies persuade most of the time not by good writing but by the interplay of sights and sounds. Or no sound at all. Joan Crawford calling her husband a rat was not half as exciting the other night as Evelyn Brent coming silently out of a door and turning her mouth on to the outstretched hand of a cop in hiding. In the same way, Haile Selassie standing up at Geneva being booed by the Italian press is a helpless figure; but the most striking thing in *The March of Time*, the single scene that gives you the most certain idea of guilt, is a tracking shot of the Japanese delegate quitting the League Assembly. There is no speech and hardly any sound, just the camera weaving and darting a yard away, step by step with this silent and frightening little man.

We have often praised the movies because they can let us see things happening all over the world. But the trouble is now that they can let us feel passions happening nowhere but up on that screen. And by showing living persons, familiar streets, we believe we are seeing what are called 'actual facts'. As far as the movies are concerned, there is no such thing as an actual fact. Anthony Eden and Joan Crawford are raw materials. They can become symbols of anything a director, a writer and a cameraman want them to be – and some things those three men may not want them to be.

I am not saying *The March of Time* has sinned in this particular case. Of course there is a worldwide feeling that collective security has broken down into a tangle of slack promises. There is a belligerent party in Great Britain which would like Eden back. *The March of Time* item is a brilliant dramatization of that feeling, and that belligerence. But it makes you wonder how mixed a blessing the movies have given to our time. It makes you back away at the prospect of what can and will be done with the newsreels in wartime.

¶ *The March of Time*, Volume 4, issue 18: *Arms and the League*. USA, 1938, March of Time.

Britain's Foreign Secretary, Anthony Eden, had resigned in February 1938 after Prime Minister Neville Chamberlain opened negotiations with fascist Italy. Other films reviewed in the broadcast included *Mannequin* with Joan Crawford and *Tip-Off Girls* with Evelyn Brent.

¶ By 1938 Katharine Hepburn had broken free from the 'high tragedy' mode that AC had complained of earlier. But the 'crazy Kate' replacement didn't please him either. This broadcast was a stray contribution to his former BBC film talk slot, now in the hands of F. Andrew Rice, of the *Yorkshire Post*.

* * *

The Baby and the Butler

The Fortnight's Films, BBC, 14 August 1938

I feel a strain of prejudice creep into my larynx at the mention of *Bringing Up Baby*. Let me just indicate its type and say you have been warned. *Bringing Up Baby* is yet another in that cycle of crazy comedies which has dashing young people standing on each other's coat-tails or walking out of a fashionable restaurant in their shirt-tails. On the corner of a Mayfair street I heard a young woman say to, I think, a young man, 'My dear, it's the gayest thing.' Well, yes, it's gay enough, but gaiety's good when it's a grace note to living. It's awful as a profession. And ever since *My Man Godfrey*, Carole Lombard, Katharine Hepburn and Cary Grant have collectively embarked on to banana skins as a career. If that old movie is your sort, so, then, is this one. But I think I'll take a nice cheerful aspirin and sit it out.

The Baroness and the Butler is about Hungary. It is, I should guess, not very accurate in its locale – you can almost smell Californian oranges creeping in behind the Hungarian mountains. Also it is on a theme of social revolt. And when the movie-men decide to take hold of a social theme, they know how to do it without leaving a single fingerprint – as witness that masterpiece of fence-sitting *Blockade*. In *The Baroness and the Butler*, Annabella is the Baroness, Henry Stephenson is the old Baron, who is also Prime Minister, Führer, or whatever they have in Budapest. And William Powell is the Butler. He is the devoted slave of his masters. But it seems that in spare moments he has been reading up on politics and has got into his head all sorts of ideas about liberty, equality and one on the house. While the family listens in to the election results the loudspeaker announces the election of a new deputy – a social democrat who is none other than William Powell. Soon Powell becomes Leader of Opposition, and you can imagine the nice kind of humour you get when they both drive down to the House together. Powell bows low, opens doors, shows his master to his seat, then retires to the Opposition benches to call the Baron the foulest names that the Hays Office will allow.

It's a good idea, and all it needs is two players who know when to keep straight-faced, to flex their jaw muscles, and lift and drop their hands. There is nobody on the screen I can think of who can touch William Powell for taking a hollow part and making the shell of it shine and glitter. He bows better than anybody alive, walks round tables and makes it seem as exciting as Douglas Fairbanks used to make a leap from a castle wall. And to lines which are not very witty and not very pointed he gives all the low emphasis of his astonishing face – all the irony and fundamental doubt of a hard-boiled owl.

¶ *Bringing Up Baby*. USA, 1938, RKO; d. Howard Hawks. Cary Grant, Katharine Hepburn, Charlie Ruggles.
The Baroness and the Butler. USA, 1938, Twentieth Century-Fox; d. Walter Lang. William Powell, Annabella.

¶ AC wrote news articles from America for the London *Times* during 1938–43. The premiere of *The Great Dictator* gave him another chance to write about Chaplin while still covering politics and the war. The year before he had contributed to Paul Rotha's film about *The Times*, *The Fourth Estate*, directing a short sequence featuring its esteemed Washington correspondent, Sir Willmott Lewis – a lively character, though AC warned Rotha that on screen he looked like 'galantined cod'.

*   *   *

Mr Chaplin as Dictator.
First Showing of New Film

The Times, 16 October 1940

New York, 15 October. While a corps of special police barely managed to handle a swirling crowd on Broadway, a distinguished audience, that included Mr Charles Chaplin himself, gathered tonight in the Astoria Theatre for the world premiere of his long-awaited film *The Great Dictator*.

Playing the double role of an unpretending Jewish barber and an unidentified dictator named Adenoid Hynkel, Chaplin mimes, rants, weeps and dances for over two hours in a typical satire and knockabout. Whether he is strutting as Hynkel or fretting as Charlie he is still, after twenty-seven years in the movies, the best comedian of our age. He starts out as the least bellicose private in the First World War, assigned to operate an anti-aircraft gun, but aims the wrong way. He wanders through a smoke barrage into the wrong army, he flies an aeroplane upside down, and finally ends his career as a soldier in a twenty-year lapse of memory.

Returned to his dust-laden barber's shop, he cheerfully goes about the task of insulting storm-troopers he can recognize only as disorderly policemen. He is finally mistaken for the dictator and cheered on to address his loyal citizenry. He takes courage and thunders a six-minute appeal for tolerance and democracy. For the barber he uses the accent of an amiable English schoolboy. For Hynkel he reserves his own resonant and melodious voice, which breaks down under the stress of any frustration into a gibberish that is an artful concoction of Yiddish Esperanto and Chaplinese. Whatever the fate of Adolf Hitler, the German people may groan to know that his speaking likeness will go down to posterity in the brilliant speeches that Chaplin delivers to 'the sons and daughters of the double-cross'.

As the dictator he sustains an incomparable parody of psychotic moodiness, a tyrant who cannot trust his intimate advisers or even his radiantly blonde stenographers. At the least brooking of his will he bursts into tears or foaming rage. Once, when his Propaganda Ministry unfolds for him a dream of world conquest, he acts out the vision in a bubble dance with the terrestrial globe for his bubble. It is a moment of ridiculous fantasy he has not equalled since the 'Oceana Roll' in *The Gold Rush*.

As usual, Mr Chaplin is his own writer, director, composer and producer. And as usual, his mood ranges from episodes that only Mr Chaplin could conceive or act to crude horseplay that would never have reached the screen if Mr Chaplin would ever allow himself to consult the judgement of another producer. But for the best part of two hours he fills the screen with the trampish elegance, the miming, the old economy of gesture that offers a new excitement to a generation that has hardly seen him, and confirms for older people the ecstatic prejudice of their youth.

Unfortunately Mr Chaplin does not build to a climax of engulfing laughter, but to a long speech that fits neither the character of Hynkel nor that of a tramp, but only of an infinitely well-meaning man whose forte is not the writing of rhetoric. A feast of comic invention peters away in an appeal for human kindness that is embarrassing as it is well meant, an appeal for human brotherhood in the naïve and imping style of a high-school prize essay. It has no place in this film. But if Mr Chaplin can be persuaded to delete the last ten minutes before *The Great Dictator* is generally released, he can then confidently offer to the democratic peoples everywhere the balm of his own impish heroism, which is a better testimony than any words he can write or say to the unconquerable spirit of the cockney at bay.

¶ *The Great Dictator*. USA, 1940, Charles Chaplin; d. Charles Chaplin. Charles Chaplin, Paulette Goddard, Jack Oakie.

¶ By 1940 AC was still broadcasting cinema (and theatre) reviews in New York, for WQXR's programme *The Stage and Screen*. But general reporting of the war and the American scene was now taking over. This is how he said farewell to criticism – a little prematurely – in his last official BBC film talk.

*   *   *

Goodbye to All This

The Cinema, BBC, 28 March 1937

Now I hear the clock ticking on the wall, and there's hardly time left to say, looking back over three years, why it has been good to see a movie once a day and why it will be good, also, to see no more movies for many days to come.

What, in all this time, have the movies given us – that we couldn't get elsewhere? If we could answer that question cleanly and clearly, I think we should know why at the moment film criticism must not claim to do too much. It's worth always remembering the word 'movies'. Because it's by movement that the cinema catches your breath and makes you wipe your eyes when a Garbo falls. Whether you like it or not, you're *in* a movie, all the time, you're not seeing a level picture grouped at a given distance. You're on trams and falling down cliffs, you're leaning back on chairs, and doors open suddenly in *your* face. It is these movements, their combinations and their effect on your nervous system, which seem to me to be the whole effect of the movies, and the reason why a bad, bad movie, if it's only moderately well put together, picks you up and carries you away as a much better stage play will not. A real movie critic will be possible when the psychologists and the eye specialists have got together and told us when and how and why we react to moving pictures. Meanwhile we can most safely talk about the movies in human terms.

The movies are not any one thing. I know this from much correspondence for which, if I never thanked you in person, I thank you sincerely now. I know from these letters that people use the movies as a drug, as religion, as a source of idealism, a source of laziness, a means to smart dressing, a means to private vows. A film critic, too, will be many things, and it's not his fault if he doesn't look at movies your way. A critic, says one famous writer, must not make judgements of better or worse, he must simply elucidate. Well, if I was capable of elucidating Wheeler and Woolsey, without making judgements of better or worse, I should not be here. I'd be up in a small room with a southern exposure drawing plans for a new and better world. And then another man says: 'A film critic must deal with them strictly in terms of their own medium, in terms, that is, of editing.' Well, there again I quarrel with the phrase, 'strictly of their own medium'. What about make-up men, and supervisors and Fred Astaire? What about the ideas that belong to the movies, the idea, for instance, that if a debutante can only take an uncomfortable bus ride from Florida to New York, she will never look at another evening gown – she'll just want to live in auto camps with a newspaper reporter? Isn't that strictly an idea in terms of movie? At least I hope it is, or there'll be nobody to entertain the coronation visitors. We'll all be on walking tours with our own particular Clark Gable or Claudette Colbert.

Until the movies develop as an art, which I'm not sure they're meant to, they'll be as large and untidy as life itself. So what hope is there that any critic can be right more than a quarter of the time? And especially, especially if he stays too long at his job. Please don't think I am falling into my anecdotage if I tell you a story. On a spring day in 1915, I was playing at soldiers with a friend of mine and, as I remember, I was angry that his infantry had knocked down and broken my cavalry – all two of them. I was going to say something spiteful and mean, as only children can, when another boy strolled along with his hands in his pockets and said, as if he was announcing lunch: 'Frank, your mother wants you. Your father's been killed.' My friend, who was about six, blushed, got up tidily, and from the look of his shoulders, as he went off into the house, he hadn't yet started to cry.

Well, that's what a film critic is doing all the time. Playing at life. Moving and arranging tin soldiers, when all the time outside is a new world. A world in which people work and make promises, love with no hope of perpetual bliss, a world today in which men commit themselves and fight for their beliefs. And sometime he must get away from a world bounded by four walls and a screen.

I think I like best Don Herold's definition of a movie critic: 'He's the lone man who sits in a Chinatown bus as a decoy for the passers-by.' That's what I like to think I've been doing all this time. And I hope that sometime you've been going my way, and Chinatown didn't seem so silly after all. And so goodbye.

REPORTER

There is a very odd, and enduring, contradiction between the prejudice of the intelligentsia that today's journalism is a debased form of literature and history, and the steady belief of historians that yesterday's journalism is one of the most authentic of documentary sources.

'Today's Wrapper for Tomorrow's Fish',
The Bedside Guardian 8, 1959

¶ In February 1942, six weeks after the Pearl Harbor attack, Alistair Cooke set out by car across America to document for himself, and a book, the country's wartime life. He reached California and the moviemakers in the late spring, weeks after Bataan, in the Pacific, had fallen to the Japanese. The book's manuscript, long thought lost, was published in 2006 as *Alistair Cooke's American Journey: Life on the Home Front in the Second World War*. After the war, AC's observations on movies and American life continued in *American Letter* (retitled *Letter from America* in 1949) and the pages of the *Guardian*.

*   *   *

1942: Hollywood at War

Alistair Cooke's American Journey: Life on the Home Front in the Second World War, 2006

In the morning, I decided to go and note the sufferings of Hollywood under total war. My appetite to get out there was whetted when I read in the morning newspapers several columns professing outrage at the new order that no American should henceforth be allowed to keep more than $25,000 after his federal and state taxes were paid. Because the American Communist Party had mooted the idea in its platform of 1928, and Mrs Roosevelt and the Congress of Industrial Organizations had been hot for it in 1941, many columnists warned that the death knell of private enterprise had already sounded over the land.

Out in Hollywood, the stars were discussing it much more realistically. They thought naturally of the upkeep of their mansions. In the commissary of a famous studio you could hear conversations between male and female stars oddly like the lamentations that sounded through the more exclusive London clubs in the 1920s, after the Socialist government had stepped up death duties and estate taxes. Some of them did not see 'how they were going to live', but with undaunted energy, agents were already beginning to figure out ways of including the palaces and entourage of their clients as essential props of their popularity and, as one studio executive said, 'hence essential to war morale'. The people who were really left high, dry and panicky were the actors' agents, who saw their best providers going voluntarily into the services or slowly but surely being picked off by the draft. Ten per cent of $50 a month was a ghastly dole for men who normally bask very handsomely in the percentage due from $100,000 salaries.

However, most of the people who work in the movies are not producers, stars, feature players or even agents. In the construction shops, men who build the sets were working to drastic new restraints. Henceforth they may use no more ironwork. Walls must be made of cotton or muslin. And every time a battleship or a lifeboat sinks in a studio wreck, it must be salvaged and used again. They were told to use nails as sparingly as possible. The government had an official to check on ravenous Hollywood consumption of synthetics and of such oddities as glycerine for tears and breakfast foods for snow. There will be fewer snow scenes till the war is over. The story editors, reacting more optimistically to the Pacific losses than anybody else, had already prepared a schedule of Pacific war movies reaching well into 1945. On the basis of official war photographs and newsreels, the camera crews concluded that the Salton Sea and its surrounding flora and fauna were astonishingly like that of Wake Island. To make the shores of the Salton Sea as realistic as possible, and also to comply with navy regulations about the security of equipment, the interested studio built an air base out there and then donated it to the navy. They were then given permission to go ahead and play all they wanted. The studios hit a difficult snag in the making of these war pictures. They naturally would want to feign a good deal of actual combat, but Hollywood, and the several-thousand-square surrounding miles that have commonly obliged as background for Spanish Loyalists, Yugo-slav guerrillas, Foreign Legion sorties and run-of-the-mill sheik pur-suits, is part of the First War Area. The protection of this vast area was sufficiently arduous without having to send reconnaissance units off to distinguish between a detachment of live Japs destroying Bakers-field and Alan Ladd and William Bendix shooting it out for the Academy Award. So the army decreed that actual combat, and especi-ally aerial combat, must be done in the state of Utah. Accordingly, the first studio to film an epic of the Air Corps had to soften up civilian tension by placing prominent advertisements in the Salt Lake City and Ogden newspapers assuring the residents that a fleet of Jap bombers being destroyed by American fighters would be no cause for celebra-tion. The war would still be on. Which, in an inoffensive way, will be a relief to Hollywood for some time to come. For it is proper to say that Hollywood was revelling in the romantic challenge of the war.

I suppose that the further you go from the actual battle line the more you have to compensate in imagination for not being part of the real thing. Romanticism may be only the illusion of distance. And the West has always had for Americans the enchantment of a paradise away from the nagging realism of the familiar. In the last century, the California real-estate men worked up a brisk religion out of this appeal, and certainly for many back-broken farmers from the Mid-west, a retirement in Southern California has in reality proved as near to heaven on earth as they ever hoped to come. But the religion is maintained even by Californians who seem to have little here below. It was a poetic event when the motion picture industry, attracted by the notorious sunshine, and the variety of natural scenery, chose Southern California as its spiritual home. It was inevitable that Holly-wood should become the temple of this never-never land. So as I walked around the studios, observed the clarion signs pointing to air-raid shelters and talked with executives who from desks of cypress, and armchairs of white leather, announced in ringing tones their dedication to ultimate victory, there did not seem to me anything tasteless or embarrassing in their attitude. Their professional attitude to life has to be thoroughly romantic and highly stylized. They showed me with engaging pride a set representing an English street complete with tavern. Technical directors – that is to say, expatriate Englishmen of twenty years' standing chronically homesick for a social plane of English life they never in fact attained to – showed me the loving accuracy they had bestowed on the hanging inn sign, the pewter beer mugs, the churchwarden pipes, the low-hanging beams. To say that this inn was unlike any English inn known to our day or Dickens's is irrelevant. Hollywood is the world's assembly-line of the romantic myth. And watching the conscientious tempo of the work going forward on war movies, you would have felt that the writers and executives and producers were honestly giving their all to the nation's war effort, even if that all produces a distortion of human behaviour even more sentimental than usual.

There is a curious disparity between the work of the writers and producers and that of the technical crew. The writers brace themselves to picture conceptions grander than usual, but the cameramen and prop men and research departments leave no labour unturned to reproduce the smallest detail of uniforms, terrain and equipment. Their diligence and calmness reminded me vividly of the air cadets at Randolph Field working in a hangar, or on a test flight or in the Link trainer. And it would not be surprising if, when the war is over, it is these men – the unpoetic underlings – whose work on war films will rescue for us whatever honesty our war films will later seem to have.

Jamming the Sombrero Back On

American Letter, BBC, 2 June 1946

Californians have many reasons to be proud of their immensely beautiful and infinitely varied state. But they do not often tell you that their
fame as fruit marketers is due mainly to hundreds of thousands of very
humble people. The business of picking fruit, of planting and irrigating
and weeding out broccoli, and tending the difficult crops that grow on
marginal land has been done in the past by people who had no choice
but to work in dizzy temperatures and to work for a few months of
the year through most of the day. White men will not do the work, so
Mexicans and Filipinos and Japanese-Americans did it. But the war has
changed all that. The Japanese-Americans were all interned during the
war, except when they were drafted to fight for the land of their birth.
The Mexicans and Filipinos saw their chance to go to factories and ship-
yards, and there they picked up some new ideas about what constitutes
a tidy wage. Many will come back because they have to, but not enough.

In Hollywood the other day, a man told me that the movie studios,
now that the war is over, can relax their enforced campaign of Latin-
American goodwill. 'During the war,' he said, 'we had to show Mexicans with shoes on, without sombreros, and they had to be pictured
as active people and good neighbours, but now we're jamming the
sombreros back again and taking their shoes off.' However much
Hollywood may try in the next few years to show Mexicans as easy-
going submissive people, grateful for any dollar they can pick up in a
fourteen-hour day, the Mexicans who form the pool in this country
of what they call out here 'stoop labour' will be unconvinced. California will be able to depend less and less on an easy supply of cheap
foreign or semi-foreign, or even native labour. There is a battle coming
here, though the battle lines have hardly formed as yet.

Testing Americans' Taste
and Thoughts

American Letter, BBC, 4 August 1946

Lately the big movie producers have been getting restless about the fate of the movies they make. They have too much money invested in their products to wait in comfort for the verdict of the box-office intake. They would like to know ahead of time if a picture is worth making before they make it. Well, there is a new outfit, a sideline of Dr Gallup of the Gallup Poll, which is called Audience Research, Inc. This organization of samplers, prophets or what have you guarantees to tell the producer what final sum of money he will make on a given movie, within 10 per cent. Now, if you ask people what makes them choose a movie, they will doubtless tell you that they choose something true to life, or they follow a particular star, or they read reviews, or, on a fancier level, they follow the work of certain directors or writers. The Audience Research people say this is all nonsense. They are not saying that people don't like to think these are the motives that send them off to the movies at unpredictable times, or even every Friday night when the girl next door is free to come and watch the baby. They do say that the name of a director only very rarely sells a film, that critics never do, that remarkable qualities of direction, acting and all the other things the critics guard so jealously turn out to be pretty unimportant to the 50-odd million Americans who go to the movies once a week and who therefore keep Hollywood in the way to which it has grown accustomed.

These researchers use an extension of the Gallup Poll, questioning scientific cross-sections of the population. But they have also invented a little gadget that looks like a flashlight and is called a Hopkins Televoter. Now this is how they go to work. You know that Hollywood more and more in the last ten years has tried out a picture, finished but not finally cut, on the dog so to speak – that is on unsuspecting suburban audiences. The audience suddenly hears it is going to see a major studio preview, or, without being warned, it is privileged to see what the studio people call a sneak preview. Into a normal audience then steals a small group of men and women that Dr Gallup's boys have selected beforehand as a typical American cross-section. Each of them holds in his hands a Hopkins Televoter, this little electric gadget with a dial and an indicator you can turn to certain words. At one extreme are the words 'Like Very Much', at the other 'Very Dull', and all the shades of feeling in between. These gadgets are all wired up to a central spot, which, like a seismograph, draws a graph. And this graph is known as a preview profile, and, if it looks promising, the company that made the movie will undertake a big advertising campaign. If the result looks hopeless, they are just as likely to kill the film.

Of course, the producers who want to know whether they ought even to begin to make a movie have to depend on some general conclusions that Dr Gallup has come to after taking polls around the country. There are some alarming discoveries here; Dr Gallup finds that a movie sells itself first on its theme, which is not necessarily the same as plot, next on its title, thirdly on its cast and only fourthly on the writing, the direction, the acting and so on. Almost a third of all moviegoers choose their movies by the sound of the title and nothing else. When you talk about this sort of thing abroad, I've noticed that what comes out of it is the suspicion that Americans are very odd fish indeed. However, the fact that Americans make some queer discoveries about human habits only proves their consuming interest in finding out how humans tick, and, I suggest, does not necessarily prove that they are odder than anybody else. And I know people who will protest that they have a superior taste in movies and don't need an electric gadget to send them off to a movie with a title that sounds to them literary, or distinguished or impressive in a superior way. I think Dr Gallup is really on to something here, and one of the results he perhaps had not bargained for is a stripping of much humbug about taste.

Movies That Are Like Life:
Brief Encounter

American Letter, BBC, 22 September 1946

I want to say something about the reaction of most of the New York film critics to the British movies that are coming over here, and to their gift, which has escaped Hollywood, of reflecting the typical and the average in human living.

The movie *Brief Encounter* has just arrived, and the critics have been wondering how people who go to the movies no matter what's on would take to a diet of movies that are like life. One of them said that if enough women saw *Brief Encounter*, 'who knows, maybe in a couple of hundred years the Hollywood version of a woman's picture might itself develop some relationship to reality'. This critic outlines the plot and goes on, 'Standard picture stuff you say.' Then she puts in italics, '*Yes, but the woman wears the same hat throughout the entire picture.*' Many other critics have gone on to applaud a picture in which, as one says, 'the heroine is plain. You would never notice her. You would never notice him. And yet, *Brief Encounter* makes it convincing that these two every-day people suffer the ecstasies and anguishes of love that we have been taught are reserved exclusively for Lana Turner and Van Johnson. This, of course, is heresy, but that's what they said to Columbus when he said the world was round.'

Somebody over here or in Britain, I don't know which, has decided that *Brief Encounter* is too special and private for distribution in the big public theatres of America, and the magazine *Newsweek* retorts simply, 'Somebody has made a mistake.' I think they have, because the decision is based on the view that people who look at movies as the land of dreams and chocolate creams wouldn't like to see real life creep up on them. Or it's based on a false comparison between the tastes of British and American moviegoers. I have been a practising movie critic in both countries, and I think they are much the same. The kind of people I like – by no means a hot-house breed – are crazy about *Brief Encounter*. They want more. They – the Americans, now – are mad that *Brief Encounter* won't be on the same screens with Jane Russell and Clark Gable. And some men in the American film business with an eye to the future are – for the first time that I can remember – genuinely worried about what for so long has been called 'the threat' of British films. Through the 30s, British films were trying to produce, and unfortunately succeeding in producing, high-school imitations of Hollywood, with dubious sound, rather uncertain glamour and American slang so synthetic that I knew Americans who went to see them just to laugh at the so-called American dialogue. But now the threat of British films is no less than the threat of reality, of humdrum truth, of adult love, entailing irritation, a grown-up conscience and the gentleness of adult men for adult women. It's no less than that.

And for the movies that have embodied this threat, for *Johnny in the Clouds* [UK: *The Way to the Stars*] and *The Stars Look Down* and *The Way Ahead* and above all *Brief Encounter*, for these an awful lot of Americans are going to be grateful to you.

¶ *Brief Encounter*. UK, 1945, Cineguild; d. David Lean. Celia Johnson, Trevor Howard.

Mr Bogart Defends His Own.
Court's Judgment on a Night Club Row

Manchester Guardian, 1 October 1949

New York, 30 September. Into a dingy midtown courtroom bristling with coatless vagrants, embattled landlords and shuffling pedlars accused of selling fruit and vegetables without a licence walked today a familiar courtroom face and figure nicely done up in a smooth grey suit and a check bow tie. His identity was clinched when the judge heaved the shoulder of his gown and heard the marshal cry, 'Humphrey Bogart on complaint of Robin Roberts.'

For the first time in the dreary common round of this petty court, the swarthy Puerto Ricans forgot about their language troubles, the irate tenants about dead rats, and the bums about their discovered nests in empty warehouses.

Mr Bogart, wearing his famous hunted look, was steered by his lawyer into the small and squalid well of the court. Tapping behind him on limb-breaking high heels came a sultry brunette, her lawyer, and a bosom companion, a round-faced blonde with large eyes and a Dolly Varden hat.

Mr Bogart, it appears, had been resting after his Hollywood labours in a merry session at a local night club in the early hours of last Sunday morning. His movie star wife, Lauren Bacall, was not with him, and by way of consolation and also as a fatherly tribute to his eight-month-old son, Mr Bogart bought from the cigarette girl a large panda – a doll, that is. Miss Roberts, a model wickedly accused by Mr Bogart's lawyer of having Hollywood aspirations, tapped over to his table and tried to take the panda from him. Knowing his rights under the penal laws, Mr Bogart held on to that which was his. In Miss Roberts's heartrending version this morning, he seized her wrist and before you could say, 'Drop the gun, Louie,' she had been hurled to the floor and suffered thereby grievous bodily harm, with three blue bruises on the chest causing unmentionable hurt to the small of her back.

It probably did not help Miss Roberts's case that she had exhibited these wounds on the front page of a local afternoon paper in photographs taken by a studio which specializes in glamorizing models with a hopeful eye on Hollywood contracts. Mr Bogart's lawyer brought all this out in a legal recital which had the judge nodding his big face in ominous agreement.

Asked to expatiate on her indignities, Miss Roberts flashed her black eyes and said she had gone after Mr Bogart's panda at the suggestion of the night club's publicity agent. Her lawyer backed this up with the remark that Mr Bogart had tangled once before with the night club's sense of decorum and been told never to show his face there again.

This might have seemed to a bystanding pedlar to be bad news for Mr Bogart. But the judge did not think so. 'You mean,' he snapped, 'that this night club did not want Mr Bogart there again and this publicity agent gets a girl to go and grab his property?' That was suddenly the way it looked.

The judge inhaled triumphantly, while Mr Bogart flexed his jaw muscles and said nothing in his celebrated deadpan way. His lawyer let slip the fact that Miss Roberts had discovered her bodily grief three days after the tussle happened. Whereupon the judge announced that according to the penal code any citizen had the right to protect his property and even to use force, but only, he cautioned, throwing up a fastidious index finger, 'sufficient force to protect his property'. He decided that there was a reasonable doubt that Mr Bogart, far from committing a third-degree assault, was not actually upholding the relevant section of the penal code.

Accordingly he hardly waited for the defence lawyer to suggest that 'this is a polite form of blackmail' before he waved a big arm and said there was not a court in the land that would prefer formal charges. The case was therefore dismissed, and Miss Roberts shook her raven hair and her blonde bosom companion heaved her chest and rolled her big, big eyes.

A cheer went up from the assembled spectators, bobby-soxers, pedlars and riff-raff. Mr Bogart nodded his expert appreciation of American court proceedings. And the lawyers, the blondes and brunettes swept out to the grinning crowd outside. There a swarm of photographers broke into frog-like stances at the foot of the steps. First came Miss Roberts and her blonde helpmeet. They paused a moment at the top of the steps, took hands and descended, like models into a salon, with a one–two, hip-swinging rhythm. This earned them the raucous boos and cat-calls of the crowd.

Hardly a minute later and Bogart himself appeared, while the traffic stopped in its noonday swirl and a wave of cheers broke from the fans. The photographers begged him for a smile and a wave and urged the crowd to do likewise, which it did in ecstasy.

There was a rush for his waiting cab. Somebody stepped on an old lady's terrier and there was the unmistakable crunch of bones. At a rough estimate, about a score of delirious fans and loungers suffered grievous bruises on the chest and the small of the back. Mr Bogart was thrown into the cab. The traffic light at Madison Avenue turned from red to green and the cab roared away. Once again, justice had triumphed.

The Other Hollywood

Letter from America, BBC, 13 July 1951

In forty years the bright lights have drawn to Hollywood many strange down-and-outs, and attracted much human flotsam; and it's no discredit to the armies of able and sensitive people in the movies, or to Hollywood as a community, that it is a city deep in human dregs. The city is thick with ne'er-do-wells of every description – ex-waitresses who will never get near a studio; fifth-rate playboys who skipped their home towns; desiccated old couples from the Midwest come to live out a hollow old age in the monotonous sunshine. Third-rate writers who will write nothing, and drift into a hand-to-mouth life. Cabinet-makers and electricians and photographers who cannot make the grade in the expert world of the studio technicians, and who wind up running small shops, or doing odd carpentry jobs or running slightly shady photographic studios. Bumptious real-estate men who came too late, when every boulevard and hillside had been bought and priced, and repriced, by smarter men. Broken-down crooners, show-girls, unsuccessful models, burlesque dancers, movie-struck high-school girls, sitting up on drugstore stools hoping that what happened to Lana Turner will happen to them, that a swift young talent scout will spot them, and whisk them out of the drugstore into the movies, and a big house and a yacht.

All day long the studios' phones tinkle with calls from bit actors, from a White Russian who would like to be an extra; from an animal trainer who owns a parrot that can whistle; from a beaten-up army officer who wants to give technical advice about the Civil War; from a woman who thinks that she might be expert at making artificial flowers. I went recently into a little factory inside one of the studios where a family did just this – they made all the flowers you see in all the rooms and gardens and landscapes in the movies. God thoughtlessly neglected to consider what great arc lights do to the natural kind. It was a beautiful sight. Every known and unknown flower from every part of the world was reproduced in exquisite detail; and in such a variety of foil and plastic and paper that it was impossible to tell further away than an inch or two that they were not the finest blossoms of the real thing.

I've tried to hint at the great wealth of jobs and skills that Hollywood requires, and unfortunately the greater wealth of incompetence that is attracted to it by pathetic people acting on the belief that too many of us hold – the belief that all you need for success in Hollywood is a little scampy skill and a lot of nerve. Alas, there's no trade or profession I know with a greater requirement to live up, every day, to the most demanding, the most perfectionist standards of work – if you want to do well and stay in your job.

This Is Cinerama

Letter from America, BBC, 10 October 1952

Something happened last week to a few hundred people in New York which I shall choose to talk about because it will be happening soon to thousands in all the American cities, and then across the ocean, and before long, I imagine, in small towns in Egypt and Africa.

What happened to an audience in New York was something called Cinerama. You had better memorize the word at once, because five years from now it will be as familiar a word as telephone. This, I think, constitutes a revolution, the second in twenty-five years. A lot of things happened in the world at the end of 1927, but only one revolutionary event. It was a picture, in a movie theatre, of Al Jolson down on one knee, crooning in black face. The revolution was that as his mouth opened, you heard sounds coming from it. It doesn't seem much today, but it was the first step in a sequence of events that took in the talkies, and television and marvels yet unheard of. Four years after that Aldous Huxley put out a novel in which he imagined the birth of the 'feelies' – motion pictures in three dimensions and natural colour, which exuded from the screen the smells of the things you were seeing, the whiff of wild lilac round the bend of a road, the sniff of seaweed as you approached the sea.

Well, we are not quite there yet but very nearly. The New York audience went into a theatre specially rigged out for last week's revolution known as Cinerama. The screen was a curving cyclorama, 63 feet wide, 23 feet high: that's about six times the normal size. It is theoretically divided into three panels, which are filled by the image from three projectors, one dead centre and two others at the side. The film was shot by three lenses on three reels simultaneously. The trick of making the images overlap is so fine that they have to sink the projectors in cement, so that their vibrations will synchronize.

The lights went out and 'bam!', suddenly there you are in the San Marco plaza at Venice. When I say there you are, I mean there are the rounded pillars – lean out and touch them – the great façades, the brilliant light, the shifting skies and pigeons fluttering into your face, so that people ducked and, in spite of arrangements to the contrary, felt they could smell 'em. The first picture was a ride on a rollercoaster. Nothing peculiar in that, except that the audience is sitting in the rollercoaster, lumbering up the clacking incline, and then suddenly there is the gaping sky, the dip down and the plunge into the end of the world. A sophisticated New York beauty, a young matron who can't take rollercoasters, never could, fainted in the aisle, thus having the exact reaction of those naïve spectators in a Paris basement in 1895 who saw the first film, a picture of a train arriving in a station. The train puffed in, towards the audience, and philosophers leaped for the nearest exit.

Everybody is saying of course that the movies have taken another giant stride forward. But the charm of Cinerama is the more exciting possibility that the movies have taken a giant stride backwards, back to the direct sensation those first people felt when they saw the creaking train of the brothers Lumière. There are some old fuddy-duddies among us who still believe the movies are at their best when they are chasing something – something physical (even if it is only Harpo Marx chasing a blonde) – rather than when they are trying to say something persuasive about the emotions of a human couple faced with death or taxes. Flaubert, Shakespeare, Dickens and a few others have had things to say about death and taxes, and California does have a tendency not to be able to add much. But Shakespeare can't put you in the Monument Valley of Arizona, put you in the saddle with Gary Cooper and give you the direct physical sensation of tearing round the mesa and through the arroyos and shooting it out with the rustlers. It now appears certain that before very long we shall actually be aboard that horse and nestle into the illusion so completely that city folks will leave the theatre muscle-bound and out of breath.

The Cinerama show the other night was a succession of scenes. A performance of *Aida* at La Scala, in which you could see the people in the first ten rows of the La Scala audience rather more fleshy and breathing than the people sitting next to you in the theatre. An aeroplane trip round some of the West, high over the Rockies, tracking through the purple and red canyons of the Grand Canyon. Ducking under the Golden Gate Bridge over San Francisco Bay. No aeroplane trip or pack trip I've ever made was more actual than this. The Cinerama people can pick their weather, fly low, shift to a helicopter.

They do not claim that they are putting on three-dimensional movies. But they are exploiting to the terrifying hilt the well-known principle of peripheral vision. The screen is so wide that you can't quite take in all of it. What you see out of the corners of your eyes is what you would see in life. So the fact that the image doesn't continue round in a full circle is an irrelevant accident. As far as the spectator is concerned it does. And for the first time in history it will be possible to transport a stationary audience to London or Cairo or Bangkok and set them down, there, and all that will be missing will be their literal presence in the flesh. They will be there with all their nerves and senses, except smell – I expect Cinerama will catch up with Aldous Huxley as soon as possible.

I don't think anyone who has been to this Cinerama show has quite recovered yet or had time to brood about the effect of yet another technological revolution on our way of life. We had this summer an example of what it means to perform the national political nominating convention in the homes and public meeting places of some 50 million people. Americans got into the skin of one of their great political institutions, and millions of them have not yet recovered. We don't know yet what the televising of the conventions will do to American politics, to elections, to the convention system itself. Some of us fear what one good demagogue with a fine voice and a rousing profile might do to the tyranny of popular government.

But Cinerama in this sense is a giant leap forward into space. And just as terrifying a prospect. The only time that I ever saw Adolf Hitler was at a big rally outside the Braunhaus in Munich in 1931. I was a student who had only just heard of him. I got jammed in there and I watched him and soon felt my heart begin to pound. He was – all morals, politics aside – a superb performer. When he got to his peroration, he ended on a practically meaningless sentence. He shouted, 'It is five minutes to twelve.' Nobody knew in his head what Hitler meant. But they felt they had been slapped on the back and a sword put in their hands. Hitler paid a direct physical compliment to the nervous system. I had to fight my frightened way out over fainting women and cheering, sobbing men.

I was glad the next morning to sit down and see it in the newspaper and know that most Germans could sit back and read, and judge the speech unmoved, unseduced by the physical experience of the thing itself. The next Hitler will not suffer from this restraint. Cinerama is wonderful and I shall pursue every show they put on all over town. But I wonder, when the politicians get hold of it, what will be the future for what Edmund Burke said was the guardian of popular liberties, 'the dignity of reflection', when the event is over.

¶ The film *This Is Cinerama*, produced by Robert L. Bendick and Merian C. Cooper, was unveiled at the Broadway Theatre, New York City, on 30 September 1952. The 'feelies' of Huxley's novel *Brave New World* still lie in the future, but the 'smellies' arrived in the winter of 1959 with *Behind the Great Wall*, a documentary in AromaRama, and a spoof murder yarn, *Scent of Mystery*, shot in Smell-O-Vision. Neither system flourished.

¶ AC wrote extensive reports for the *Manchester Guardian* on the Alger Hiss perjury trials of 1949–50, the subject of his book *A Generation on Trial*. He spent fewer columns on HUAC investigations into other aspects of Communist 'infiltration' into American life, but did cast an eye on writer-director Robert Rossen's friendly appearance before the Committee on 7 May 1953, and later wrote feelingly about the blacklist. Here, his attitude towards all parties is cautious.

*   *   *

A Hollywood Ex-Communist.
Admissions to an 'Un-American' Inquiry

Manchester Guardian, 9 May 1953

New York, 8 May. The House Un-American Activities Committee, now known as the Velde Committee after its chairman, has just finished a series of hearings here investigating Communism in the entertainment industry.

It has heard nineteen witnesses, seven of whom Representative Velde called 'co-operative'. With its last witness the committee again struck pay-dirt. He was Robert Rossen, director of the prize-winning *All the King's Men* and of the later *The Brave Bulls*, who has had no film work since June 1951, when he swore he was not then a Communist but claimed his constitutional right of silence when asked about his Communist past. He told the committee yesterday that he had refused to answer about his past because he was loath to name associates who might have left the party.

However, in the past two years Mr Rossen said he had done 'a lot of thinking', and had decided that no individual can 'either indulge himself in the luxury of individual morality or put himself against what I feel today is the security and safety of the nation'. He had gone to a government agency and told them everything he knew about the Communists.

Yesterday he admitted that he had been a Party member for ten years before 1947, and must have paid, in dues and contributions to rallies and the like, 'easily' $40,000. He called off the names of fifty-seven Hollywood persons whom he had known as Communists during his time as a Party member. He maintained that 'a great many issues the Communist Party fought for were basically very good issues', and he thought that a wartime writers' congress, with headquarters in Hollywood, had 'done some very good things'. But he left the Party finally because 'the ideals you look for are just not there. None of the things are being fought for but are being used as a means to an end.'

He had come to the conclusion that for a witness to claim the protection of the Fifth Amendment (which shields a citizen against self-incrimination except under indictment by a grand jury) was 'a boogy man', for the simple reason that 'I don't believe you can be incriminated by telling the truth.'

In this series of hearings, as in many others before it, it is remarkable how invariably the 'unfriendly' witnesses are people who have cited the Fifth Amendment as grounds for refusing to answer whether they have been or are now Communists. The continuing strength of this and the other two Congressional committees investigating Communism is that the overwhelming majority of the witnesses called before them either admit to membership in the Communist Party or cry persecution and claim their right of silence when the Communist issue comes up.

In other words, the House Committee is evidently working on far more accurate evidence than it was in the days when liberals and nonconformists of various sorts feared they might be slandered by it.

There is widespread, though increasingly tacit, criticism of the tone of the committee proceedings, but it is getting harder to prove on the record that innocent liberals, or men whose only crime is heterodoxy, are being maligned or slandered in public hearings.

Senators Jenner and McCarthy and Representative Velde are now able, if only through the penitent admissions of reformed Communists, to quote impressive statistics showing that nearly all the witnesses they call have a record known to the Federal Bureau of Investigation or to the committee's investigators or both, of active membership in the Communist Party. This is a great change from the Communist hunt in the mid-1940s.

It does not dispose of the fundamental question of a citizen's right to mend his ways without public confession. But as time goes on, if and when the Democratic Party rallies itself to a full-blooded opposition, it will be on this fundamental issue, and not on wolf cries and imputations of wholesale slander, that the opposition will have to stand.

¶ Robert Rossen returned to film-making after his HUAC evidence, but chose to work outside Hollywood.

The French Line:
Morality Squad at Work

Manchester Guardian, 31 December 1953

New York, 30 December. In St Louis yesterday three members of the police department morality squad appeared in line of duty to guard against any disturbance of the peace that might be caused by the first screen appearance of Miss Jane Russell in three dimensions.

About 4,000 citizens of Missouri, whose state motto is 'Show me – I'm from Missouri', went into the theatre, looked Miss Russell over and came out again in good order. It is still a moot point whether their morals were impaired, and the morality squad is meeting today with the head of detectives and a prosecuting attorney.

The movie bears the dubious title of *The French Line*, and was not approved for exhibiting by the so-called Breen Office, which administers the morality code to which the Motion Picture Association of America voluntarily subscribes. This is the second time this year that a studio has gone ahead and filmed a script after the Breen Office found it unacceptable. The first offender was a comedy called *The Moon Is Blue*, in which a seductive girl warned a New York lone wolf that seduction (she actually used the word!) was no part of her plans for the evening. This movie was banned by the Roman Catholic Church but did a brisk business among Protestants and unbelievers.

The case of *The French Line*, considered as a morality lesson, is much more complicated. Miss Russell is innocently endowed with certain natural advantages which an English judge several years ago found impossible to censor on the grounds that they constituted an act of God. In her current movie, Miss Russell wears, if that is the word, a French-line bathing suit and does a dance sequence which the Breen Office believes will certainly bring in the cops to any theatre where it is shown. However, in private life Miss Russell is the leader of a weekly Bible class and although the casual patron of her new movie may think she is enjoying herself in a light fantastic way, Miss Russell's performance actually represents a triumph of art over personal ethics. She agrees with the strictures of the Breen Office on her performance and refused to appear in person at the movie's first showing. The St Louis incident looks like an early foray in another imminent battle between the forces of light and darkness.

¶ *The French Line*. USA, 1953, RKO; d. Lloyd Bacon. Jane Russell, Gilbert Roland, Arthur Hunnicutt.

Is US Television Killing the Movies?

Letter from America, BBC, 10 June 1954

Last Monday evening something happened on Broadway that used to happen every night during the war. The lights went out. The week before an air-raid siren went off in midtown. It is, I think, a symptom of the general gloom about Geneva, and the feeling of helplessness over Indochina, that these two events could occur to me at the same time; and that the air-raid sign, though it made only a few people duck for cover, caused many to say: 'I guess this is how it will come.'

It turned out that they were only cleaning the siren, lubricating its pipes, so to speak. But I haven't truthfully said what happened on Broadway. The lights didn't just go out. We had a brownout. During the war, this was a nightly reminder that the carefree sparkle of Broadway and its pleasures was dimmed, or ought to be, for the duration. At eight or nine o'clock every evening the big neon advertising signs – what are called in the trade 'spectaculars' – and the illuminated movie titles, sometimes a block long, went out. All that were left were the marquee lights, the regular street lights and illuminated signs immediately under the theatre marquees or in the lobbies. It was a sober sight to us, though it used to impress visiting Britons fresh from the blackout as that blinding light which will precede the Day of Judgement. They used to stagger around in Times Square trying to get their bearings, until the effect of the brownout had worn off. Their normal vision was never restored until they got on to the side streets or up dark alleys.

The brownout last Monday, sharp at nine o'clock, had nothing to do with air-raid precautions. It was a protest put on by the theatre owners and people in the movie business against an extra 5 per cent amusement tax which the City of New York was about to impose on them. Since then the city council has passed the tax and it looks as if it will be tagged on to every theatre ticket after July 1. Now this is in addition to the 10 per cent amusement tax imposed throughout the country by the federal government. This is purely a New York City tax. The theatre people, the movie men, especially, say that a levy of 15 per cent on their business is just about enough to bankrupt it. That could be pardonable hysteria in a prosperous time, but the main point is that New York City is the showcase for all the new movies. A good deal of the selling power of a movie is built up in a long New York run. The theatre owners (by which I mean movie theatres) say there just won't be any long runs in New York if this tax goes on. In fact, they expect there'll be the most disastrous falling-off in movie attendance.

All over America this has been a pain and an omen to the movie industry. Since 1950, the paying audience for movies has been going steadily – at first violently – down. It's now down by about 30 per cent. The horrendous novelty of 3-Dimension, so called, gave the industry a brief shot in the arm last year, but 3-D now sounds as much of an old slang phrase as the 'flapper' or the 'New Look'; and the same trend has re-established itself again: fewer and fewer people are going to the movies. And this in a four-year period in which the national income is higher, the number of people in jobs greater, than at any period in American history.

The effect on the professional movie colony of Hollywood is striking to anybody who looks beyond the popularity and the income of, say, fifty or sixty stars. Feature players who have been doing nicely for ten, or even twenty, years suddenly don't appear any more. There is a lot of doubling up of casts, and economical commuting of actors between studios. About 50 per cent of the writers on long-term contracts have been fired, and there's been a general paring-down of technical crews, and rehearsal time, and costs.

The men who run the industry are loath to identify the villain of this strange situation, and are almost suspiciously insistent that television is not the whole story. But they do say the *whole* story, implying that television is an awful pain in the exchequer. It has not been possible, until this last winter, to measure just how formidable the competition of television is. Because last summer and autumn the transcontinental network for television was completed. The most striking novelty of the American landscape today, to anyone who knows it pretty well, is a little box about as big as a prairie school-house. These boxes are trim and white and you see them every thirty miles, as rhythmic as telegraph poles, as you cross the country, whether you go by the south, the three middle routes, the two northern routes across 3,000 miles. They are the microwave repeater stations, that pick up and carry the television image into the laps of the next section of the people. The result last season was that the number of television sets in this country jumped from about 19 million to now over 30 million – that's one set for every five people, or two sets for every three families, covering 252 stations. We used to think – and, unhappily, the movie boys used to think – as late as three years ago that it would be years before people in the Rockies and the Sierras and the desert would have television. Everybody had movies, but now everybody doesn't have movies. Last year, suburban movie houses started to close in many big cities; then the main movie houses in many more small towns.

We may be going along on a false assumption here, on the oldest logical fallacy, which says that because something happens *after* something, it happens because of it. However, when the movie people try to defend themselves or keep their courage up, they nearly always slip into saying that if only Hollywood will make better and better pictures they can easily compete with television. My own view is that the best movies lie outside the argument. Television is not going to interfere with the audience for *From Here to Eternity* or *High Noon*; an interesting point by the way is that television in New York is not holding back the crowds for *Genevieve*, which is now in its third month at a theatre that does not often boast of such successes. But any studio that makes one *From Here to Eternity* or one *Genevieve* in a year is pretty proud of itself. Hollywood did not come to great richness because of one or two smash-hits. The movies that kept the black ink flowing in the account books were the saleable little B-films, which might be nothing as art but were entertaining enough for a lonely bachelor, a weary cowboy, a couple on their night out. But now people don't have to get dressed and stand in line for this sort of entertainment. And it seems to me the biggest threat of television to the movie industry is that people can now stay home and see bad movies.

It may be dangerous to generalize from the habits of one's own friends, but I have done a brief galloping poll among people of very different sorts. And without quite rationalizing their habits, they say that it has to be a very special, a much praised, movie, to get them out and paying money into a box-office. If you then say, 'So you've stopped seeing movies,' it comes out that, on the contrary, they see as many, if not more, movies than they have ever seen. But they see them on television. If you are a merciless enquirer, as I know you would want me to be, the significant fact comes out that a lot of people are very hazy indeed whether the movie they saw last night on television was in fact a movie or a live play acted in the studio.

I have been associated in the past two winters with a television programme [*Omnibus*] which gave a great deal of energy and skill to learning the peculiar needs of plays and acting and direction for television. One Sunday, I remember, we set the whole of Ravel's *Mother Goose* suite to a sort of play or fantasy. We had barrels of actors, playing all the characters in the *Mother Goose* tales. Some scenes took place in an underwater tank. Well, they weren't exactly taking place in a tank, but it looked that way. They were on a stage simulating the ocean floor; then the cameras add a ripple effect and it looks like an underwater scene. We had several sets that are known as matting areas, draped entirely in black velvet. The actor – Hop o'-My-Thumb let's say – stands at the top of a flight of stairs against a black curtain. One camera photographs him. Another camera photographs fish in a tank, and ocean vegetation and a toadstool. Hoppy jumps from the top of the steps on to a platform. The two images are synchronized before you see them, and it looks as if Hoppy is hopping from a rock on to the toadstool. That and all the other weird and tricky effects which had to be caught right the first time, in forty-five minutes, and which looked fine and dreamlike on the screen, practically killed our crew for a week.

The next morning a friend said to me, 'Say, that was a really knockout movie you had on yesterday. Who made it for you – Disney?' This remark set off a howl of pain from anyone who had worked on the show. But the more acute howl of pain, it occurred to me afterwards, might well come from Hollywood. And now, to add to these troubles, in the past six weeks millions of people from coast to coast have had at their elbows an incomparable mystery story, a gripping trial, a hilarious entertainment and a first-class political brawl – all in one; and on tap twice a day, from ten in the morning to twelve thirty, then from two till five thirty. I mean the investigation which Senator McCarthy's committee is holding into his row with the army. You may doubt the truth of the phrase that people had this 'at their elbows'. Don't Americans do any work? Yes, indeed, but not since the Baseball Championships in October have so many people got married, so many mothers been sick, so many grandmothers died – that's the way the office staff tells it. And somehow, in the unlikeliest offices, television sets have sprouted or been hired. The secretaries bring their lunches in, and claim an early lunch hour in order to catch the last hour of the morning's proceedings.

There are no television programmes conceived in the imagination which can hold a candle to these hearings. And by now we know Mr Ray Jenkins better than Spencer Tracy, and the army's counsel better than Mr Micawber, whom he might well be. The country has come to see and hear Senator McCarthy for six hours a day in motion, in anger, in sarcasm, in righteousness and in anxiety. The result has been – from public opinion polls – that there has been a heavy decline in the numbers of people who are for him and a big jump in the now sizeable majority that is agin him. But, whatever the political results, it is hard not to watch him. For he is a first-class actor, and it is an awesome thought that his permanent fame may come to rest not on the few or many Communists he may throw into gaol, but on the fact that he threw Gary Cooper and James Stewart out of work and Hollywood into bankruptcy.

¶ The Senate's public hearings, prompted by acid fall-out from McCarthy's claims of Communist infiltration in the United States Army, were the first to be televised live across America. Over thirty-six days some 80 million people tuned in (far more than the audience in December 1952 for AC's presentation of *Mother Goose*).

DiMaggio and Monroe

Letter from America, BBC, 14 October 1954

The Monroe–DiMaggio breakdown is easily dismissed as just another Hollywood marriage. It's true enough that over twenty, thirty years Hollywood has developed certain mores and customs. And the world jumps to the conclusion that love and marriage in Hollywood constitute something like a religious heresy, a shameless cult mocking the true faith of marriage and children. I have no hesitation in saying that this is mostly moonshine and is brewed from a compound of ignorance and envy. The casual, sometimes brazen inconsequence of love in Hollywood is no different from the social life developed in all countries and all ages by a minority of rich people whose riches alone help them to do with impunity what people with a job to watch must either do with dreadful discretion or convert into nothing more harmful than a daydream. What is commonly thought to be the chronic immorality of Hollywood is no different in kind, and no more exhibitionist than the high life of the French and Italian rivieras, of the West Indies, the Hawaiian Isles and – name your resort. It is far better publicized, but that is simply because the playboys and playgirls of the Riviera are unknown to newspaper readers, whereas the Hollywood stars suffer from the unfortunate distinction of representing the first world mythology.

The gods and goddesses of the Greeks were not much known outside the Mediterranean, and were never seen in the flesh. But the mere announcement of Marilyn Monroe arriving on platform five would cause a riot anywhere in the world. She was mobbed on arriving in Tokyo last year more embarrassingly than she was on leaving San Francisco. I was fascinated and amazed to hear in London this summer that the Teddy Boys, like the later Roman senators, go in for one of a series of haircuts modelled on their idols. One of them, a newspaper told me, was the Tony Curtis. Now, there are no Teddy Boys in this country and if you were to go into a barber here and ask him for a Tony Curtis I don't think he'd have the vaguest notion what was on your mind. The fact that London has a haircut known to a minority, known to anybody, as a Tony Curtis only goes to show that all the publicity about movie stars does not emanate from this country.

One of the big surprises to a new celebrity – and to movie stars hoping to 'get away from it all' in Europe – is the painful discovery that they behave the way a lot of people expect them to behave. And one of the inevitable developments in Hollywood in the past decade or so is that when a studio has a big star on its books, it is more and more inclined to write into his or her contract certain cancellation clauses which come into force at once if the star gets into any sort of scandal. Of course, we all have such clauses operating in our contracts with our bosses. Respectability, or the fear of it, holds an unwritten contract with us all. But until ten or fifteen years ago movie stars were rich enough, and sufficiently isolated from the life of the city of Los Angeles, to be able to afford to flout respectability. They no longer can do it. To the major studios a promising actor or actress represents a very expensive investment – of grooming, publicizing, romanticizing, to say nothing of salary – and at best it is an investment that doesn't pay off for several years. For every find that turns into a star, there are hundreds that don't justify the original investment. So now the studios are covering themselves, in response to what can for once be accurately called 'popular demand'. It is the popular demand for a hero and heroine to act that way in real life. The beginning of this demand, I think, was the marriage long long ago of Douglas Fairbanks and Mary Pickford. A Frenchman called it 'a poetic event', since it realized the ideal daydream of a whole population. The breakdown and the subsequent effect on the box-office was a shocker and should have warned the movie men that their creatures were now expected to behave by more rigid standards than the public sets itself when it's at home, so to speak, and in its carpet slippers.

I don't think there's been so much talk, from the unlikeliest people, about a movie marriage since the Pickford–Fairbanks idyll as there has been the last fortnight about Marilyn Monroe and Joe DiMaggio.

I hope I can manage to get across to you that this marriage, when it suddenly burst on the world – an elopement naturally – nine months ago, was equally a poetic event. Marilyn Monroe was not, like Miss Pickford to an older generation, the World's Sweetheart, or as one English author wrote nearly forty years ago, the kind of girl everyone wanted for his sister. Miss Monroe is more the type of girl every man would want for the sister of the boy next door. But she is not a Hollywood sophisticate. She was a poor girl, an orphan, brought up in an orphanage, and towards the end of the war she was a war-factory worker – a tousled, cheerful, lonely working girl, pretty as a kitten. It is not hard for millions of such girls to identify themselves very readily with her.

So who did Rosie the Riveter marry? She eloped with one of the two or three greatest baseball players there have ever been; nobody but the Yankee Clipper himself, a melancholy modest man who loped after a high ball in slow motion and plucked certain homers from the upper atmosphere. The Yankees' famous number five, who came up to bat at difficult times, bent over and looking no more heroic than Buster Keaton, his eyes flashing less like a Galahad than a turtle. He would let his bat swing back as idly as a spare leg, and when the runs were needed most he would whack them on his day as nobody has done since the immortal bambino – Babe Ruth. A couple of years ago he had a run of bad luck. For years he'd had trouble with his back and some sort of nagging pain in his heel tendons. He was in and out of the game, and when he came back in he looked gloomier than when he went out. But for three or four years he was untouchable. Then his heel started up again, and various ailments, and at last he hit a sensationally bad batting streak. He asked to be shelved. And the next year he retired, still in his thirties. Then he met Miss Monroe over a plate of spaghetti on a blind date. And they eloped. The perfect fulfilment of two ambitions: the average American boy's dream of being a baseball hero, and the girl next door's dream of Hollywood.

So they moved down to Hollywood, and to Joe 'down' is the word, not only from his beloved San Francisco, but from any sort of life that made sense to him. He was suddenly surrounded by voice coaches and dancing teachers, and press agents, and telephone calls for pub-licity stills, for magazine covers, for calendars, for interviews, for decorators wanting to do over the living room or sell you a mere thousand yards of Piranesi print curtains. And the object of all this concern was a wife who worked hard in a calling where you go to bed at nine and get up for work at five in the morning. It was all hopelessly bewildering, and one day Miss Monroe announces, right upstairs, right over your puzzled head, that she is going to file for divorce. Her lawyer comes dashing over one morning and delivers the papers to Joe, sitting there on the living-room sofa. He behaved very well, said the lawyer, 'took them very complacently and decently'. Then he got up, hiked his packed bags into his car, while 200 newsmen, photographers, radio and television hounds were mashing the flower beds and ruining his lawn, breaking off branches of trees to get a better shot. They asked him if he was going to make San Francisco his home. He came as near to a snort as a diffident man ever will: 'San Francisco,' he said, 'has always been my home.' And he drove off away and north from this madness like the prodigal son.

I tell you this story in its social outline and leave you to write your own moral. But don't ascribe it to Hollywood, whose divorce rate is hardly higher than that of Bradford or Kensington. Put it down in an age of television, aeroplanes, publicity and universal movies to the overwhelming conspiracy of fame against two ordinary and engaging young people who pay a rather high price for the only extraordinary thing about them – her prettiness, and his old knack of hitting a ball into the grandstand.

The Dispatch from Muskegon

Letter from America, BBC, 12 May 1955

Now, the dispatch from Muskegon is about the latest thing in drive-in movie theatres. You know that in summer they're a very popular feature of the countryside. You drive into a big field, line your car up with others facing the screen and park against any of the hundreds of little iron posts. You pull a microphone out of the post – or speaker – slip it through the side window and hang it in the car. And you sit back, tell the dog to lie still, and watch the movie in what is known as modern comfort. On hot nights, it can be a lot of fun. Though I think it's more fun still inside an air-conditioned movie theatre. Since air-conditioning is universal now, you would think drive-in theatres would have gone bankrupt. But not so. Apparently there are people who just love to see a movie from their own car, looking through the windscreen. Of course, you have the advantage, when it rains, that you can turn the wipers on, whereas in indoor theatres they don't supply wipers. Well, now they've really refined this country pleasure. The dispatch says: 'Drive-in patrons in Muskegon, Michigan, can now see the movies from a heated, glass-enclosed gallery – a sort of building. They leave their cars outside and occupy the gallery seats.' Isn't that where we came in?

A McCarthy Legacy.
Stars and Their Shadows

Manchester Guardian, 26 June 1956

New York, 25 June. The Fund for the Republic, an independent child of the Ford Foundation that was born to wrestle with problems of civil liberties, published today a 600-page report, in two volumes, on 'blacklisting', a practice which the fund concludes is now taken for granted in every part of show business except the New York theatre.

Everyone who has had only a casual acquaintance with the routine of casting movies or television plays, with hawking a programme for sponsorship, sooner or later becomes aware that there is either a very underground system of excluding 'controversial' performers, or that the moral climate of our time is remarkably stable and enervating. A bright-eyed producer or an alert casting manager will pluck from his memory 'just the type' to play Cyrano, a baseball manager, a drunk, George Washington, or what have you. A telephone call to the actor's agent establishes that the man is available and eager. He is a dues-paying member of the proper union. He has just had, or is perhaps still enjoying, a successful run on Broadway. His name is pencilled in and the satisfied director goes out to lunch.

When he comes back he finds a note to call the producer, or the sponsor, or a minor official of the network that carries the show, or another minor official of the advertising agency that got the sponsor in the first place. He may find on his memo pad an unfamiliar name from the small staff of a man who publishes a bulletin, procurable by subscription, which lists the alleged 'Communist-front' affiliations of actors who once were Communists, or who appeared before congressional committees, or who joined one of the innumerable 'people's' groups since identified by the Attorney General as

Communist fronts, or who simply gave their talent during the war for any one of hundreds of 'emergency' benefits for 'anti-fascist' refugees, for veterans of the Spanish war, for aimless or harmless busybodies who had a protest and a 'cause'.

Until about a year ago the upshot was predictable. The actor was hastily told he was 'unsuitable', or the agent agreed to let the sleeping watchdogs of Americanism lie without being refuted. Today the word is likely to come through, by equally devious but 'reliable' channels, that the actor has been 'cleared', is no longer 'controversial', and is therefore well qualified to hit the cymbals in a televised jazz session or to impersonate a drugstore clerk whipping up a milkshake.

The shower of quotation marks in the preceding paragraph is not accidental. We are in a twilight zone between the protected area of the law and the no man's land of slander and scurrility. Who patrols this land? Who are the obscure anonymous policemen who so sedulously sift the harmless actors, writers, musicians, dancers or the sheepish conformists from the goats? How systematic are the precautions taken by uniformly discreet men at their desks in an advertising agency, a soap firm, a network production unit or a Hollywood studio?

These are the questions the Fund for the Republic set itself to answer. To do so it shrewdly appointed as the editor-in-chief of this report a journalist so 'uncontroversial' as to be a Roman Catholic layman and a former editor of *The Commonweal*. Mr John Cogley has done a masterly and spine-chilling job. His staff began in January 1955 to collect facts in Hollywood and New York, the capitals of movies and television and radio. It interviewed 500 people, including watchdogs, victims, Communists, penitent Communists, union leaders, advertisers, producers, journalists, publicists of every political wing. It bolstered a reporting job with a legal study and a survey of 'morale in the radio and television industry'.

Its conclusions are depressing. Several hundred performers of one kind or another have been out of work for years because of the blacklisting custom. Some are known Communists, some have run close to contempt of Congress; and these are perhaps the only people whose misfortune one can suffer without much damage to the conscience. They are the minor Fuchses, the garrulous Red Deans of show business who have had to face the ire of most Western societies which have painfully discovered of late that total freedom of expression, if it leads to action, is a rash thing to allow to men enlisted in an international conspiracy, whether they are writers or electricians.

But this seems to be by far the smallest group. There are many, many others who see no sin in having mildly radical political opinions. Many more evidently had no political convictions at all, but gave their services free to some vaguely identified worthy cause. The retribution has been devilish, and – this report makes very clear – it has been systematic. The entertainment industry, the report concludes, has allowed outsiders working for their own profit to set up a security system of their own outrageously outside the law: which advertisers and networks and film studios have then from laziness or cowardice used as the arbiter.

The report has 'brought in no indictments and has offered no recommendations'. It has merely listed in dreadful detail the legacy of McCarthyism: which is the acceptance by otherwise responsible men of the doctrine that the law is an untrustworthy punisher of subversion; that rumour is to be believed from any source unless it can be overwhelmingly refuted; that a man's reputation is only spotless when it can be guaranteed by self-appointed moral guardians of the extreme Right.

The moral of these depressing volumes might well be the one James Thurber appended in one of his wonderfully trenchant Fables now appearing in the *New Yorker*. In the current issue there is the lamentable case of a mongoose who didn't want to fight cobras or anything else. 'The word went around that the strange new mongoose was not only pro-cobra and anti-mongoose, but intellectually curious and against the ideals and traditions of mongoosism.' Thereupon strangers who had never laid eyes on him 'remembered that they had seen him crawling on his stomach, or trying on cobra hoods'. He said he was trying to use reason and intelligence, but he was told that 'reason is six-sevenths of treason' and that 'intelligence is what the enemy uses'. In the end he was tried and condemned to banishment.

Thurber's moral is – 'Ashes to ashes, and clay to clay, if the enemy doesn't get you your own folks may.'

¶ Following publication of his assiduous *Report on Blacklisting*, John Cogley was hauled before the US Congress's House Un-American Activities Committee for interrogation, just like the entertainment figures the volumes documented.

How Television Has Hit the Cinema in the USA

Letter from America, BBC, 29 July 1956

The *Wall Street Journal* has taken one of its periodical looks into the movie business. It confirms what I gathered in casual private conversations in Hollywood in the spring. I heard that the industry has earned 40 to 45 per cent less than it did last year. I heard it from a prominent director, whose pictures incidentally are doing wonderfully well all over the world. And it could have been that, in the incomparable human manner, he was feeling sorry for the other bigwigs who did not have his knack. I do not know that big round figures covering a whole year are reliable things to go on. The fact reported by the *Journal* is that there was a 15 per cent drop in revenue from moviegoing this spring, and that the movie men are now biting their nails with anxiety over what the summer will show. This in itself is a new reflex.

In the rich, carefree days before television, summer was always accepted as a time for fishing, swimming, clambakes and fish fries, county fairs; when the old folk rocked and philosophized on the porch and the young folk were off making hay, in various forms, around the countryside. But since television built its forests of antennae on the roofs of 40 million homes, summer has turned into the best time for movie attendance. This is really an eye-opener. It does not mean that more people are going to the movies in summer than used to go in winter. It means that there is an absolute, and apparently unrecoverable, drop in the moviegoing population in winter. The night air is crowded with television programmes; and at the weekends, when the movie houses used to be jammed, the networks seem to lump all their best programmes together.

American television is a teeming, frantic medium, and some of it, of course, is trash. But much absolutely first-rate stuff, of all kinds, comes out on television in the evenings and the weekends. A plethora of good plays, finely directed; that was inevitable. But in the last three years, the networks have been gobbling up all the talent they can find not only in ballet and music and vaudeville and comedy and every conceivable form of show business; they have been scouring the research institutes, and psychiatric clinics, and universities, and industrial labs, for acknowledged experts who show a gift for communicating to a huge audience their knowledge in medicine, science, psychiatry and in all the fields which the movie people gingerly approached, in an occasional short, as 'documentary'.

At the weekends, the choice is almost suffocating, whatever your taste. You can leap from an adaptation of George Orwell to one of the big money 'quizzes'; from a programme on astronomy to a survey of American ballet; from an actual operation seen on the heart or the brain to one of a series of serious dramatizations on the history of, let us say, the great Adams family. You could, for instance, flick your dial on a Sunday afternoon and jump from seeing the Metropolitan Opera doing an unplayed Mozart to a performance of *Macbeth*; with another flick of the wrist you were listening to Dr Benjamin Spock, the most distinguished of American paediatricians, leading a group of mothers through a tricky stage of childhood care; a quarter-hour later, you would have a choice of a play by Paddy Chayefsky, a circus from Chicago, a press conference with Adlai Stevenson or the sight of the present Supreme Court – in a moving dramatization – listening to Chief Justice Warren read his historic judgment on segregation on 17 May 1954.

The movie people now seem resigned to the fact that, as the top man at RKO puts it, 'there are a lot of upper middle-aged and elderly people we are never going to get back to the theatres', except possibly for some very big and successful film. The decline in winter moviegoing is therefore so serious that the summer is now looked on as the harvest season, when the studios garner all the profit they are going to make. Summer in television ranges between the fairly good routine comedy and the vaudeville and the awful; and it surely will be a dreadful day for the movie people when television starts to set the same sort of standard in summer as in winter.

The movies, of course, have been plagued by the general prosperity. The costs of production have gone up like a rocket. The *Wall Street Journal* has checked, and accepts, the figure that the weekly attendance at movies in this country has gone down from 90 million paying customers ten years ago to 50 million today. Another decline of, say, 10 million would pretty soon force some of the studios into bankruptcy. The movie people themselves admit this.

Hollywood's famous luxury is certainly resting on a precarious base when a banker on the board of a major studio can confess, as one did to me a week or two ago, that the profit margin in his company, which is a big one, is so slender that 'we'd be really in the red if it was not for the sale of candy and popcorn in the lobby'. It is a fine thing, is it not, when the success of a great entertainment medium depends not on the actors, or the writers, or the skill of the camera work or any of the arts by which a movie can seem as moving as, but more tidy than, life itself, but comes to depend on how much popcorn you buy in the bright lobby before you plunge into the enchanted darkness.

As a routine remedy for its troubles, the industry has been building more and more drive-in summer theatres. They never caught on much before the war, but since the so-called peace they have multiplied all over the country. You drive along an eight-lane freeway or a country road and off to the left you see a huge billboard, its white screen facing an open field and a forest of spaced poles like little tombstones. They are the stations up to which you drive your car, pull a little loudspeaker off the top like a cap, hoist its cord into your car, and prop the speaker up against the side window or the windscreen. You then sit back in your car and watch the movie without having to wonder what little Fred and Susie are doing in the dark of an audi-torium. They are snugly with you in the car, and so is Rover, the family dog. The drive-in movie is probably the only invention which has increased one type of audience: the country family audience, the small farmer and his brood, the summer folks, the young spooners, the rumbustious teenagers. Of course, it assumes that every family has a car. And in a country where there is a car for every two and a half human beings, the assumption is correct enough to act on.

However, there are only 4,000 'drive-ins', and they cannot make much difference between the national profit and loss of the studio. So what are the big studios doing? They are beginning to weed out the opulent middlemen, to the great pain of many an associate producer who has rarely made a picture, the so-called front-office men, the armies of publicity chiefs and production assistants earning two or three thousand dollars a week – for what, the studios are at last sensibly asking. They are also leasing or selling their old successful movies to television. They are thinking of coming back into the studios for production and cutting the big costs of going on location. They are plunging into the gamble of cutting out B-films and small budget films, which would take nobody away from his television set, and pouring all the money into elaborate, big-budget movies. Things like *Moby Dick*, and *War and Peace* and *The Ten Commandments*. This sort of movie costs a fortune, but if it clicks, it *makes* a fortune. And these are not the sort of spectacle that television can afford to put on, or, having put on, can make very impressive in black-and-white on a 21-inch screen.

There is one change, one remedy, which has a desperation so shameful about it that even now the biggest studios cannot for their pride conceive that it might be the answer. It is to stop making movies altogether except to sell to television companies. All the big studios are doing it on the side. But they are nervous about it. They dread the day when there will be as many television sets in Europe as America. They fear that trying to marry television and keep your own purity at the same time is a hazardous proposition. They dread the thought, which comes to them in nightmares, that maybe the young will seduce the old, that in allying yourself with the enemy you may easily get swallowed up in his army and soon look as pathetic in your old Hollywood uniform as a fading opera star, or a seaside ventriloquist or the old, proud actor-manager, who dared, in the infancy of the movies, to scorn them as fly-by-nights that would never replace his living presence.

Hollywood Stars on the Rack.
Magazine Articles under Legal Scrutiny

Manchester Guardian, 21 August 1957

New York, 20 August. He that hath wife and children, said Bacon, hath given hostages to fortune. In the last month this old saw has come to Hollywood as a spectacularly painful truth.

It had no point in the 1920s, when movie actors hoped to be mistaken for fugitives from the Foreign Legion, and when the actresses hid their spouses in order to further the romantic legend that they gave their days to seeking new conquests and their nights to enslaving them. But the movie actress who first decided that children are proper things to flaunt has a lot to answer for. She was nursing a bull market in peccadilloes. She would attract, sooner or later, the attentions of the seediest sort of private eye, that is to say of the blackmailer. She made inevitable the Hollywood trial that now has the country panting more obscenely than it has done since Governor Grover Cleveland, the Democratic nominee for President, admitted his contributions to the upkeep of an illegitimate child and so tuned the fork for the Republican campaign song:

> Ma! Ma! Where's my Pa?
> Gone to the White House, Ha! Ha! Ha!

Confidential magazine boasts a circulation of 4 million readers, but there must be millions more. Its running reports on the sexual shenanigans of Hollywood are so bold and highly coloured as to attract not only the swooning fans to whom Rock and Tab and Marilyn are bywords but the sort of substantial businessman who fears that someone was looking, and the type of severe matron who grabs the despised magazine at the hairdresser's to bone up on

11. 'It was the end of the Chicago fire, and for fifteen minutes we had watched the studio production department embarked on its annual field-day.' The climax of *In Old Chicago*.

12. 'I hold that the Marx Brothers are as subtle as my bicycle, but they move quicker. And anyway, as Groucho might say, I haven't got a bicycle.' Groucho Marx in *A Night at the Opera*.

13. 'The simple, inexplicable characteristic of natural stars: you cannot take your eyes off them.' Humphrey Bogart and Lauren Bacall in *The Big Sleep*.

14. 'Fairbanks' unique grace and zest . . . an athlete without strain.' Douglas Fairbanks in *The Iron Mask*.

15. 'The perfect fulfilment of two ambitions: the average American boy's dream of being a baseball hero, and the girl next door's dream of Hollywood.' Joe DiMaggio and Marilyn Monroe, briefly married in 1954.

16. 'He filled an empty niche in the world pantheon of essential gods. If no cowboy was ever like him, so much the worse for the cattle kingdom.' Gary Cooper in *The Westerner*.

17. 'That jaunty, bouncing, cocky little figure, successfully pretending to be a scamp but rarely managing to conceal the candid, decent Everyman underneath.' James Cagney with Mae Clarke in *Lady Killer*.

18. In his film talks AC made no secret of his crush on the actress Loretta Young, captured here among the studio foliage of *Zoo in Budapest*.

19. 'When Chaplin took to anyone he was wide open from the start.' A shot from AC's movie *All at Sea*, filmed in 1933 in California on Chaplin's yacht.

20. 'We had a marvellous evening . . .' AC and his first wife Ruth, recently married, flanked by Chaplin and Paulette Goddard at the Coconut Grove nightclub, Los Angeles, in 1934.

21. AC in convivial mood at a drinks party with the 'lovely rascal' Lauren Bacall,
a good friend.

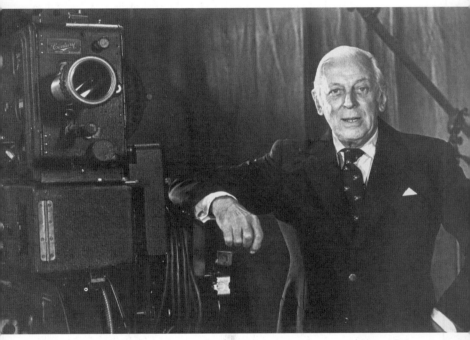

22. AC in the 1980s, standing by one of the movies' dream machines, a Century 35mm film projector.

the debaucheries she is duty bound to describe to the parish council.

It is these circumspect readers, recruited from the censorious middle class, that have thrown the movie studios and their boards of directors into a state of apprehension that is pitiful. The movie stars who have brought million-dollar libel suits against *Confidential* may be trying to wipe a stain from their honour. But to their owners in Wall Street they are lucrative properties depressing their dividends in the courts.

As a legal issue, the present trial is simple: California has its own law of criminal libel, defined as 'the publication of defamatory matter with malicious intent . . . An injurious publication is presumed to be malicious if no justification motive for publishing it is shown . . . If it can be proved that the matter charged as libellous is true, and published with good motives and justifiable ends, the party shall be acquitted.'

The movie stars and singers whose evidence before a grand jury led, last spring, to the indictment of *Confidential* are seeking to show that the published stories about them are untrue and therefore justify the charge of the grand jury's bill, which is for 'conspiracy to commit criminal libel', with malice aforethought. The defence is determined to bring the victimized stars to court and make them admit that the stories are true. It has under subpoena about one hundred stars, some of the first magnitude; and their domestic anxiety, swollen by the anguish of the studio financiers, has only to be imagined to be pitied.

The human ferrets and scavengers who haunt the court, and the millions beyond who will sniff its findings, have been hoping day after day that the presiding judge would allow this strategy of the defence. Yesterday he dealt a blow to it. He refused to admit the testimony of a night-club singer who said she was indeed the houri on the rug in an article which the prosecution had chosen not to put in evidence. Judge Herbert Walker ruled, in fact, that 'no evidence will be admitted regarding the truth of articles other than those read into the record'.

Early in the prosecution's case the court was diverted by a dramatic reading of twelve amorous episodes which the principal characters are on hand to condemn as fiction. These stories will have to be proved or disproved. The judge, however, made the excruciating point of saying that in excluding yesterday's story as irrelevant he was not stating a principle. He promised to keep everybody on the rack by judging each new story, each new exhibit, on its merits. Once they had grasped this refinement, about eighty actors and actresses who saw themselves suddenly out of the surf were back treading the water of their chronic anxiety. There remain a stoical thirteen, who presumably will have to suffer their day in court and so stand for Hollywood's good name.

¶ In the event, only Maureen O'Hara and Dorothy Dandridge stood up to refute the lurid claims of *Confidential*. In early October, facing a deadlocked jury, the judge declared a mistrial. The State of California agreed to abandon charges against the defendants; *Confidential* agreed to stop hounding the stars. Robert Harrison, the proprietor, sold the magazine the following year.

The Death of the Movies?

Letter from America, BBC, 2 February 1958

Last Monday the *New York Times* got hold of a report that was secret until then. Since it's been published, the awful truth is out and hiding it will not hide the very dire plight that it reveals. The report is a continuing survey of the market for movies in the forty-eight states and a survey of the comparative audience for television – or rather for the home audience for old movies.

Now, let's go back a little. Nineteen fifty, it seems, was the last big profitable year for the movie industry. In the very year that we were cockily dismissing television, television began to eat away at movie attendance. By 1954 it was so bad that the movie industry decided if it could not beat television it had better join it. The movie companies showed trailers on the air; they allowed their top stars to be interviewed; they gave them freedom to pursue a second career on television. Some of the studios rewrote their old successes for television; and in the advertising intervals boosted their new films.

The result was that attendance fell off by 17 per cent. In the long run the result of this courtship seems to have been the seduction and downfall of the movies. It led to a step, which this report says was a fatal one. The studios decided to sell to the TV networks for a whopping lump sum practically all the talking movies made before 1948. In the last year or so we've had them available, at our elbow, every night in the week – any time between 5 p.m. and three in the morning; with the result that movie attendance took another disastrous nosedive by about 15 per cent.

In the same period the amount of time the public spent watching the old movies on its TV set rose 500 per cent. The report hesitated to sit and brood over this dreadful comparison. It went out and asked people how often they used to go to the movies, and how often they go now. It discovered that among old moviegoers the percentage who thought of going to the movies but didn't rose in the last year from 60 to 76 per cent. Now this amounts to a loss in theatre admissions of about $10 million a week. The public now spends four times as many hours staying home to look at old movies as it does going out to see new ones. In the last quarter of last year movie attendance dropped yet another 7 million a week.

The report ends with the mournful, bell-like statement that if this trend continues for another nine months or a year, most theatres and studios in the United States will face bankruptcy, and that if Hollywood were rash enough to sell to the TV networks the movies made since 1948, it would be a death blow to theatres and to production.

I'm sure that the movie industry won't go to its doom quite as simply as that. The industry as it was for a quarter of a century, with powerful studios financing their own product and coaxing big stars with long-term contracts, that went for ever, a few years ago. But to hear that the movies are in radical trouble, and could pass away, is a shock and a shame. We have been knocking the movies for so long that it's alarming to realize how long we've enjoyed crying 'Wolf' – on the usual assumption that no wolf ever lived in these parts. I feel a little ashamed myself, rather like those people who perpetually moan over the absurdities and inefficiencies of democracy till they wake up one morning under Hitler and find it's too late to say they were only kidding.

I am deeply repentant about all the times I've sneered at the movies. The movies were one of the joys of my youth, like bicycles and arguing over Roosevelt and radio. Remember radio?

¶ AC wrote several reports of Oscar ceremonies over the years, always from the safe distance of his television set in New York. In 1958 *The Three Faces of Eve* was among the films honoured; he does not mention his own minor contribution as the story's onscreen presenter.

*   *   *

Annual Parade of Leading Film Stars. Oscar for Alec Guinness

Manchester Guardian, 28 March 1958

New York, 27 March. The Academy of Motion Picture Arts and Sciences (a title that should frighten no one, since it takes in Anita Ekberg as well as montage) held its thirtieth annual prize-giving ceremony last night in Hollywood. For the first time, the Academy spurned the advertising offers of automobile and lipstick companies and chose to sponsor the show itself. It thereby invested $850,000 of its own money to light, photograph and telecast the image of a stageful of stars whose personal services would otherwise have been available, one way and another, for about $3 million.

It was a sacrificial feast all round, suffering most of all from a severe rationing of the sort of talent – in singing, dancing and gag-writing – that could obviously be peddled elsewhere at the usual fancy going rates. It was a sadly amateur affair, giving the impression of a shipload of stars marooned with their floating scenery on a desert island, who discovered too late that they had failed to carry a quota of writers. There were five MCs instead of one: James Stewart, Rosalind Russell, David Niven, Jack Lemmon and Bob Hope. Only Hope kept his joke machine in normal running order, but then his gag-writers stamp out laughs like licence plate manufacturers in Detroit. There were several production numbers from old Academy winners, sung by stars uncannily chosen for their bathroom tenor.

There was a funny little cartoon history of the movies done by Disney and presided over by an unctuous baritone grafted on to the uvula of Donald Duck. There was, thank heaven, Mae West, grunting and sighing as shamelessly in her sixties as she did the night her show was first raided on Broadway.

Nearly all the men were boxed and delivered in what passes in America for white tie and tails, a uniform that made familiar faces seem to be dangling above giant cardboard cut-outs of a pack of stevedores dressed up for a wedding. The women – the Kim Novaks, Anita Ekbergs, Joan Collinses, Lana Turners and all – slid, wriggled, swung and insinuated their way on to the stage as if their God-given bodies were drugged with some devilish essence of beauty.

Fred Astaire waltzed on in genuine tails, trig as a fish, and Gary Cooper loped to the podium on the even keel of Wyatt Earp about to dispose of the entire male population of Dodge City, Kansas. These two provided the breathless moments, the only hints that we were in the presence of unimaginable talent.

But what about the awards? These maudlin, funny and solemn moments must be noted, because they add up to a stifling hour and half before we come, around midnight, to the only awards anybody gives a damn about, the choice of the best picture, director, actor and actress. Innumerable worthy technicians had dropped by and received the little golden spacemen, known as Oscars, for talents embracing a new automatic light print and the discovery of yet another unholy refinement of the 60-foot colour screen.

At last Gary Cooper announced that the best movie was *The Bridge on the River Kwai*. Thereafter the *Bridge* swept the board. It has the best writer, the best director (David Lean), the best scoring, best film editing and – to everyone's ultimate relief – the best actor, Alec Guinness.

At the very end comes the Oscar for which a million girls would give their all: the best actress of the year. It went to Joanne Woodward, the girl from Georgia who never had even a feature part till Nunnally Johnson threw her the triple threat of Eve White – Eve Black – Jane White in the movie of *The Three Faces of Eve*, the celebrated case of multiple personality.

In the one touching moment of this $850,000 epic, Miss Woodward could not restrain her unrehearsed tears at realizing an experience she had 'day-dreamed about since I was about nine, I guess'. She waved limply at Nunnally Johnson, a wry sandy-haired man, a Robert Benchley with a Georgia accent, the last impish descendant of the incomparable cut-ups of the 20s. What he thought about this luscious shindig would win another Oscar in another country, in another time. As it was, he too sniffed at the sight of the girl he had bullied and bet on, all her talent in shreds now, her nose as red and damp as his, two simple Southern fugitives trembling at a ball in Babylon.

¶ On 15 September 1957, at the height of the Cold War, Nikita Khrushchev, leader of the Soviet Union, arrived in the US on an official state visit, and made headlines the next day by telling journalists at the National Press Club, 'We shall bury you.' For the *Guardian*, as it was now known, AC tracked his eventful progress from Pittsburgh and Coon Rapids, Iowa, to California and the heart of Hollywood.

*   *   *

Showing Mr K the 'Real America'. Hollywood Union Rules May Spoil the Scenario. Pittsburgh Snags, Too

Guardian, 12 September 1959

New York, 11 September. Mr Khrushchev's American timetable, which the State Department published this morning, reveals a fascinating compromise (in the host's favour) between the premier's known inclination to farms and factories and the irresistible tendency of American cities to throw distinguished visitors a municipal 'banquet'.

Mr K will be the guest at two agricultural experimental stations, one business machine computer plant, one hybrid corn company, three official luncheons and eight civic dinners.

The 'final plans for the Pittsburgh visit', it says here, 'have not yet been firmed up or finalized': which could be a phlegmatic hint of the trouble the State Department is having in trying to arrange that Mr K shall not be touring the steel capital of America when the loyal steel workers, now on the longest strike in the industry's history, are either picketing the factories or paring the family budget and begging off the payments due on the automobile, the refrigerator, the deep-freeze and the second television set.

The State Department's only other miscalculation was a rather spectacular one in timing Mr K's visit to Los Angeles. Like every other visitor in the world, Mr K would like to see a movie being made. But his one-day visit falls on a Saturday, and for the past two years the union rule has been absolute that no shooting can take place on Saturday or Sunday.

Desperate negotiations are now proceeding between the State Department, the union and the Twentieth Century-Fox production company to see if a movie crew now in production can be coaxed into working on Saturday the 19th at triple pay. The president of Twentieth Century-Fox disclaimed all knowledge today of any such plan, but battle dispatches from the coast say that if it costs the company its profits Mr K will positively mingle with Frank Sinatra and the comely chorus now filming *Can-Can*. No capitalistic considerations must stand in the way of Mr K's seeing 'the real America'.

Mr K will receive an official luncheon from the Motion Picture Association of America. The struggle for seats by Hollywood idols is said to exceed the boldest shifts of their idolaters. Mr K will make 'a motor trip to points of interest in the Los Angeles area' (Tour of Stars' Homes A Specialty – $2), which may be the high spot of his whole odyssey, revealing as it will 5,000 square miles of 'the real America', compounded of drive-in shoe-shine parlours, tamale stands, 'family funeral homes', horizons of plastic slums and suburbs and more second-hand car lots than the Soviet Union will achieve in the Communist millennium. After that he will come down to earth and such humdrum realities as San Francisco Bay, more dinners and learning new tricks with hybrid corn.

The Script That Got Away.
Mr Khrushchev's Propaganda Tour
at US Expense. Los Angeles Outburst

Guardian, 21 September 1959

Los Angeles, 20 September. The world capital of make-believe was a rueful place this morning. It is at the moment making eighty movies, seventy-five of them for television. Every one of these scripts, no matter how deeply trivial its plot or revolting its message, has been scanned by X-ray eyes for the slightest error in a date, in the acoustic level of the sound, in such vital aesthetics as having a man who comes into a room with a brown felt hat leave with the same quota. Yet Hollywood looks back today on the most garbled production in its fifty years' experience. It is bewildered and guilty over the script that got away.

The formal details had been planned by the city government, the movie studios, and the State Department. No detail of Mr Khrushchev's arrival – the route of his motorcade, his dietary preferences, the protocol of the seating arrangements at lunch, the rehearsing of the scene he was to see being shot – had gone unplanned.

He came in at an obscure corner of the airport and the mayor of Los Angeles greeted him in the cryptic, cool manner that has become almost a mark of patriotism among the American officials who have the misfortune to be cast as his hosts. He was whizzed so fast over the boulevards between the airport and the Twentieth Century-Fox studio that not one Angelino in a thousand could have guessed, without prior knowledge, that here was the chairman of the Council of Ministers of the Union of Soviet Socialist Republics and not, say, Marilyn Monroe on her way to a dress fitting.

He was shown what any other distinguished tourist would have been allowed to see. He saw the dancing girls of *Can-Can*. He was actually seated at the same table as Gary Cooper, Eddie Fisher, Marilyn Monroe and James Mason. The supreme accolade was reserved for his wife: she was seated next to Frank Sinatra. American hospitality can go no farther.

'And yet, and yet . . .' as the old silent movie captions used to say, the production blew up in the faces of hundreds of skilled politicos, directors and protocol experts who had written it. Nikita Khrushchev, the humble shepherd boy who grew up to play the starring role in the lurid melodrama known to the papers here as 'The Hangman of Hungary', retraced his spiritual ancestry and suddenly turned from the home-town boy made good into a frightening 'baddie'.

He began, with amazing magnanimity, by greeting Spyros Skouras, the president of Twentieth Century-Fox, as 'a friend and brother before Christ'. He ended by recalling again the futile invasion of his country by soldiers of America, France, Germany, Poland and Britain, by briefly catching himself in an apology for such a tasteless memoir, and then by swelling the veins in his neck in protest at the State Department's denial of his wish to go down to Anaheim and make a tour of Disneyland. (The Russian security men were against it, and Mr Khrushchev agreed not to go, but in public he tactically decided to change his mind.)

'What do you have there – rocket-launching pads? Is there a cholera epidemic down there? Have gangsters taken control of the place? Your police are strong enough to lift up a bull; surely they are strong enough to take care of gangsters?' But no, the State Department could not possibly promise to 'guard my security'.

Unhappily the State Department was right. Not for nothing had the Los Angeles police been issued with a pamphlet of instructions for the safety of Mr Khrushchev that ran to seventy-five pages. He did not get to Disneyland.

'This situation is inconceivable,' he bellowed. 'I thought I could come to this country in peace, not sit in a closed car in the smothering heat under the sun. I thought I could come as a free man.'

The movie stars could not have been more uncomfortable if they had been sitting there in nothing but their mascara. Miss Monroe ventured that Mr Khrushchev's speech 'was interesting'. Winston Churchill could not have done it better.

This, it turned out, was only the beginning of the catastrophe of a nightmare of miscasting. Mayor Norris Poulson, of Los Angeles, is an admirable Californian, an alert host and a patriotic citizen. But he, too, tore up the script and played Frankenstein to the monster.

Mayor Poulson's sin was to mention again the delicate verb 'to bury', which Mr Khrushchev thought he had interred once and for all at the National Press Club in Washington. 'We shall not bury you,' cried the mayor. 'You shall not bury us . . . But if challenged we shall fight to the death to preserve our way of life.'

Mr Khrushchev's face was, in Miss Monroe's memorable word, 'interesting'. He does not take this sort of talk from Gromyko, let alone from such political midgets as the mayors of host countries.

'If you want to ride on this horse,' he said, trotting out one of those marvellously laborious Russian idioms, 'we accept that challenge. I am talking seriously . . . It is a question of war or peace . . . I have not come here to appeal to you . . . I have not come here to beg.'

Nor had he come to America to be shown 'your might' or to be left 'shaky at the knees . . . Our rockets are on the assembly lines and on our launching pads.' Mr Khrushchev clinched the historic melancholy of his visit to the City of the Angels by thinking aloud that he 'might go home'.

The only mystery left, in this factory of thrillers, is why the travelling Russian reporters so faithfully report back home that America 'welcomes the premier' and applauds his words. The visit is already a pathetic throw of the dice against the croupier, not a tour of America to see what America is about but a free campaign tour provided by the State Department, an incomparable advertisement at the American expense of the glories of Communism and the coming violent decline of the Western world.

¶ AC's next *Guardian* piece reported that the dancing girls from *Can-Can* 'left Mrs Khrushchev grey with shame', while her husband called the film 'pornographic trash'.

First Night for Doomsday:
On the Beach

Guardian, 17 December 1959

Tonight a good many citizens of sixteen countries, and the Antarctic exiles in Little America, will walk into a motion-picture show and reel out in a depression profounder than anything they have experienced from 'the world of entertainment'. They will have witnessed the total and final eclipse of our civilization in the five months after the end of the first nuclear war.

Not to be carried away at the start, we should simply report that *On the Beach*, the movie made from Nevil Shute's novel, is holding a simultaneous premiere in London, Paris, New York, Madrid, Berlin, Rome, Stockholm, Zurich, Johannesburg, Melbourne, Tokyo, Lima, Caracas, Washington, Chicago, Los Angeles, Toronto, Little America – and Moscow. Stanley Kramer, who produced and directed the film, planned it that way from the start. In a statement remarkably unlike the movie producer's usual endorsement of his product, Mr Kramer says that 'I intended the film to be seen on all continents at the same time, because I wanted to create a film for people in the power of their mass, a film that might make people everywhere feel compassion for themselves.'

What they will feel as individuals is not to be guessed at. But unless the Japanese, the Venezuelans and the Russians are made of exotic clay, they will share the common feeling of all the people who have seen this picture in private showings (the United Nations secretariat, many ambassadors, businessmen, journalists and the Soviet Cultural Commission) that *On the Beach* is something quite unique in the history of the movies: a political event of the first order, brought home to the bosoms of ordinary people with the intimate force which, of all the popular means of expression, only the movies can command.

Its story is as clean and unsentimental as a skull. The nuclear war is over and the radio operator of an American submarine, cruising in the Pacific, picks up no response from Europe, Africa, Asia or America. Only Melbourne comes in with the bell-like inference that human life has been obliterated everywhere but in Australasia. By expert calculation the surviving continent has five months left before the drifting radioactive cloud will plough it, too, into the universal grave-yard. The submarine heads for Melbourne, and the rest of the story is about the life of that city before the end comes: the first child sickens, the population queues up for suicide pills, the human animals retire to their lairs, and the last shots are of the empty streets of Melbourne, a flapping Salvation Army banner, the ultimate relic of human energy or belief. The submarine crew prefers to die as close to home as possible. It puts out eastwards for America.

The spectator emerges in spiritual shock but the optimism of the flesh soon asserts itself. No stimulant could be finer than the human bustle of the sidewalk, the quick return to friendship and nocturnal mischief. There is no doubt, I think, that the immediate emotional effect of the film could provoke a pandemic of pacifism more threaten-ing to the 'military posture' of the West than the 'peace at any price' campaign of the 1930s was to the cause of British recruiting and armament. Our dim consolation must be that the United States government, for one, has peered into the prospect of doomsday and is divided only about the way to delay or confine it. The political parties are now so absorbed in peddling their appetizing surplus to the 1960 voter that their public statements about war, peace and the defence of the homeland are almost negligible as disinterested guesses of the alternatives ahead. But in the last three weeks three independent research teams here put out their findings, and whoever takes over the White House and the next Congress will have to ponder them. One was done by Johns Hopkins University at the invitation of the Senate Foreign Relations Committee, another by the Research Insti-tute of Stanford University and the third by the Rockefeller Brothers Fund.

They all agree, in approximate terms, that a nuclear war in the next decade is more likely than not. They severely warn us that the military decline of the United States in the short span of fifteen years has left it 'open and vulnerable to direct and devastating attack'; that the disarmament studies at the United Nations and Geneva may 'blind the United States to the possibility that a Soviet Union with a clear superiority in the arms race will use it to blackmail or attack its major opponent without warning'; that 'the mutual annihilation theory' (as we see it realized in *On the Beach*) is actually too 'comforting' since it assumes that 'both sides completely accept it'. In spite of the mutual reassurances to this effect of President Eisenhower and Mr Khrushchev, the Stanford report concludes that 'there are plausible, even probable circumstances in which the leaders of a country might decide that war was the best alternative', chiefly because they will have calculated that a huge and dispersed population could certainly survive and within ten years at worst repair the political and economic damage to its functions as a nation.

The report presumes a frightful slaughter, possibly of one-third the American population but of only 10 or 20 million Russians. It figures that if all the survivors were exposed to a hundred times a normal amount of radiation the number of 'seriously defective' children would be only 1 per cent higher than it is today; and that while the leukaemias of strontium 90 would be horrible they would be 'well within the range we are accustomed to'. The survivors might expect a medium lifespan between one and six years shorter than the normal. The plain deduction from the Stanford Report is that the Russians are much better able to evacuate their city populations and to sustain their economic and social life after an effective counter-attack.

From these and other shivery calculations, the reports reject the consolations of the 'balance of terror' theory and conclude that the American capacity to prolong its attacking power is at best in doubt but will be wholly inadequate unless the Strategic Air Command is uprooted from the Omaha cave and kept perpetually mobile, unless also the city populations of the United States are given civil defence training at least as thorough as the twenty to forty hours' instruction now compulsory in the Soviet Union, and unless the continental United States is adapted to the indefinite evacuation of 80 or 90 million people.

If these hypotheses seem almost as grim as the closing sequence of *On the Beach*, they are the least that responsible military men must go on. The White House view accepts these possibilities but holds that gradual disarmament is attainable by mounting proof that mutually profitable agreements with the Soviet Union can be made and kept. The Pentagon view is that there is no practical alternative to winning the arms race and convincing the Russians that the United States will not yield to nuclear blackmail. The third view, implicit in these three reports, is that the American people are today criminally unaware of the sacrifices to their comforts that are essential to match or efface the Soviet missile advantage, so that the 'balance of terror' may become a reality the Russians will respect.

Whether the millions about to be shaken by *On the Beach* will be moved to accept the realities of their survival may be doubted. But the film will have done a service to the Western world if it stirs a large number of them to translate into political action the cool scientific warning that few men alive today can count, in the dawn of D-Day, on a life much longer than a thousand breaths.

¶ *On the Beach*. USA, 1959, United Artists; d. Stanley Kramer. Gregory Peck, Ava Gardner, Fred Astaire, Anthony Perkins.

¶ In 1961 AC began to contribute surveys of developments in the arts for the *World Book Year Book* series, issued annually by the *World Book Encyclopaedia*. This is his apocalyptic assessment of the state of the American film industry, written late in 1962.

*   *   *

The End is Nigh

'Alistair Cooke on the Arts', *The 1963 World Book Year Book*

I seriously doubt whether anything useful can now be said about the development in America of the motion picture. The main trend is brutally clear. The industry is more than ever an industry, and the pathos of its present plight is its recognition that it is failing in the first duty of an industry: to stay out of the red. It appears unlikely in the extreme that Hollywood will ever again regain the flux of artistic vitality and commercial success it achieved in the 1930s and 40s. It has been bankrupted by television and is now no more than a factory for the insatiable appetite of the networks for marketable sensations.

There are only two big studios,* and they are both in dire trouble. Both of them long ago abandoned the long-term contract, the stable of stars, directors and writers, and the willingness to let fledgling movie-makers put out sharp and good little B-films along with the necessary 'epics'. Like the hero of Dostoevsky's *The Gambler*, they

* MGM and Twentieth Century-Fox.

are trusting to a final desperate wager to repair a lifetime's habits of improvidence. *Cleopatra*, like *Mutiny on the Bounty*, is a frantic throw of the dice, the sinking of millions in a gamble for solvency. Whether or not it works, it is a sad symptom of the malaise of the American motion-picture industry.

Dignified Hollywood Awards
its Oscars

Guardian, 10 April 1963

New York, 9 April. The thirty-fifth annual presentation of the Oscars, whereby Hollywood honours its own, took place last night before a high-style audience in Santa Monica Auditorium and a beer-and-pretzels populace of something like 80 million on the outside looking in.

The ceremony was distinguished for a cluster of 'firsts'. Gregory Peck won his first Oscar; the television ceremony was uncluttered by funny men, inept cartoons or exhibitionist blondes; and it ended on time. For the first time also, no adult female wept on cue. The winners took their statuettes with the dignity of Doctors of Letters receiving their little scrolls.

With urbanity pressing in on him on all sides, the master of ceremonies, Frank Sinatra, was a prisoner of his surroundings. He made a few desperate leaps to get out – calling women 'chicks' at one time, and referring to an absent friend as 'a drinker's drinker' – but a glacial silence chilled these shafts and he was otherwise reduced to behaving with straightforward good taste and good humour. There were old-timers present who thought things had come to a pretty pass when no recipient called on his mother to bear witness to the nursing of his talent, when no shoulder-straps broke, no comedian appeared in little-boy shorts, no 15-per-cent-of-the-gross producer promised to return to his grocery store if he could not make movies of blinding courage and integrity. But to the midnight millions looking on, the whole show had the agreeable frankness of a trade exhibition, in which superior artisans received their due and left the stage with the least possible pretence of being Trappist converts.

Most of this surprising maturity must be due to the television director of the ceremony, Richard Dunlap, who worked with clean sets, showed dress design sketches instead of fulsome models wiggling on stage and used a charming chandelier as a point of rest instead of the huddling claques, the jazz drummers, the bouncing cleavage of other years.

There are, to be sure, some conventions that can be flouted only at the risk of open rebellion. Mr Sinatra was compelled to defend Hollywood against the annual charge that it is decamping before the Italian invasion. (The Academy Awards ducked that one last year by giving its prize to Sophia Loren, thus joining the enemy instead of fighting it.) The Academy has to honour at least one child actress, and it justified this chore last night by picking a superb one, Patty Duke, for her performance as a blind-mute in *The Miracle Worker*. She alone was allowed to indulge the time-honoured habit of catching her breath into the microphone, venting an honest tear, and saying 'Thank you' with a strangulated uvula and a crooked eyebrow that bodes ill for her future. Also, the Academy must spend at least half the programme handing out awards to sound engineers, special effects contrivers, music scorers, art directors and film editors.

All but one of these prizes went last night to *Lawrence of Arabia*, which thereby added a gambling suspense to the dull necessities by teasing the audience into making book on the probable sweepstake winner. It was, of course, *Lawrence of Arabia*, for by the end Private Shaw had walked off also with the best director (David Lean) and the best picture. The only other lookers-in were *The Miracle Worker*, which as well as Miss Duke had Anne Bancroft as the best actress; *Sundays and Cybele*, best foreign film; *The Longest Day* for best black-and-white photography and best effects; *Divorce – Italian Style*, best screenplay; and *Sweet Bird of Youth*, best supporting actor (Ed Begley).

Only Mr Peck appeared unshaken by the deafening sophistication of the evening. He thanked the writer, the director, the producer, the cast, the cameraman, heaved an old-time sigh for God to give him strength and gave humble thanks, too, to his wife and family and friends for 'their moral support and affection'. It is possible that Mr Peck confused Mr Peck with his heroic role in *To Kill a Mockingbird*, that of a Southern lawyer defending a Negro against the wrath of a small town. If so, he shared the misapprehension with the Academy's voters, who refused to be dazzled by the sardonic brilliance of Marcello Mastroianni in *Divorce – Italian Style* and plumped for Mr Peck's rather plodding performance of the American hero we should all very much like to be right now. It may be one useful measure of the white man's guilt towards the Negro that Mr Peck this morning is the All-American hero.

¶ Three weeks before the opening of Twentieth Century-Fox's *Cleopatra*, already famous for its tangled production history and financial excesses, AC reported on the company's shareholders meeting in New York. He passed over his own small part in the *Cleopatra* enterprise: partly on the basis of his patrician nose, he'd been invited to test for Julius Caesar by the film's original director Rouben Mamoulian. Cooke declined. The role went to Rex Harrison.

* * *

Mr Zanuck Triumphs.
Talk of a Dividend

Guardian, 24 May 1963

New York, 23 May. After all the ribbing that Twentieth Century-Fox has had to take in the last year, for the abdication of its Greek dynasty, the succession of the Old Pretender (Darryl F. Zanuck), the desperate bid of a company trying to recover a $40 million deficit by spending $34 million more on a single picture, it is only fair to report that the company made a modest profit in the first three months of this year.

This announcement, made by a flushed Zanuck to a reeling audience of shareholders, produced a storm of applause that could be dubbed into *Cleopatra* to boost the decibel volume of a Roman circus.

When Mr Zanuck held up his hand, as a mad hint that the best was yet to be, the audience froze in incredulity. The company even hoped, he crooned, for a 'dividend, when we are logically justified'. The rafters of the old town hall, which have heard some inflammatory statements in their time, shivered and creaked. It was a wonderful tribute to the resilience of private enterprise that a company could plunge $74 million into the red with the express purpose of justifying a dividend.

Once the shareholders had recovered from this big moment, some spoilsports inevitably wanted to know: 'How come?' Mr Zanuck provoked a whine of rising inflections with the news that the least possible revenue from *Cleopatra* that could pull Twentieth Century back into the black was $62 million. (Only one picture in motion picture history – *Gone with the Wind* – has ever earned so much.) Where, the hecklers wanted to know, had the other $28 million gone?

Well, the studio, which was idle all last year, was making two pictures and another dozen would begin by the fall. But if the costs of *Cleopatra* could be written off already, so as to let the studio show a profit of $2.25 million for the first three months of this year, weren't the costs of the new pictures also written off in the same way? Perhaps, somebody ventured, the hidden deficits were explained by high salaries for unmentionable persons?

Mr Zanuck didn't quite follow. So, somebody followed him right into his own home. Why was his salary (of $150,000) $50,000 higher than that of the President of the United States? And why was his 28-year-old son suddenly 'Chief of Production'? Mr Zanuck grimly replied that executive salaries (of other people) had been cut in half, that his own would be drastically slashed to $125,000 a year, and that the production chief, who happened to be his son, 'was held in the highest esteem by other companies'.

The only really raucous notes – graceless boos from envious females, and whistles and groans from the others – came when the secret was painfully unveiled. Miss Elizabeth Taylor's salary for *Cleopatra* was $1.7 million, but she had also been promised 10 per cent of the gross revenue (money which often turns into dividends). If the film grosses its necessary $62 million, Miss Taylor will be paid for this single, breathtaking performance $7,125,000.

'Who made this ridiculous contract?' some boor shouted.

Mr Zanuck kidded them not. 'It was,' he said, drooping slightly, 'her going rate at the time.'

Cleopatra, a Working Girl's Dream.
Only the Snooty Displeased

Guardian, 14 June 1963

New York, 13 June. Cleopatra barged into New York last night on her poop of beaten gold, and 10,000 New Yorkers on the streets outside yearned to be with her.

That is the only proper measure of the biggest, loudest, shiniest, heaviest (600 lb per print), most rainbow-hued film in history, which was originally budgeted for $1.2 million and has a single desperate purpose: to recover the $42 million it actually cost.

All considerations of aesthetics, historical accuracy, truth to life, dramatic power must obviously be put aside before the compelling need to salvage Twentieth Century-Fox from the Red Sea into which *Cleopatra* plunged the company, and to set it on its feet again, on dry land, with a few honest dollars and a loaf of bread.

Consequently, all the halfway celebrities with names to hawk were invited to abide by a timetable which would bring their faces and voices to the breathless millions of television. A banker who took 200 seats was asked to invite not so much the most beloved of his personal friends as the company presidents, big-time lawyers, cereal and mattress tycoons who might do the film 'most good'.

Twentieth Century has a telephone listing for a department of 'publicity and exploitation'. In the next year the exploitation branch will be put to its finest test, for the company badly needs about an extra $20 million to be on its feet again.

All the first omens were benign. The financial chivalry of New York was in the audience and was visibly stunned by a pageant that seemed less like a motion picture than a nine-ring circus and fashion show staged in the ballroom of the Americana Hotel. There were few tears to soil the glistening pancake-base of the ladies, but there were rapturous little bursts of applause for every one of Miss Taylor's hundred or so costumes, which are sure to dictate for the next year or two the absolutely compulsory outfit for intending seducers from Hong Kong to the Rue de Rivoli.

The waving cops on Broadway were a good deal more strident than the lounging state troopers of Tuscaloosa, and the barricades were more rigid than the small fences that kept the Alabama students away from Governor Wallace's last stand. When it was over, the jewellers and brokers and senators and 10-per-centers retired to several of the town's tony hangouts, and the first consensus was that Twentieth Century would survive.

This was something that the producers had been telling us, with suspicious resonance, for a year or more. After the unveiling, though, they were the most sceptical of men. They noticeably began to twitch and sweat towards 1 a.m., and there was a run on the morning papers.

By three this morning the producers had little cause to worry, for the mass-circulation papers were agog with adjectives that might have been manufactured by Twentieth Century itself. *Cleopatra* 'ranks among the few film classics', stated the *Daily News*, is full of 'high drama ... burning ambition' and 'enriches our love of beauty and art'. 'Tremendous is the word,' boomed this evening's *Journal American*. Even the *New York Times* surrendered to a 'brilliant, moving, and satisfying film ... a surpassing entertainment, one of the great epic films of our day'.

Higher up the intellectual scale, where the air is rarefied and the paying customers fewer, the *Herald-Tribune* deplored 'a monumental mouse' and covered a page lambasting the 'clichés and pompous banalities' of the dialogue, the 'fish wife' voice of Miss Taylor, the impression that 'she is really carrying on in one of Miami Beach's more exotic resorts'. At best, concludes the brave Miss Judith Crist, 'a major disappointment, at worst an extravagant exercise in tedium'.

But it is not the critics or even the producers who will ensnare the millions. It is the fairly widespread suspicion that two of the stars were enacting in private a blowzy but absorbing parody of the tale of Antony and Cleopatra. It is, above all, the very quality of Miss Taylor that Miss Crist so smoothly belittles.

Elizabeth Taylor walks with kings but at all times she keeps the common touch. She may be billed as the Queen of Egypt, but she is the universal working girl who dreamed she played *Cleopatra* in her 'Maidenform' bra.

¶ *Cleopatra*. USA, 1963, Twentieth Century-Fox; d. Joseph L. Mankiewicz. Elizabeth Taylor, Richard Burton, Rex Harrison.

AC's last sentence displays his intimate knowledge of the Maidenform company's popular, and much parodied, advertising campaigns. The film gradually recouped most of its cost, but Fox remained in financial straits until the release of *The Sound of Music* in 1965.

Men Zsa Zsa Did Not Want to Meet

Guardian, 21 August 1970

New York, 20 August. Zsa Zsa Gabor, a Hungarian sexpot of indeterminate age, is as permanent and beloved a character of the Hollywood–New York scene as Fanny Ward was of the London–Riviera merry-go-round in the 1920s. Zsa Zsa, as even doormen and bus drivers call her, is a large blonde with a striking resemblance to an iridescent meringue. She is all sugar and spice and flashing jewels, and it is reported has a heart of pure 24-carat. She is in New York more steadily than usual because she is appearing in a play called, appropriately, *40 Carats*. Zsa Zsa never does anything by halves.

Yesterday she missed the matinee because she was upset by a spectacular happening that occurred very early yesterday morning in the lift of the Waldorf Towers. This is the very plush annexe of the Waldorf Hotel, is a residential wing, and has housed at various times ex-President Hoover, the late General MacArthur, and now is the New York home of the Duke of Windsor – and Zsa Zsa.

She finished her Tuesday-night performance and joined her daughter and the daughter's boyfriend at one of the few remaining nightclubs. Then they all drove to the Waldorf in her black Rolls. They waited by the private elevator that takes the very rich and famous to their private suites. When it came the Gabor trio entered, and just as the lift boy was about to close the gates two men stepped smartly in. They were yesterday described as 'well dressed' but later Zsa Zsa amended the description to see them as looking 'like B-picture American gangsters (with) big ties, open shirt collars and pointy shoes'.

Once the door was closed they pulled out guns, pinned the lift boy, pointed the other gun at Zsa Zsa, and asked to disembarrass her of one 36-carat diamond ring, valued at $500,000, a $100,000 turquoise ring and ear-rings priced at $30,000. They then told the lift boy to return to the ground floor, where they hopped off, but not before pressing the button for the thirty-fourth floor, where Zsa Zsa retains her suite.

None of these gems is insured, and Zsa Zsa, alternately lolling and bouncing around her suite yesterday, had bitter words for the security system at the Waldorf, which the Waldorf has bitterly refuted. They have to admit, however, that they do not normally employ two robbers with open shirts and pointy shoes as escorts in the Tower suite lift.

Frankly, Zsa Zsa confessed, she was scared: 'Even (the late General) Patton would be scared here. They waved black guns in my face and said they would kill me.' The prize catch, the $500,000 ring, was, she explained, 'a gift from my third and a half or fourth and a half husband'. The half, she explained, refers to her first husband, a press attaché in Istanbul, where Zsa Zsa lived for a time before the Second World War.

The robbers got away and the mystery of their presence in the hushed corridors of the Waldorf Towers is unexplained. The other mystery is the chronic one of Zsa Zsa's age, and in her excited account of the happening to a reporter, she seemed as concerned to get those figures right as the price and jeweller's specifications of the stolen items. She was written down as 'Miss Hungary of 1936', but corrected this to read '1942, not 1936, darling'. A little later on she amended 'Zsa Zsa Gabor, 46' to '42, darling'. The jewels may be found, but Zsa Zsa's vital statistics have eluded reporters down the years.

In her autobiography, she tells of escaping from the Nazis by the Siberian railroad, crossing the Pacific, and arriving penniless in Hollywood with, at least, the credentials of a girl who had had an acting career in Budapest for some years before the outbreak of Hitler's war. Her book also darkly hints that on a moonlit night long ago she was delivered to Kemal Atatürk and became his very dear friend. If her present calculation is correct, she arrived at Hollywood at the age of eleven. Turkey's president, certainly a legendary iconoclast of social conventions, died in 1938. He evidently cherished her as an adorable nine-year-old.

¶ AC's library contained a copy of Zsa Zsa Gabor's autobiography, *My Story*, signed 'Alistair Always & Always Zsa Zsa 1960'.

Festivals of Blood and Guts

'Focus: The Arts', *The 1977 World Book Year Book*

I mentioned in last year's 'Focus' that while fewer Americans go to many movies, more Americans than ever go to, say, three or four movies a year. Thirty years ago that would have guaranteed the bankruptcy of the industry. And it has meant the end of the half-dozen or more big Hollywood corporations, financing and producing hundreds of films a year with huge resident staffs and a stable of stars under contract. It has also meant undreamed-of fortunes for independent (sometimes one-shot) companies that have the luck or cunning to exploit the seemingly insatiable hunger for violence and brutality.

In 1975, the few movies that half the population saw were *The Godfather* (parts one and two), *The Exorcist*, *Earthquake*, *The Towering Inferno*, and *Jaws*. In 1976, the itch for making films with a visceral shock spread to otherwise intelligent and gifted directors. We had the appalling end-sequence of *Taxi Driver*, in which the hero, who is presented for half the film as a sensitive young man disturbed by his experiences in the Vietnam War, suddenly is revealed as a psychopath who goes berserk with a hand-gun in a brothel. He sprays every human in sight at point-blank range and the screen is glutted with broken bone and rivers of blood, as the large metropolitan audience (when I saw it) whoops and cheers. The juicy moments in *Grizzly* are the ripping of a man's arm by a bear and the decapitation of a horse. *The Omen* begins as an apparently respectable film about the private ordeal of an American ambassador with a disturbed son. Very soon, the son is made out to be the Devil reincarnated, capable of transfixing a meddlesome priest with a bolt of lightning made actual as a sword, of throwing his mother out of the window to her death, and of causing the very visible decapitation of an inquisitve reporter.

Like *Taxi Driver*, *The Omen* tricked its family audience into thinking it was going to see a serious psychological study of ill-health, till both of them turned into festivals of blood and guts. At last report, *The Omen* was said to be vying with *The Godfather*, *Gone With the Wind*, and *The Sound of Music* (the valentines of an innocent era) as one of the all-time box-office successes. Toward the end of the year, we began to see themes formerly relegated to slummy hard-core pornographic theatres burgeoning in full-length feature films in downtown theatres: the themes, the actual sight and sound, of rape, disembowelling, even defecation.

Television has not yet dared to go so far. Because, so goes the standard argument, it is a home theatre available to youngsters help-less to know what they might see. But there are very disturbing signs indeed that the networks are committing themselves more and more to the two genres that pay off most lucratively: situation comedies and violent police plays. The television critic of the *New York Times*, not normally an alarmist of the faintest hue, wrote a bitter piece in September 1976 accusing the networks of so obsessive a concern with their advertising revenues that they are turning down such proposals as a series of 'family classics', to be underwritten by AT&T, and are packing the airwaves with dramas in which 'there isn't a single prob-lem that isn't settled by violence, a single characterization that isn't transparently sexist'. Later in the year, a federal judge ruled that the networks' own tradition of restraint, whereby sex and violence is barred from television during the so-called 'family viewing' hours between 7 and 9 p.m., is a violation of the First Amendment. The judicial argument is now at hand for any parent who wishes to assert the 'right' of an eight year-old to watch rape on the home screen. It is one more example of what, to this critic, is the almost lunatic stretch-ing to which the doctrine of free speech has recently been subjected.

The Video-cassette Recorder

'Focus: The Arts', *The 1978 World Book Year Book*

The television networks are now threatened by a technological invention that could give life to their old enemy, the movies. The video recorder – using a cassette or, imminently, a disc – is transforming the home television set into a recorder, a projector and, quite possibly in the stormy future, an exhibitor, replacing the motion picture theatre and pre-empting the networks' revenues from film re-runs. The video-cassette recorder was introduced in 1975. It boasted, correctly, that the owner could watch one channel while recording another, and could then watch *All in the Family*, or *Upstairs, Downstairs* or the Cotton Bowl game whenever he or she chose. Within a year, there were 25,000 owners of the Sony Corporation's Betamax recorder, not yet a threat to the networks' captive audiences of some 75 million TV set owners. But when NBC showed *Gone With the Wind* on two nights, it was remarked that all the blank video-cassettes in the country were sold out. In theory, at least, 25,000 homes can now see *Gone With the Wind* as often as they please. Two film companies – Disney and Universal Studios – promptly sued Sony for violation, or depreciation of copyright, claiming that the films they owned would be drastically devalued. They are demanding that Sony be restrained from selling any more Betamaxes or any other similar recorders. So far, the response of Sony, and that of the onlooking American, European and Japanese manufacturers, has been one of confident boredom. The cost of a Betamax has been halved, the sales have tripled in one year, and stock analysts predict that by 1980 the video recorder industry will register a 1,000 per cent increase over the sales of 1976.

Lawyers are sharply divided over the validity of the movie companies' lawsuit. Some say that new and binding legislation is called for. Some say that a movie company, or any other production company, can no more prevent a householder from recording a television programme than a picture magazine can prevent Eastman Kodak from selling film to amateur photographers. In the meantime, the Europeans, the Americans and the Japanese are proceeding with refinements that will produce cheaper and longer-running tapes, and will allow a separate recording unit to be attached to ordinary television sets.

But, at the same time, Philips and Sony, the two pioneers in video recorders, are promising that a cheaper and finer device, already in advance testing, could make the home-recorded programme as popular and inexpensive as a long-playing phonograph record. It is the video disc. In this system a laser beam scans the indentations on the blank record and converts them into an electron beam that composes the picture. The disc revolves 1,800 times a minute and should produce sound many times more accurate than that produced by a 33⅓ long-playing record. The industry sees an early prospect of having two-hour feature films available to the public for $10. This promise in turn opens up the prospect, surely alarming to the networks, of having the motion picture industry bypass the networks as the exhibitor of the first parts and selling directly to you, the TV set owner. There are other, at present unimaginable, revolutions: the direct sale, via cable television, of programmes to the viewer by means of a computer that reads your choice of channel, unlocks it to you and bills you later for your choice. Hitachi of Japan is already working on a video three-dimensional colour disc.

Where all this will end knows – as *Time* used to say – only God. But it certainly promises an early revolution in the distribution and exhibition of most forms of home entertainment and education. There are network officials who affect not to be disturbed. There are others who regard it all as a 'fascinating challenge'. There are glum stockholders who translate 'fascinating challenge' as 'hell – on a 1,800 rpm wheel'.

PEOPLE

We met at the Carlyle, not far from his home at Fifth Avenue and 96th Street. Mr Cooke was well known at the hotel and was treated with the deference due to a legendary fellow in his eighties. I knew it was going to be an interesting day when a Babbitt-like fellow approached the table and, addressing himself to Mr Cooke, said, 'I know you, but I can't remember your name.'

'Bob Hope,' Mr Cooke said. He chuckled softly as the interloper backed off in confusion. 'I do that all the time. They know I'm not Hope, but they don't know what to say, and they leave.'

Frank J. Prial, 'Wine Talk: A Twilight Nightcap with Alistair Cooke', *New York Times*, 7 April 2004

¶ Alistair Cooke's contacts with Hollywood personnel began at the top in the summer of 1933 with Charlie Chaplin – the star subject among the interviewees for his 'Hollywood Prospect' articles, published in the *Observer* during September and October. A general strike called by the International Alliance of Theatrical Stage Employees (IATSE) was under way at the studios, but nothing interfered with this serious lunch exchange between the living legend and the interviewer – least of all the swordfish. Chaplin was then in the early stages of work on what became *Modern Times*.

*   *   *

Charlie Chaplin Talks

'Hollywood Prospect', *Observer*, 10 September 1933

On four successive days genial, indulgent motion picture officials had, with a rather shocking deference, shown me over the typical, presumably prosperous studios. The strike had apparently blighted their luxurious labours. A girl in make-up, an occasional secretary in white ducks, were ambling around bare lots. Most of the studios were rather obviously 'carrying-on'. Emergency crews were battling humbly to learn a code of signalling, a camera, a director's whims. Later I was to see a return to what America must always, after President Harding's inspired coining, call 'normalcy'. That is, to the several hundred extras, to the Roman soldiers, the Christian maidens (for convenience, on one lot, always referred to as 'the hoods'), the dozen cameras, the small busy army of secretaries, doormen, technical advisers, supervisors, all hailing each other with a rapid, purposive cordiality I can recall in only one other place, the Braunhaus, in Munich.

When I visited the Chaplin studios I was prepared for a discreeter, a slightly more ashamed organization. There is, however, one secretary and one stenographer. There is a room with a *Who's Who*, a motion picture annual, a pile of letters, an odd print, and a caricature of Chaplin. Over a dowdy mantelpiece there is a fading sepia photograph of a young man in a four-inch collar, possibly some pleasant, enthusiastic ordinand, smiling out from over a desk on which he is signing an evidently historical document. By his side is a secretary in a buxom blouse, a dark skirt, flounced sleeves and that expression of grey demureness that women seem to carry in all photographs taken before the war. The ordinand, I peered to discover, was Charles Chaplin nearly twenty years ago.

A little dazed by the prospect of history in Hollywood, I am led outside and shown the lot. The lot is the Chaplin street. There is nobody about. The place is very still and deserted. But at any moment you expect a chesty man in a striped sweater to throw a plate from a window. Or, better, for a small black body to hobble round a corner. I look for signs, and see only the frank, immortal legends, 'Men's Clothes', on another 'Hats', on the corner 'Flowers'. And there is still the Thames Embankment, on which he prevented that inspired suicide of Mr Harry Myers.

I ask in a whisper if there are many projection theatres. I am shown it, a room not unlike a mission schoolroom, with an upright piano, a few chairs, a small screen and 'the Throne', a shiny horse-hair chair from which the great man sees his daily rushes. Like most international artists, Chaplin has to suffer cloying legends. Unlike others, most of them seem to be true. From the projection room it is a step to an outhouse, where hangs the world's mustiest suit, a green, torn costume, the cracked boots, the battered hat. Ether is their only protection. One feels that in this country they should be insured at a fabulous price, and that there is probably a special department, the Chaplin Outfit Protection Department. But in every detail this studio is a Hollywood apostasy. And the suit is apparently there for the stealing.

Soon, they say, the empty street will be packed with the Chaplin everymen and everywomen; there will be tireless rehearsals, anxious, thoughtful delays. In the second week in September a new film will be in the making.

To Chaplin the most vital thing in Hollywood is the next Chaplin film. Many of us may regret the easy conquest that makes him right in thinking so. For artistically, his ideas for a film still remain more exciting than the finished products of most others. We made no pretence of talking about much else. Lunch mattered much less. Gesticulations, frowns, grunts, sudden broad smiles, quick puckered meditations, became the accompaniment for an occasional formal nibble.

'Is it to be again a sound, but not a talking, film?'

'Yes. But much more this time it is to face the proper use of sound.'

I ventured on hoping he would never make a talkie.

'No, I'm practically certain I shan't. Not that I object to talkies. I like them enormously for other people. But my own technique has been finding itself for a good many years and to have him talk would be a fundamental intrusion.'

'Him', or 'the little man', is the Chaplin character, who is to Mr Chaplin as separate a person as any other.

'Do you agree that sound has made it much easier to make a bad film?'

'Oh, decidedly. And I for one am not going to take the risk by taking on another medium.'

'Do you agree, too, as a general maxim, that the more modes of expression one introduces into any art, the more difficult it is to make a complete statement?'

'Yes, indeed. Who is to write my dialogue if I allow that little man to talk? But I'm not complaining. I'm not sadly rejecting a desirable novelty. I don't want it. I like, I enjoy, the limitations of the non-talking film. I think every art must have binding conventions.'

'And yours?'

'Mine are not prescribed from the outside. They are simply the ways I like to tell a story. For instance, camera angles have not much to do with me. Mine is essentially a naïve technique. Of course, I admire others enormously.'

'Such as?'

'Well, you saw *M*?'

'Yes.'

'There was a masterpiece of composition and rhythm very different from the ordinary thriller. The essence of what was dramatic in a morbid character without the morbidity. And a lot of its mastery seemed to me to be in the beautiful distance at which Lang kept his camera. And one recurring angle, especially had just the right . . .'

'Coolness?'

'Coolness and control. That was it. But a device like that doesn't belong to me.'

'Because your view of the Chaplin figure is meant to be consistent?'

'It should be if it's to be a good film for me. But other directors, other styles. People are stupid about that sort of thing. They still won't recognize there are different stories, different styles, different ways of telling the same story.'

'All valid for different genres?'

'Exactly. You see, I still see everything through a proscenium arch. Because, I suppose, the cinema is still to me a mysterious, evening peep-show. I want a complete break with the actual life about us . . . even when I'm sweating to reproduce it.'

'In saying that, do you admit that your own impulse is towards naturalism?'

'No, not necessarily. I'll use anything I happen to know I think would be relevant. I'm not much concerned about form. In every art there has been since the war such a chaos of forms I think it's better to use what you understand, even if it's a medley. I don't mind if you mix naturalism, and stylization and pantomime, anything if the make-believe is strong enough.'

'Most critics write about you on the assumption that you are confessedly devoted to pantomime.'

'I know they do. It's too narrow a definition. I'm glad you've mentioned that. I'm always hearing it. I should be very sorry if there was no more to my work than pantomime.'

'Yes, pantomime has been loosely used for the visual definition that is peculiar to clowns. Would you agree that clowning is not so much a profession as a point of view, and that your work is essentially that of a clown?'

'Certainly. And clowning is possible in lots of styles, and in different forms, too, not only in comedy.'

With this principle established, we could pause to swallow our swordfish. But Chaplin was now hot on the scent of 'the little man'.

'I don't worry about where I'm going to photograph things. I know the form I like. But I do worry over the material inside it. And my material is the humour I'm exploiting.'

'It's true, is it not, that you often abandon work on a picture for a week or two until you have elucidated some "business"?'

'Oh, yes. I cannot go on unless I feel the humour is true to that character, to what I've got to say through him.'

He looked up a moment, slowly forked his dessert, cocked his head querulously, and shaking his head went on: 'The end of *City Lights*. Oh dear. A month after its release I groaned. There was a mixture of styles.'

'In direction, you mean?'

'No, in acting. It was really immoral. You remember I was outside the flower shop. When in rehearsal I suddenly saw the girl through the window I was so excited at the idea of playing it very pitifully, rather grandly, with a gaunt, heavy make-up, that I had one print made of it like that. But then I didn't abandon it entirely. I liked the sudden awful tragedy of the little man's face. And for the final take I still couldn't resist "acting" it. It was fun to take it that way, but it was much too deep for him. The end was all right, when she's feeling his face. He was still simple, blank, puzzled. But I made him a profound character, profound to himself, I mean. Oh, it was bad, bad, and just cheating.'

From the flurried stroking of his hair and the expression of his eyes, I gathered there can be no one alive who hates Chaplin more for that misdemeanour than Chaplin himself. He put his napkin on the table, looked embarrassed and amusingly sad. Then he suddenly brightened.

'Now, the new film . . .'

And he was off talking rapidly, laughing, singing – the restaurant was now empty – telling me sequence by sequence about the new film. At five o'clock we left our lunch. Up in a garden in Beverly Hills there was more room. So he went on, acted all the characters, mimed with that compact dancer's body, paused, improved, rejected an idea, excitedly improvised a new one, threw up his hands and laughed as hugely as I, guffawing on the grass. At twilight, he too sat down, exhausted.

It is sad that none of that demonstration, no word of the exposition, may be recorded. I had the rare privilege under oath of secrecy. Once the idea of the film is known it will be slickly copied, parodied, cheapened. And other funny men are less scrupulous about the time they take to make a film. With terrific labours I am told this one will be ready in the spring, perhaps before. Six weeks is, on the contrary, a long time for the making of the weekly Hollywood masterpiece.

It will be as palpably funny as anything he has done. But it is more than a personal comedy. For the first time on the screen, I think, it resolves this particular superficially comic phenomenon into a social comedy that is genuinely contemporary and, I think, sometimes profound. As they may guess who have heard Chaplin talk about the history of anarchy, about pantomime, Marx, the Haymarket Riots, Chaplin in social satire will be no joke.

¶ AC's other Hollywood interviewees in 1933 included directors Ernst Lubitsch at Paramount and Frank Lloyd at Fox, a studio whose acreage was sufficiently big, Cooke wrote, for England to consider it a county: 'Foxshire would be visible on the map.' After Foxshire, he met the crusty British character actor and former cricketer C. Aubrey Smith at his home, shortly before Smith reported for duty on *Queen Christina*. He also visited the Warner Bros. ranch, one of the locations for RKO's *Little Women*, where he met the director George Cukor and Katharine Hepburn, and was introduced to an American ice-cream icon.

*   *   *

Messrs George Cukor and C. Aubrey Smith

'Hollywood Prospect', *Observer*, 15 October 1933

One afternoon I had spent at the Fox Hills Studios, strolling round Trafalgar Square, Birdcage Walk, the intervening garden and Berkeley Square. During the next I was watching the gentle Mr Boris Karloff bowling medium-paced off-breaks while gracious English matrons chided Airedales on the edge of the boundary. Being now vaguely aware of Hollywood as that corner of a foreign field that is for ever England, I could only think it thoughtfully patriotic of Mr C. Aubrey

Smith, when I visited him, to be 'pottering' about the garden. But he is no longer 'Round-the-Corner Smith' or even the Englishman in whose honour the Los Angeles City Council gave to Hollywood its superb cricket ground. He is, at seventy, the unquestionable choice whenever a studio requires 'a distinguished Englishman' to look at once important and natural without benefit of the Hollywood monocle and the Hollywood cravat.

Tenniel has drawn him miraculously in his picture of 'The White Knight'. Some dull casting director should be permanently branded for supposing there could be another for the role in the now proceeding production of *Alice in Wonderland*. He had just completed his performance of the actor foil to Miss Hepburn's charming stage-struck girl in *Morning Glory*. He was about to begin work in the new Garbo film. He came to the movies at sixty-five and I approached him as being the stage actor who could summarize with most conviction the case for the stage actor in films. I asked him what advantages there were in a preliminary stage-training.

'The stage actor has a better confidence. His work is surer, it has more definition. He can be more certain of his detail. And after one picture, he knows the right 'pitch' of his part, the maximum effective strength he can use in playing it.'

'What personal disadvantages has the screen for the stage actor?'

'Oh, lots. He has precious little room to move about in. And if you're my size, so little of you shows! It's this cursed narrow angle.'

A point had been raised I had hoped to provoke. Sucking my mint julep as guilelessly as I could contrive, I asked: 'Do you want a bigger screen?'

'Yes, by all means. They'll soon have it.'

'So that it will have the look of a proscenium opening?'

'Yes. And then the actors will look in the right proportion.'

Pondering that last sentence, and the heresy that to me it embodies, I mentioned 'the narrow angle' to Mr George Cukor one hot afternoon when we were out on location at the Warner Brothers' ranch with the cast he was directing in *Little Women*. I lamented the current confusion between making films and making photographic records of stage plays.

'Oh, yes. I think you're right about the large screen. It would encourage stage direction.'

'Fatally encourage?'

'Yes, I suppose.'

I elaborated the force of the adverb by hinting that several Russians, for instance, had made excellent films without stars, without actors, without a discoverable plot, scenario or text that can be separated from its direction and camera treatment.

'Oh, yes, montage,' said Mr Cukor, 'is all right for them. It's too tricky for us. I've been in pictures for four years, and still have to stop myself focusing and grouping as I did for the stage. I admit I and theatre directors like me – Mamoulian for example – would be the first to confess we have a lot to learn. But we have a special function in films like this – adaptations from novels and stage plays – where to know the difficulties of stage presentation is to be readier to see where the camera can overcome them. I grant you that stories written for the screen should be impossible to perform elsewhere. But here, for instance, I'm trying to make a careful visual reproduction of a story that thousands of people know by heart. The temptations are not merely technical ones.'

'You mean it might be thought smart to guy *Little Women* in 1933?'

'Yes, or take it very solemnly and make it heavy and sentimental. Really, it's charming and unpretentious.'

Having a natural prejudice against plays and pictures that the critics call 'charming and unpretentious', I was prepared to doubt the pretensions of *Little Women*. But charming, if obviously charming, it will certainly be. There was Laurie's house. And there was Jo's, perfectly rebuilt. Miss Hepburn was kicking her legs on the grass, reading aloud 'the dawg it was that died'. Trees were there, and sunshine, and powerful floodlights.

Only the birds were missing. Suddenly, one swooped low and carolled with gusto. There was instant chaos. The production was abandoned. Assistants swore, cameramen breathed hard, the 'grips' ran around with stumps of trees, newspapers, hammers, waving them to chase away the offending reality. Because – a bird does not sound like a bird. It sounds like a Santa Fe train going through the Mojave Desert. Or like a Nazi pronouncing Dollfuss. To reproduce a bird-whistle it is necessary to have highly skilled men trilling through an instrument at a respectful and calculable distance from the microphone.

This bird unwittingly protested on my behalf. Since actual reality is impossible, why the reverence and ingenuity to imitate it? But Mr Cukor was adamant. I bit peevishly at the 'Good Humor' Miss Hepburn had thankfully provided. (A 'Good Humor' is an ineffable block of ice-cream coated with chocolate and stuck on a wooden holder, a delicacy the British Empire must discover or surely perish.)

'Don't mistake me. I want the movies to remain the movies. But soon some of them may legitimately take over the themes and methods of the theatre. Besides, there will soon be the stereoscopic screen.'

Then, truly, the actors will look 'in the right proportion'. I recalled the horror of Chaplin's face when I discussed the stereoscopic screen – 'how indecent, how loathsomely sophisticated, depriving us of the one illusion we must cherish'.

But Mr Cukor and Mr Smith were unshakeable. Theirs is undoubtedly a view to respect. But it was not mine. As I scrambled down the hills of the Warner Brothers, I had no aesthetic consolations. Only two human, unmentionable ones: I reflected that Miss Hepburn had given me a 'Good Humor', and that Mr Aubrey Smith must be the only English cricket captain – possibly the only man in Hollywood – who has played against Rugby, Oxford, the Players, Australia and Katharine Hepburn in one lifetime.

¶ AC responded warmly to the homespun American humour of Will Rogers, whose sound films were hugely popular in the US. Following Rogers' death in a plane crash with aviator Wiley Post on 15 August 1935, and with *Life Begins at 40* newly released, Cooke paid his tribute as soon as his BBC film talks resumed after the summer.

*   *   *

A Remarkable Man

The Cinema, BBC, 16 September 1935

At this point it is hard to have something to say which, like this remarkable man, shall be human and sensible at the same time. Even in America his character was so regional that a man from Texas might sit uncomfortably in a Maine cinema and be saddened by the exploitation of a great man as just another film actor. Hollywood knows its America less than most American cities and it's hard to know what they could want to make out of a man who was the bone and humour of the South-West.

This kind, fair cowboy, who, hearing some smart aleck trying to be witty about finance, would go on picking his teeth and casually define a holding-company as the people you give your money to while you're being searched; this man who preferred to talk an Oklahoma dialect that to you and me is just quaint and foreign, would have had no difficulty at all in capping the suavest asides of Oscar Wilde or Max Beerbohm. It is one of the remarkable, and remarkably American, things about him that he enjoyed their status as a national wit, that every morning about 50 million people opened their newspapers and turned straight to the highest-paid feature there has ever been in journalism – those half-dozen sentences he managed to cable every day from wherever he happened to be. And several million American citizens, aroused against the idea of losing the Philippines, had only one morning to read Will Rogers's remark that 'the Philippines wanted their freedom bad until they sent a deputation over to us to see what it looked like. Now they ain't so sure.' And the Philippines might well have thanked Rogers for the remark. There was a time when Rogers had been watching cricket here and he wrote: 'Every time I go to Lord's they're taking time out for a meal, for tea or lunch. And all their games get drawn. Now if I had my way I'd line all the players up before the game and say, "Now, fellers, no food till you're through."' Or that time when Rogers cabled from a revolt in Cuba and said: 'I sure like Cuba better than the United States. Their democracy's got us beat. I know every boy in the United States has a chance to be President. But here every boy *has* to be President.'

Such lines as these, written up as film dialogue, lose half their humour when another word is spoken, and when the character speaking them doesn't share his background with his audience. Only once, in *State Fair*, which some repertory theatre might now well revive, was the Rogers character introduced, built up and set moving organically in a milieu that to us strangers was fascinating as a curiosity. In *Life Begins at 40*, the Pitkin novel adapted to the screen, there is no remarkable direction; Rogers dutifully enacts his limited *moues* and shrugs – he was never a very good actor – and again he suffers from being kept too near to the camera for a man whose visible character was obvious in his body and carriage. But the Rogers flavour is there, the cowboy Goethe that never gets recreated in his acting. And if we have now to look on this picture as part of his family album, it will bear even that sentimentality. For it is a personality that, wept over, still remains the image of a remarkable man.

¶ *Life Begins at 40*. USA, 1935, Fox; d. George Marshall. Will Rogers, Richard Cromwell, George Barbier, Rochelle Hudson, Jane Darwell.

¶ By 1939 Chaplin was preparing *The Great Dictator*. AC applied his memories of Chaplin's daily routines in an extended profile written for the *Atlantic Monthly*. After publication, he wrote to Alfred Reeves, Chaplin's manager, wondering about Chaplin's reaction. 'He did not express an opinion at all about it to me,' Reeves replied; 'I liked it all right as a "dramatic composition" but "factually" not so much ... We hope to see you again some day, and perhaps you will find time to drop in on us for a cup of tea.' But their paths now rarely crossed – the last time in a London restaurant during the 1960s.

*   *   *

Chaplin at Work and Play

'Charlie Chaplin', *Atlantic Monthly*, August 1939

Nearly everybody who has met Charlie Chaplin seems to recall the moment vividly by the physical shock of taking his hand. You expect a small man to have a small hand; but it is not until you have doubted for a moment whether it was flesh you held or some ivory knickknack that you look at its grinning owner and say, to yourself, he certainly is a tiny man. His feet are in scale, peeking out like mice from under high-held trousers. He is a little over five feet high, and his hair is piled like a melting snowball on a monumental, you might almost say huge, head. His hair has been greying since his mid-twenties, and according to Henry Bergman, his oldest actor friend and adviser (who has been in every film Chaplin himself has made), it turned white in a day and a night in 1928 when a crisis in the day's shooting of *The Circus* coincided with the breakup of Chaplin's second marriage. However that may be, it is white and thick now.

He is neat without being prim and moves with noticeable economy, more like a gymnast than an actor. Like a gymnast, he hops through a daily game of tennis which has given Fred Perry a reasonable workout. With this daily tennis nothing and nobody must interfere. Chaplin possesses excellent health, but is anxious about it all the time, and he has a gymnast's sensitiveness to minor ailments.

When he is enjoying himself, which is mostly in his own home, he walks continuously around and between the furniture, flinging up his hands, throwing back his head in a mocking gesture, talking volubly, speculating about the president's gold policy – whatever the cause, expressing dejection, expectancy, pathos, delight and scorn. After several hours of this gruelling tension, he will practically disappear into a big chair and begin to sip pints of cold water. In such breathing spells you can get a good look at the original face which few motion-picture fans can imagine without its surmounting mop of black ringlets, its square moustache and its doughy complexion.

He has a well-modelled tanned face with small ears set almost flat against a stiff brush of hair, a small straight nose, the long convex clapper which is what most comedians seem to have for an upper lip and a very firm, balancing chin. It is a large head, its bone structure massive for the body it rests on, but there is nothing heavy about the features. As in most mobile faces, the activity is all in the eyes and mouth. He has light grey eyes and a mouth that can do anything. In acting out some grim anecdote, he will freeze his eyes and look like a death mask. A second later the eyes are almonds, the mouth a curling semicircle, and he is Pan. Or he blinks warily, tugs nervously at his wrist, inclines his head at an angle, licks an uncertain upper lip and is a melancholy sketch of the Duke of Windsor. On his feet again, he will mimic any and all the people he has met and remembered; it may be a Japanese cabinet minister or Ramsay MacDonald, an inspired drunk, Roosevelt or a current film star. Or he takes up a position with his arms outspread, waiting to receive a cape, slumps his firm shoulders, breathes heavily and is suddenly the patrician buffalo which was Edward VII – whom he once saw in a newsreel and marvelled at.

His personal living is about as extravagant as that of the average feature reporter. He gets up, eats, mooches around the piano, hits off a theme he fancies for his next film, reads for an hour or so, wanders round the garden, reads a lot more and plays tennis, has two or possibly three people he likes in to dinner. His living room – and when he's alone it's the only one he uses – is a homely thing. It is not subjected to periodical style changes and has rarely seen anything so formal as even the rambling kind of cocktail party that writers give – nothing remotely like the celebrity parties thrown by foreign correspondents, for example. It is a lived-in room. You have no misgivings about mauling the cushions; they have been well creased. The sofas have been sat on through many an all-night talk. The piano is open and slightly out of tune.

He is very English in his desire when a job is done to stretch his toes out in the acres of leisure over the hill. Security has come to mean the right to eat when he chooses and to have room to wander around, humming old tangos, playing a piano accordion; it means not being bothered by a calendar or Hollywood's strident personalities. He has difficulties here. Newer stars are often piqued at Chaplin's indifference to their fame or their parties. He goes to the movies possibly once a month and knows the names of fewer film stars than any soda-jerker in the country. He assumes another privilege that has brought him a lot of angry criticism: he does not care about time and the responsibilities set by a clock. If he is due at a party or a concert and is interrupted by a book or a friend, the odds are he will settle down with either and the engagement will never see him. At midnight he'll go out in search of food.

As the years have gone by he has kept a few close friends and grown tired of saluting the other great and near-great. There was a time when he particularly envied artists and writers what he supposed to be their special and civilized life. He wanted to meet famous men – Einstein, H. G. Wells, Aldous Huxley, Chaliapin. He met them, and Wells became and has remained a good friend. His other friends are a doctor, a movie director, a sea captain and one or two journalists. From his present wife he has had a companionship he never had before, and since she happens to be an extremely able hostess he thankfully leaves the mechanics of the household to her. When he gets depressed about anything, he likes to worry his bone in private. Mrs Chaplin has the sense to leave him alone when he is in that mood.

His matrimonial troubles were spread across the nation's front pages, not because they were more tangled than other unsuccessful marriages, but because, being an idealist, once a marriage had failed he had neither the heart nor the patience to see it briskly disposed of. He shares the Englishman's moony quest for an ideal relationship; he also shares the national distaste for admitting failure and has balked, as the English still do, at the unsentimental practicality of the divorce court.

He enjoys as much as anybody else the woven contradictions of his own personality, and will talk frankly about his feelings and his prejudices and attentively listen to suggestions about why he has them. He suffers fools with cheerful patience. He probably would be as intolerant as anybody else if he did not know that he has this ability. At fifty he is at the age to savour not so much what he has done with his life but the foolish things he knows how to avoid. 'There's nothing so enjoyable as discretion,' he once said to me. 'When you get to be over forty, it's the great virtue.' He admires reckless crusading in others and he takes naturally to men with a grouch. But, if it's all the same with you, he checked out of evangelism more than a decade ago. He is amused now by the thought that twenty years ago he was officially listed as a dangerous radical. The telegram from the Soviet on his recent birthday, lauding his artistic chores in behalf of the revolution, was greeted laughingly by a Charlie Chaplin who is a determined democrat, an anti-royalist, a good businessman and no longer as earnest as he used to be.

He hates night clubs and jazz, is bored by streamlining and efficiency experts. He has never bothered to search out for his staff rising young cameramen, film editors or ambitious graduates from major studios. During the interval of two or three years between films, his studio, a large rambling lot with a few bungalows and a small office, is quiet as a tomb. He keeps on full pay a half-dozen studio employees – his manager, a stenographer, his projectionist, a cutter, a janitor. If they can bear the monotony of loafing around the studio for a year or two they are free to play billiards, talk, smoke, do a little carpentry perhaps and occasionally project an old film. But they know their time will come. They are kept in reserve like the National Guard, leading a peaceable community life in the pleasant intervals between wars. There comes a day when Mr Chaplin drops in to inspect the general staff. He wanders through the crumbling streets that made a town in an old film. He stops to examine the disrepair of the window frames of the houses. He gazes down into the arid cement basin which was his suicide's intended grave as long ago as *City Lights*. He pokes around the dismembered hull of a ship in *Modern Times* and sits down to rest on the stony bosom of the *City Lights* statue, lying now on a broken plaster elbow. He starts to envisage where new streets will be built and where the interiors will be shot. He is ready to collect the dividend from the energy his staff have been storing all that time. They must be on hand now night and day for the next two or three months, for though life may still go on outside the gates of the Chaplin studio it can have no further meaning for them until a new film has been shot, recorded and packed away in cans for the New York premiere.

Only in the last two films has he ever worked from a script prepared beforehand, preferring always before then to shoot 'off the cuff' – that is, by improvising on the set from a general idea or a situation roughly imagined. With the coming of sound films, this became a ruinously expensive procedure. Silent film was expensive enough, and Chaplin had been accustomed to waste several thousand feet of it on the hard way up to a perfect scene. But nowadays to waste a thousand feet is to waste about twelve minutes of sound recording, high voltage and the mounting expense of a necessarily larger crew. So now Chaplin produces a shooting script first, like anybody else. This entails a delay of about nine months in shooting. But it also means that the legendary nervous tension which formerly ate up the weeks and months of unlucky actors on the set is now transferred to the ramshackle one-room bungalow, in a corner of the studio, where Chaplin works with two scriptwriters. The shooting is quicker and smoother, and most of the temper is taken out on himself.

When he starts to write a script he goes on a schedule that never falters until the film is finished. At a quarter of ten every morning, his car rolls into the studio. Out from it jumps a nervous Chaplin in a cap, white slacks and an angora sweater. He walks off rapidly to the bungalow and greets the writer he has employed for the film, his assistant director (this time his brother, snatched after a long exile from the Riviera) and the massive old friend, spiritual uncle and adviser, Henry Bergman. The room they work in reflects Chaplin's deep distrust of elegant surroundings whenever there is anything serious to be done. If it was ever wallpapered, the paper has expired into mildew. It is a small room containing three wooden chairs, an old table, about a half-dozen books with peeling backs and an ancient upright terribly out of tune. It has a window, an assortment of ashtrays and worn oilcloth on the floor. It is probably about as luxurious as any of the rooms Chaplin rented in the boarding-houses of pre-war England.

Here they stay till early evening, late evening or midnight. A scene may be sketched out in an hour or a week. Days go by as they thrash over a detail, and a sentence scribbled hopefully on Monday morning is still unfinished by Friday. In these days of deadlock, Chaplin is liable to pick up the script, curse the studio and the bungalow, pack his assistants into a car and take them all back home. He has been known to regard lunch as a devil's device to break the continuity of all good human work. The point of retreating into the mountains is to come to grips with a crisis and slay it. To this end he will lock himself up with the writer and director and give his Japanese servant stern orders that he is home to nobody and will not answer the phone. He calls his studio and tells his faithful and wiry little manager Alf Reeves, who managed him in the early vaudeville days, that he is out to anybody who may write, call or cable. The next day Reeves tells a friend, or a stockholder in New York, once a United Artists' director phoning from a corporation meeting in London: 'He can't see you, and he can't talk to you.' Alf puts down the telephone, shrugs his shoulders as he has done in the Chaplin employ for thirty years, and remarks, 'I'm on the blacklist, too.'

When Chaplin started to brood over the script of his present film (to be called *The Great Dictator*) the Los Angeles police were ineffectively using all the routine methods they knew to get in touch with him. They had a little matter of a subpoena to discuss. One Michael Kustoff was optimistically claiming that Chaplin had used his story in *Modern*

Times. The process servers started by walking up to the front door. The Japanese servant shook his head and politely slammed the door. They tried going in with the laundry; they posed as doctors and Western Union boys. Finally, in February of this year, the federal courts gave up. Judge McCormick ruefully signed an order to allow the subpoena to be served by publication.

Meanwhile Chaplin sat in his living room slowly composing pages of script. Last month he finished it, and this month will begin the second stage of the storm-and-stress period that precedes his films. He will begin the shooting. And it is on the studio floor surrounded by a milling cast that you can appreciate what his work means to him, and why, by ordinary studio standards, it is so slow in being born.

The average movie director rehearses painstakingly enough up to the moment of the 'first take'. He may shoot a scene as many as three times, and only one take will be used in the version the public sees. The average director may think of art in his whimsical moments, but he has also to think about the studio overhead. It is perhaps unfortunate for Chaplin's productivity that he pays his own bills and is doggedly prepared to waste thousands of dollars to get a scene the way he wants it. When the rehearsals are over – and a tiny scene has taken an hour or a day – the cast soon learns that this is only half the battle. For, with lights burning and cameras grinding and electricity sputtering away at a fearful price, he will still shoot a difficult scene as many as twenty times. It was estimated that during the actual shooting of *Modern Times* he was spending about $1,000 an hour. The final version constituted about a fifth of the total footage. The original length of *City Lights*, as a mere stretch of celluloid, would have reached from Hollywood somewhere into the Mojave Desert, if that would have helped. Chaplin hacked it down to one tenth its original size.

Many critics will say he could have blotted out another thousand feet and lost little. But that is an artistic comment and is curiously irrelevant to Chaplin's intentions, about which he is single-minded and immovable. His sole concern is with his own view of the Chaplin tramp character and what it can effectively do to an audience. Before *Modern Times* appeared almost any well-wisher might have begged him to delete those pre-war subtitles written in that strangely sentimental declamatory style: 'Cured of a nervous breakdown but without a job he leaves the hospital to start life anew.' But at the moment they were of a piece with his idea of *Modern Times*. Like many another artist, he turns out his best and his worst with equal zeal. It's only a year or so after the film is out that he groans at the worst and is comically unmoved by the best which the Chaplin cultists are still clutching to their bosoms. Nothing can now induce him to see *Modern Times*: he regards it as a sorry botch. When a film has been screened, it is deader than last Sunday's rotogravure. He accepts any amount of criticism of it for the reason that he is no longer interested. But while it is in the making it must be thought and dreamed about, lived with, played with, talked over, through and around.

From the actors and the crew he requires a rock-like patience. If he spies an inattentive actor from his chair on a high ladder he will flare in terrible rage, and two minutes later turn with a tired, incredulous smile to his cameraman and say, 'Can you imagine me, losing my temper like that?' The moment he recovers his temper is a moment so warm and amiable that people who have sworn to leave his employ for good and all promise themselves, 'Just this once.' The intervening crises are about as tense as any in Hollywood.

It is an odd coincidence that the two Hollywood directors who discipline their working crew to the limit of exhaustion should be the old and the new reigning comics – Chaplin and Disney. There are well-authenticated stories of artists in the Disney studio breaking down in tears before Disney's merciless insistence that a certain animal should have a nose just off *retroussé* or that a kick in the pants must be drawn in twelve and not sixteen frames of film. If rightly drawn, this means to Disney an audience satisfied without strain. To the animators and draftsmen it means blood and tears. Chaplin is equally hard on actors, property men and continuity girls, demanding that everybody should follow the inconsequent flight of his own ideas and hunches. But he is as hard on himself. If he gets an idea which he guesses will establish a character, he will produce novelettes of description and shooting script till the thing is clarified into a mere one or two shots.

A typical crisis, which took about three weeks to resolve, occurred in drafting *City Lights*. He had a hazy but attractive idea of a blind flower girl sitting on the sidewalk selling a flower to a poor man whom she must mistake for a rich man. His assistants patched up sequences that suggested the general idea. They were shot, argued about and destroyed. Chaplin strode all over the studio, working himself up to a pitch of anxiety which refused such homely details as food and rest. He tried every conceivable formula employing girl, flowers, sidewalk, rich man, poor man, $5 bill, expensive automobile. He shot these fumbling scenes and then wondered how the girl could be aware of the automobile. At the end of the third week, he suddenly conceived the vital detail – the slamming door of an automobile. In the finished movie, the incident flowed like water over a pebble, smooth and simple for all to see with no hint of the groaning pressure that had been applied. All that happened was that the poor man approached the girl, bought a flower and gave her his last dollar bill. While he stood waiting for his change, and while she was fumbling for it, she heard an automobile door slam and the purr of a luxurious car. She hesitated, said, 'Oh, thank you, sir,' and the tramp, not wanting to break this pretty vision but sad about his vanished change, backed away on tiptoe.

Audiences recognize such expositions as 'typical Chaplin' magic, ways of mating plot and character into effortless quicksilver. Behind them, however, may be the story of a fired actor or scriptwriter, distressed visits to the doctor and the exhaustion of the Chaplin health and temper.

Many ambitious writers and directors have tactfully suggested that much of this clarifying process could be shared, but though Chaplin will listen carefully to theories of this and that about film-making, first and last he trusts his own instinct and is careful to employ writers not noted for their personal style or invention. When a film is shot and he is running it over for editing, he will leap up in a split second to indicate exactly when a scene should end.

When he is choosing a theme or incidents for a projected film he will consider anybody's ideas. He even becomes an enthusiastic convert. But only as long as the evening lasts. The next morning, as unsentimentally as an executioner, he snuffs out the beautiful idea. Once when he was considering producing a short film to precede his feature film, a friend told him the old French legend of 'Our Lady and the Tumbler'. It is a slight and tragic sketch of a medieval tumbler who, on his way to the next village, rests in the shadows of a nunnery. He is awed by the sight of a nun counting her beads. The Mother Superior catches him and he is thrown into a cell. At night he escapes into the chapel and in gratitude falls on his knees before the Virgin's image. He is ashamed to offer his ignorant prayers. So he decides to present, for the Virgin, the best show of his talent. He throws himself over and over. Wet and panting from going through all his tricks, he finally attempts the best and hardest tumble known to his time. He breaks his back and dies. And the Virgin comes down and blesses him in his death trance.

Chaplin read it and started one warm summer evening to sketch the script. It is an incidental of the trade he excels in – which was that of a clown before he was a film star – that he is an agile acrobat, can navigate the high wire, and skates with professional grace. He started to act the first efforts of the poor tumbler's gratitude. He mimed a whole scene of wonder at the ritual serenity not of this world, the half-comic realization that he was ignorant, the slow self-questioning, then the quick flicker of ambition to show the only skill he knew. He was, for positively one evening only, every shape and name of humility.

The next morning he sucked his teeth and tossed away a newspaper. He said, 'Yes, it's a beautiful idea – for somebody else.' He could not be persuaded out of the conviction that film fans do not pay their quarters and shillings and francs to see the experimental art of Charles Chaplin. 'They come to see *him*,' he said, and 'him' to Chaplin means the little tramp. Ideas are good to play with, and especially ideas which can be visualized into acting. He plays with them as a violinist lingers over a cadenza, but he always knows where cadenzas belong and whether they can be played at all in the key of Charlie the tramp. He always thinks and talks of that shambling figure as he might of an absent friend in delicate health. 'He' must be coaxed and planned for and tended to give the best his admirers expect of him. It is Chaplin's greatest fear that he may lose his acute sense of what an audience expects of him. To avoid that he will gladly sacrifice new conceptions and tear up painfully composed scripts which might turn into any other art than his.

And yet he is now spending all his fruitful days and nights in composing the character of a dictator. Those who have seen him recreate scenes in the life of Napoleon have no fears for his popular reception as a dramatic actor as remarkable as he is as a comic. But his moment of trial will come the first time the new Chaplin face appears on the screen. If the audience accepts the new role, his dramatic career will not be threatened. If they clap the familiar moustache on to it, and read the old slyness into the unfamiliar features, then the little tramp may seem an impertinence and the new character an impersonation that failed. He has taken three years to plan this tricky parallel. But *The Great Dictator* will be more than an artistic risk. As a business venture it has called for considerable daring. Chaplin has never minded losing the German and Italian revenue. He has scorned to publicize the simple error those countries make in identifying him as a Jew. This time his choice of theme almost certainly blights for him any prospect of showing the film in Poland and Portugal, in most of South America, in the admiring Soviet, and in Japan. Japan is problematical. It loves Chaplin and still on his birthday holds a ritual parade of a hundred Chaplin figures through the streets of Tokyo.

If, through some unforeseen quirk of British foreign policy, the word 'appeasement' should raise its haloed head again, Chaplin would resign himself to the possible British suppression and go right ahead with his double characterization of a dictator and a bum who gets mistaken for him. For at fifty he still has in abundance the obstinate passion to do exactly what he wants to do. This intractability is the mainspring of his artistic consistency. He may prize discretion now in his personal and social relations. But his work is in a world of fantasy where ideas must be wooed slowly and won for what they are worth. And when he wants to do something hard enough, the sight and sound of an emerging film are well worth to him the loss of his digestion, a friendship or two, a million dollars or the blessing of the British Foreign Office.

¶ The 'Our Lady and the Tumbler' idea dates from 1934, when Chaplin was considering several short films. AC was enlisted to help, but no films resulted. He later drew upon this *Atlantic* profile for the Chaplin memoir in *Six Men*.

¶ AC never warmed particularly to the films or personality of Alfred Hitchcock (from 1939 another British import to America). But as these two radio vignettes prove, he kept a quizzical eye on the director's doings.

* * *

Ho! Buicks!

Mainly About Manhattan, BBC, 19 January 1939

In Manhattan the new Hitchcock movie, *The Lady Vanishes*, has been voted by the critics as the best directed movie of 1938. I have never known an audience in a movie theatre anywhere applaud so wholeheartedly together as the Broadway audiences are applauding *The Lady Vanishes*. There is just one moment, however, in that film where a great laugh rises from the American audience, which positively does not happen in England. When the train is switched which the Central European crook is chasing along the road by the side of the track, a great shout goes up from the startled audience. The two cars come along the road, and half the audience is smitten with astonishment, and cries, 'Ho! Buicks!' You know that Americans will often accept ridiculous plots in stories provided the material details are precise. They had been thinking – the poor fools – for an hour that *The Lady Vanishes* was taking place in our own day, until the sudden vision of those two ancient Buicks. The idea of extremely smooth and well-groomed European spies of 1939 using such a car is almost, for the Americans, the biggest laugh in the picture.

The First Comment on
American Life

Letter from America, BBC, 2 November 1969

It must have been thirty-one or two years ago that Alfred Hitchcock, the English film director, first descended on the United States like the mountain come to Mohammed. In his first week in America he achieved the rare privilege of a full-page photograph in the then-new illustrated magazine known as *Life*. It showed him in the one chair they found that would accommodate him, drawn up cosily to the fireplace in his New York hotel. But the fireplace was a fake – no flue, and therefore no wood, no coals. It was there simply for decoration, and Hitchcock got off his first comment on American life. Nowhere, he suggested, was there a private place to curl up and gossip. He was shown staring – at a distance of about two feet – into the cold, flameless void, and the caption on the picture read: 'Disappointment in American fireplaces'.

¶ From 1938 to 1940 AC collaborated on several projects with the Museum of Modern Art's burgeoning Film Library in New York. He gave lectures in Columbia University's Film Study extension course, organized with MoMA. With the Library's curator, Iris Barry, he arranged a successful film season in 1940 devoted to his childhood's favourite athletic hero, Douglas Fairbanks, who had donated his film collection to the Museum early in 1939. And for MoMA he wrote the short book *Douglas Fairbanks: The Making of a Screen Character*, analysing the screen character of 'Doug' from three angles: popular philosopher, athlete, and showman. Lecturing on 20 December 1939, a week after Fairbanks' death, AC had presented himself as a 'very dissipated example' of the Fairbanks influence: 'I spent a lot of time, between the ages of nine and twelve, in a gymnasium. I used to go about five nights a week – which is why I am round-shouldered today. The trouble with Fairbanks, of course, was that instead of getting us into a gym to do elementary body-building, he sent us to the exciting equipment of the gym, so that by the time I was fourteen, I was pushed off horizontal bars on the doctor's orders. But I did learn to do some tricks, and it became a pleasure for anybody who had some training to identify the things he could do with what Fairbanks was doing.' Robert Fairbanks, Doug's brother, pronounced himself 'immensely pleased' with AC's book, and hoped he would write a full biography. But he never did.

* * *

The Making of 'Doug': The Athlete

Douglas Fairbanks: The Making of a Screen
Character, 1940

Many and varied were the dilemmas of 'Doug' over a score or more of his pictures, yet there was a regular technical formula for a Fairbanks triumph. It was the galvanizing of a cheerful young American into a sort of campus whirlwind who extricates himself in a final scherzo of energy to win romantic and material success. For the audience it is a beautifully deceptive act of flattery, suggesting that all that is needed to clear up the stagnation of city life, a capture by Moroccan bandits, or a cabinet crisis in a South American republic, is the arrival of an average healthy man. What is nowhere suggested, and available only on painful thought to the holder of an insurance policy savings account, is the fact that aside from his impulses, which were those of a popular evangelist, 'Doug' was a person of superbly responsive physique and of quite extraordinary grace and initiative.

Nowhere was this more evident than at the crises, in his movies, when he appeared to be cornered. One of the special excitements of watching Fairbanks at bay was the knowledge that he was no more earthbound than Superman, his 1940 counterpart. In the most typical films (especially in *A Modern Musketeer*, *Bound in Morocco* and many times in *The Mark of Zorro*, *The Three Musketeers* and *Robin Hood*) there was a delicious moment when he would fall back before his adversaries, not in retreat but to gain a second in which to reconsider the resources of a room as a machine for escape. Most romantic melodramas have these ominous bridge passages and they are usually resolved in a single conventional plunge to escape – a decisive revolver shot, a flicking off of the lights, the fortuitous collapse of the villain by an unknown hand. Fairbanks would not have been the incomparable 'Doug' if he had not provided the most characteristic pleasure of his films in just these crises. And 'Doug' could not have held the popular imagination so long if he had lacked the extraordinary physical rhythm and grace of Douglas Fairbanks.

Fairbanks took up gymnastics in New York. It is pretty obvious from his movies that he became a first-rate all-round gymnast with a preferential talent for horizontal bar and pommel-horse. By the time he went out West he was a superior swimmer and horseman. He managed to win over the moderately sullen crew of the Triangle studio by his apparent willingness to take serious physical risks, a sign of comradeship very rare in the actors they had been used to, who more usually resented location shooting because there was no hotel. By the same willingness, he was also occasionally a nuisance – holding up shooting once for a night and day while he wandered off to learn trapping from a forester. He made the maximum use of every outdoors specialist he came across, astounding the Frontier Day stars of the Cheyenne, Wyoming, rodeo by his courage and aptitude for roping and bronco riding. He practised some sport every day for nearly twenty years and practised most whenever he could get professional coaching. Unsatisfied with the respectful boxing and wrestling practice he was getting in Hollywood, he sent East for Bull Montana, who trained in a New York gymnasium where Fairbanks had known him as a fighting equal unmoved by the dignity of actors. His studio soon became an athletes' mecca. World champions came there to pose first and teach afterwards. College track and swimming teams went home in a daze after being photographed with the movie hero who, in 1922, had paced Bob Simpson, then the world's champion low hurdler, and had given a good account of himself in an all-round competition with Brutus Hamilton, the American decathlon champion.

He made friends with the aeronaut in *The Lamb* in order to learn to fly a biplane. For *The Mystery of the Leaping Fish* he annexed the 'professor' and learned what he could of underwater tricks. For *The Three Musketeers* he was faced with the prospect of having to play reasonably well a man known to literature as 'the greatest swordsman in France'. His fencing had always been, if anything, better than his horsemanship, which was better than first-rate. In *The Three Musketeers*, according to a former French foils champion, he moved easily into the championship class. In training for the same movie, he put up an unofficial challenge to the amateur record for standing high and broad jumps. For *The Gaucho* he learned to throw the *bola* and pictures of a casual practice period show the easy rhythm of perfect relaxation, the mark of a natural athlete.

He could amuse himself and his friends by doing what are called 'feats of strength' and there is a snapshot or two of him weight-lifting. But he was watchful of this sort of training. He was trained not to show off biceps but to develop his body to a virtuoso pitch of responsiveness. Even professional gymnasts need apparatus and are clannishly leary of uncertified ropes and fences and invitations to perform without well-resined hands. Fairbanks's glory, the mystery of his visual fascination, is that he could throw all the textbook tricks on the makeshift apparatus of ordinary life. He appears to the moviegoer to be a sort of Ariel, leaping where he has a mind without any of the natural checks of gravity. But there is not a leap, a turn or a change of terrain which cannot be precisely named in the gymnastic jargon. It is simply that these things are normally done on a horizontal bar, or on parallels or on a trapeze. To Fairbanks the limb of a tree suggests a hocks-off; a narrow lane with high walls is a risky, but workable, set of parallel bars; a spear is a pole to vault with.

This spontaneous identification of shape with function seems to be a faculty of comedy in more fields than the gymnastics of Douglas Fairbanks. It is essentially the same gift, and engenders the same pleasure of surprise, as when Chaplin – newly employed in a pawn-shop – is handed a watch and instantly uses a can-opener on it with exquisite skill; or when, hungry, he sees an old shoe and miraculously the shape of the sole is a fish and the arc of nails is the plan of bone strategy that the best-mannered fish-eaters know all about. Fairbanks, too, produces the effect, when let loose on a landscape or cornered in a room, of revamping the stubborn natural fixtures of the world we live in to match the highly specialized needs of his dilemma. It looks like reckless gaiety, and one critic has dully said the secret of Fairbanks is that he knew how to assert himself. But to assert yourself in any art with a mite of distinction, it is necessary to have something to assert. A hundred comedians since the movies started have groaned and grinned and asserted themselves to the limit of their glandular command. Their unflagging mediocrity, and Fairbanks's unique grace and zest, are still unexplained. Fairbanks was able to give the appearance of casual self-assertion for much the same reason that Weissmuller can smile and crawl at the same time, or DiMaggio can lope to the diamond.

This is why Fairbanks held the senses as Eddie Polo, the favourite 'athletic actor' of his day, could not. Fairbanks was, even under stress, an athlete without strain, and in his most daring leap there is the assurance of reserves. But mainly it is that virtuoso use of the land-scape as a natural gymnasium whose equipment is invisible to the ordinary man, the use of his own body as a crazy but disciplined bow on something that turns into a handy fiddle, that made him an enchanting image, whatever the plot was saying – and when the story was saying something about a girl in danger, or the need for courage, offered a technique unknown to actors to enforce its romantic spell.

¶ A lively and prominent British film critic in the 1920s, Iris Barry had found a second niche in New York as the curator (1935), then the director (1947–50) of the Museum of Modern Art's Film Library. AC remembered her fondly in a portrait piece following her death on 22 December 1969.

✳   ✳   ✳

To Iris Barry (1895–1969)

New York Times, 18 January 1970

She was a brassy little girl in Birmingham, England, who shocked her grandmother by spending every spare hour at the movies, when the movies were a thin cut above the poolroom. She shocked the rest of the family when, having spent the First World War in a succession of unladylike jobs (shipping telephone poles for the Post Office, ordering machine guns for the Ministry of Munitions), she made a profession of her vice and became the first woman film critic in England.

In the heyday of the flapper she was one of the most beguiling of the breed: a small trig brunette with an Eton crop, a pair of sceptical violet eyes and a belly laugh that responded like a Geiger counter to the presence of a stuffed shirt. She was always long on mockery and short on tact, and when she demanded more money and a trip to Hollywood from the *Daily Mail* she was, as she put it later, 'severed rather forcefully'. She decided, on her own, to get to the way-station of New York, and for a time she practised the pathetic routine of a genteel English girl on a casual visit to America who, in fact, was down to the one-room walk-up and whatever snacks the escort can pay for.

But she always landed on her own or somebody else's feet, and first she ran into a patron in Philip Johnson, a sponsor in Alfred Barr and a husband in John E. Abbott of Wall Street. These three complemented her vague but grand design, which was somehow to have a private film collection and yet be on hobnobbing terms with the Warner Brothers and the gods and goddesses they employed. Johnson moved her into a 53rd Street brownstone, then masquerading as the young Museum of Modern Art, and set her cadging books from the libraries of bankrupt tycoons which she sold for books on painting. Barr recalled she had been a founder member of the London Film Society and thought she would be 'better employed doing something about a film collection', a rather grandiose promise given by the museum in its original manifesto about which nothing had yet been done. Out of the blue, or a cocktail acquaintanceship, came John Hay Whitney, who put up the money for a preliminary study of what a film collection might be. By now she was married to John Abbott, and the two of them first wangled a fat grant from the Rockefeller Foundation and then, with Whitney's *entrée*, whisked off to Hollywood and for a year or more explored the tedious mysteries of projectors, staff, storage vaults, raw film stock, copyright, and pierced the more formidable barrier of Hollywood's indifference to its stockpile of old movies and its suspicion of the non-commercial showing of any of them.

There were interminable battles with corporations, lawyers, banks and all the other keepers of the cash register who awoke with a bang to what was then the pleasing new concept of 'residuals'.

This was the way the Museum of Modern Art Film Library (now Film Department) began. Iris Barry was its inventor, crusader, first curator and subsequently its director. Very few of the fans who drop by to catch the early Fairbanks or *The Birth of a Nation* have ever heard of Iris Barry or, I am sure, give a passing thought to the Laocoön coils of stock holdings, proprietorship and dumb greed through which she had to slash her way towards her vision of a regular parade of the motion picture's past for you and me on a grey afternoon. But there it is. She died in France three weeks ago, full of years and unquenchable humour. It is a good time to recall her pluck and cunning and energy.

For all the hundreds of thousands who now accept the Museum Film Department as an inevitable amenity of New York City, she was their pioneer public servant. She would have laughed herself sick at the thought.

¶ Will H. Hays, who served the Motion Picture Producers and Distributors of America as its first president from 1922 to 1945 and inaugurated the Production Code, died in 1954, just as the Code's impress on studios and exhibitors weakened. For the *Guardian* AC contributed a wry obituary of Hollywood's first moral watchdog.

*   *   *

Will Hays: An Appreciation

Manchester Guardian, 9 March 1954

Will Hays was the Moses and Daniel of Hollywood's public morals for a quarter of a century. But before he became a moralist he was a successful lawyer, a decisive witness before the Senate committee investigating the Teapot Dome scandal, an active politician, and national chairman of the Republican Party. He was one of the first such chairmen whose success in a Presidential election campaign was automatically rewarded with the position of Postmaster General in the incoming cabinet. But his name did not become a byword until President Harding released him from his chores with the mails and sent him out to the City of the Angels to beckon the flapper down from the dining-room table and set her in the path of the Ten Commandments.

The 'Hays Office' was for twenty-four years the movie producers' voluntary arbiter of their new-found standards of taste and virtue. His intervention came none too soon. The triumph of the Prohibition

Amendment had the wholly unexpected effect of making American society obsessed with the need to procure the alcohol it could formerly take or leave.

Hollywood began to ride high, wide, and handsome on a tidal wave of bathtub gin. There was much ado about the death of a young actress after a Hollywood party and the following suspension from film-making of a popular comedian, Fatty Arbuckle. This horror touched off a passion for reform in several states and mobilized the anger of the Roman Catholic Church, the powerful women's clubs and the Southern Baptists. The movie-makers were alarmed to see the market for their product shrinking so fast that they were faced with the obvious choice of bankruptcy or a spectacular house-cleaning. It was at this point that the industry decided to take the baseball cure and look around for a reforming 'tsar'.

Will Hays, a little saturnine man whose lantern jaw was held at permanent half mast below a collar the height of a beer mug, did not at first glance look like the Lord's anointed. But in the mores of the 1920s he was an ideal choice. A Republican, an elder of the Presbyterian Church, a 33rd-degree Mason, a member of the National Council of the Boy Scouts of America, an Elk, and a most loyal servant of the Loyal Order of Moose, he was exquisitely qualified to distinguish at the drop of a cocktail glass the goats from the sheep. Virtue alone would have been powerless to subdue the general frivolity, but Mr Hays was an astute politician, and within a year or two a code of production ethics was drawn up and after intermittent relapses was so cleverly applied that while the movies were provoking enough to get people inside the theatres, they were no longer 'suggestive' in the statutory sense. The churches were placated, the movie colony confined its debauches to its own homes, the women's clubs abandoned their boycotts, and the box-office boomed.

¶ As a critic in the 1930s, AC frequently encountered Humphrey Bogart scowling in gangster films. Their first real-life meeting, recalled in his book *Six Men*, took place in 1952 on the convention train of the Democratic Party presidential candidate Adlai Stevenson. This sparked a firm friendship with Bogart and his wife Lauren Bacall. AC's *Guardian* obituary, following the actor's slow death from cancer of the oesophagus, became the springboard for his later writings on Bogart.

*   *   *

Bogart and the Age of Violence.
An Idealist in Hollywood

Manchester Guardian, 16 January 1957

Miami, 15 January. Thirty years ago, towards the end of the first act of one of those footling country-house comedies that passed in the 1920s for social satire, a juvenile in an Ascot and a blue blazer loped through the French windows and tossed off the immortal invitation: 'Tennis, anyone?' Possibly he did not coin the phrase, but he glorified the type, if wooden young men with brown eyes and no discoverable occupation can ever be said to go to glory, on stage or off.

This young man, whose performance the late Alexander Woollcott said 'could be mercifully described as inadequate', yet seemed to be cast by fortune for the role of a Riviera fixture. He was the son of a prominent New York doctor. His mother was a portrait painter of socialite children. He himself dawdled awhile at one of the better private schools and was intended for Yale. Intended, but never ready.

Twenty years later he coined another phrase, with which the small fry of the English-speaking world brought the neighbourhood sneak to heel: 'Drop the gun, Looey!' Could both these characters be Bogart, the cryptic Hemingway tough, the huddled man in the trench coat who singed the bad and the beautiful with the smoke he exhaled from his nostrils? They could. Could any actor, no matter how lucky in his parts, how wild the gamut of his ambition, swing so successfully between the poles of make-believe, represented by 'Tennis, anyone?' and 'Drop the gun, Looey!'? He could and did. He was always content to nestle in the camouflage of any fictional type that came his way, provided the manager paid him and left him to himself, a very complex man, gentle at bottom, and afraid to seem so.

It is fair to guess that far back in the Lonsdale era he was always his own man. He no doubt stood in the wings in his blazer chuckling acidly over the inanities on stage, just as he lately complained that he could not walk the streets of New York without having truck drivers and corner brats spring their forefingers and give him the 'ah-ah-ah-ah-ah-ah' tommy-gun treatment. On Fifth Avenue two years ago a wholesome young cop testing shop doors at two in the morning moved up on him from behind. 'Everything all right, Mr Bogart?' Everything was fine, and Bogart sighed after him: 'It does no good. I haven't played a gangster or a dick in nine years.'

But this was his most famous self: the two-faced cynic who robbed the banker and the gangster with equal grace, who was sometimes a heel and sometimes a big-city stand-in for the United States Cavalry, but who was always the derisive foe of the law in its official forms. And this character was suddenly very precious in the age of violence, for it satisfied a rather desperate need of the engulfed ordinary man. When Hitler was acting out scripts more brutal and obscene than anything dreamed of by Chicago or the Warner Brothers, Bogart was the only possible idealist likely to outwit him and survive. No Ronald Colman, Leslie Howard or other handsome boy scout, but a conniver as subtle as Goebbels, a very tough gent who in the end would be on our side. The enjoyment of this character from Glasgow to Singapore was assured by the supporting artistic fact that here was a universal type of our rebellious age but one that never appeared in life quite so perfect, never quite so detached in its malice, so inured to corruption, so self-assured in its social stance before the diffident, the pompous and the evil.

It would be tempting – and the French will be tempted – to write of the Bogart character as the archetype of the Outsider, but he packed in fact the more explosive social threat of the Insider gone sour. He was, in short, a romantic hero, inconceivable in any time but ours.

The way he came to achieve this character and its renown is a pretty irony, and he himself put it all down to luck. Bogart was just as old as the century, and by the mid-30s he was getting to be a little too scarred for a juvenile. He would undoubtedly have faded into the kind of feature player who never stars and makes a compensating fuss about the size of his name in lights. Robert Sherwood had written *The Petrified Forest*, and was looking around for what would now be called an 'offbeat' piece of casting for the part of the listless killer, Duke Mantee. Against the advice of his friends, who remembered Bogart from his tennis-racketeering, Sherwood picked the ageing juvenile with the scar, the odd lisp and the look of implied derision. He was an instant star and was soon whipped out to Hollywood for the movie version. And that led straight to *Dead End* and the glory road.

It proved again, what actors rarely admit, that the stars in their courses are nearly always set by the casting director. A new view of an old face was all it took to change Wallace Beery from a slant-eyed villain into a lovable cuss, to turn Myrna Loy from an 'inscrutable' (as the word is understood in Oriental melodramas) into a chin-up wife for William Powell, himself transformed by the same insight from a gunman into a teasing combination of smooth operator and faithful spouse.

Soon the word got back east from Hollywood that Bogart was living out his screen character in a running series of marital brawls. 'The battling Bogart', the columnists called him when his divorce came up. 'Battling Bogart!' groaned his oldest theatrical friend, Clifton Webb, recalling a few weeks ago the shock of this fantasy. 'Why, any woman could walk all over him. The man's a softie and, I might add,'

– reflecting on the last and ghastly year of Bogart's illness – 'a very gallant one.'

This true remark points to yet another 'offbeat' role that no producer had the wit to discover: the character of Humphrey Bogart himself. Only once, in *Casablanca*, did the audience see a decent approximation to the unfooled man, whose wryness was the mask of an incorruptibility he mocked. He drank and blasphemed and tolerated, even fattened, the newspaper myth of a locker-room tough guy.

But sometimes the hard shell cracked. He advised young actors to 'take the big part, but hold off the big house and the Cadillac, or you'll be the studio's slave'. The only point in making money, he said, was 'so you can tell some big producer to go to hell'. When the McCarthy era was incubating in the congressional hearings on the 'Hollywood Ten', he recklessly flew to Washington to defend their right to think and say 'anything they damn please'.

When it was murmured by the studio heads in 1952 that an open embrace of Adlai Stevenson might possibly weaken the bonds of a contract, Bogart and his wife, a female chip off the same species, packed their bags and toured with the Stevenson train. They bowed in small New England towns at all hours and ducked out on the observation platform only when they were asked. They openly scoffed at the Presidential fitness of 'the big General'. Bogart was scoffing when he died. These were chance cracks in the armour plate he built around his integrity, a word he would have scorned to use.

One is always reading in obituaries of men who could not abide cant and fearlessly denounced it. Bogart never denounced it. In a score of meek disguises, it was as plainly offensive to him as a bad smell. This made him an impossible man to make up to, to cozen or to bully. He had the deadly insight of a drunk who is beginning to get troublesome and whom you hope to appease with cordial approaches. Such men pause in their garrulousness long enough to say quietly, 'You don't like me, do you?' So he was also not a man to flatter or, what was harder in his last year, to sympathize with.

Before I saw him last I had had, from a surgeon friend, the dimmest prognosis of his condition. And I was very loath to go up and talk with him. He had just made his will and he spoke of it, and his illness, with an entirely unforced humour – neither with complaint nor with a brave absence of complaint. It is hard for actors to avoid the dramatizing of their emotional life, whether grossly by 'living the part' or subtly by sentimental deprecation. Bogart was merely himself, a brave man who had come to terms, as we all may pray to do, with the certain approach of death.

In sum, a vastly more intelligent man than most in the trade he practised, a touchy man who found the world more corrupt than he had hoped, a man with a tough shell and a fine core. He invented the Bogart character and it fitted his deceptive purpose like a glove. By showily neglecting his outward forms of grace, he kept inferior men at a distance. For he lived in a town crowded by malign poseurs, fake ascetics, studio panders, the pimps of the press. From all of them he was determined to keep his secret: the rather shameful secret, in the realistic world we inhabit, of being a gallant man and an idealist.

¶ AC first met Nunnally Johnson in New York in 1940, when they both participated in a Museum of Modern Art presentation of *The Grapes of Wrath*, just released – one of the writer-producer's most notable films in a successful career spent largely at Twentieth Century-Fox. But their close friendship dates from *The Three Faces of Eve* in 1957. Needing an authoritative voice to establish the factual basis of his drama about a multiple personality sufferer, Johnson invited Alistair to introduce the film to audiences, in his own words, on camera. Filming took twenty minutes; Cooke's agent negotiated an extravagant fee of $7,500. From *Eve* onwards Johnson was his closest Hollywood friend, and a frequent correspondent. One of his letters (15 December 1957) ends with the mock slogan: 'Leave the dishes in the sink tonight, Mother! There's a Nunnally Johnson production in town!' In fact, Johnson's wit was self-deprecating, and always dry. AC gave an address at his funeral in 1977. Re-using one striking phrase, he also contributed a foreword to the book of Johnson's letters edited by the producer's widow, the former actress Dorris Bowden. Tom Stempel's biography, *Screenwriter*, was published in 1980.

*   *   *

For Nunnally Johnson

Funeral service address, 29 March 1977

A year or more ago, Nunnally – in my presence – turned to my wife, with a characteristic look of alarm, and said: 'Now, Jane, I want you to do something for me. When I go, I know that that husband of yours will do one of his sneaky BBC talks about me, and I want you to see to it that he doesn't get away without saying something *good* about me. Just get him to set the record straight – let him report that I was pure, and good, and noble, totally unselfish, intrepid, had the physical courage of a lion and was a devil with the women – just the facts.'

So, at Dorris's request, I am keeping that promise to him. And I will try to be brief. Because Nunnally cherished lucidity and pithiness, and I have the warning reminder of his last suggestion about how to improve the *New Yorker* magazine. He thought they should get out a new title page and at the top of it have a scroll, and inside the scroll, in Tudor Gothic lettering, inscribe the legend: 'If it's in the *New Yorker* – It's Too Long.'

This occasion is bound to be, for us, an unforgettably sad memory. Because we were greedy for his charm and humour, and now feel cheated of a few more years of them. But soon there will come a flood of unforgettable happy, even hilarious, memories. And, I suppose like many of you here, I could regale you from now till midnight with priceless lines that only Nunnally could have coined. But I realize that you have your own. However, there's one memory I should like to share with you, because it has kept coming back to me over and over in the past, for obviously unconscious reasons. But I can only guess that, for me, it expresses a quality that Nunnally had more than any humorist I have ever read or known: a unique combination of kindness and mischief. We tend to toss the words 'wit' and 'humour' around indiscriminately. Unlike the wit, whose target is always somebody else, Nunnally was a true humorist in the Mark Twain tradition, whose target was usually himself. Nobody since Robert Benchley has put on such a wonderful performance as a bewildered mouse in a world of tigers and jackals.

A dozen or more years ago, Dorris, Nunnally and I were on a holiday in Copenhagen. Nunnally was never very comfortable in foreign parts. There was once a move to live in Switzerland. He went there to scout the possibilities but soon turned them down. 'Nobody told me,' he said, 'that they talk Swiss!' Well, in Copenhagen, there came a day when, while the wolf was not actually at the door, there was always the prospect that he might be. And against that day, Dorris thought it would be prudent to be provided with a protective fur coat. Nunnally wouldn't go with us to buy it because he said his religion – whose name escaped him for the moment – prohibited him from accompanying females on shopping expeditions. So Dorris and I went off together, and pretty soon she was rustling among the skins, sometimes getting hidden by them, giving the impression of Little Orphan Annie lost in the jungle. Eventually, she made her choice, and I was sent off to collect the treasurer.

I came on him sitting on the terrace of the Hotel d'Angleterre with a very woebegone expression. 'You know something?' he said. 'If you sit on the terrace of the Hotel d'Angleterre in Copenhagen long enough, you won't see a goddamn soul you know.' We went off back together to the very chic furrier and Nunnally took out his chequebook. But by that time Dorris had changed her mind. She couldn't decide whether to switch from the mink stole to the sable wrap or the blotched leopard or the spotted lynx. And Nunnally put on a big show of having had his meditative therapy disturbed. He slumped into a sofa and took out a cigarette and heaved a great sigh. And I said, 'Cheer up, Nunnally, you remember what Othello said?'

He said, 'No, what did he say?'

'"Ah, that we call these delicate creatures ours / And not our appetites."'

Nunnally said, 'Don't look at me. I'm just a poor white boy from Georgia. Who am I to contradict a black general who quotes Shakespeare?'

There is surely no need to mourn for such a man, who guarantees his own immortality with the rich life he still lives in the memories and hearts of his friends. And for Nunnally – ailing and frailing these many years with such incomparable gallantry – surely last Friday was a release, was the arrival in port after a long storm.

The last time I had the sad honour of saluting a man in this way was over twenty years ago. And the man was H. L. Mencken. Now, even to think of a funeral service for Mencken was almost to blaspheme his memory. For his writings had given abundant proof that he took a bilious view of such goings-on. And his will actually stipulated: 'Let there be no whooping and gargling over my bones.' His instructions were followed. 'I should prefer,' he wrote, 'that a few friends who are disposed to think kindly of me might gather in some congenial place and celebrate my ascension into heaven with the aid of the greatest single American invention – namely, the dry martini.'

I once told Nunnally about this and he said, 'Wonderful! Just wonderful!' So if we are to sprinkle any drops on *his* bones, I think he would prefer them to be juniper drops. As for funeral baked meats, there is only one dish he will absolutely demand to be put on the heavenly menu. And that is grits.

All I can say is, that if he had had a gravestone, I should like to have seen it chiselled with this simple sentence: 'If the English language had not already contained the word delightful, we should have had to invent it for him.'

Georgia Boy at the
Hollywood Bash

'Mr Pepys in Hollywood', *The Letters of
Nunnally Johnson*, 1981

What sort of unpretentious man could stumble into this sort of eminence? In his splendid taped memoir of Nunnally, Tom Stempel makes the shrewd point that a small-town boy from Georgia who had lived through a Norman Rockwell childhood ('that is why Norman Rockwell is my favourite painter') took away with him 'the values he was escaping from. Throughout his life, there was a tension between the desire for the order and stability represented by the idea of home and the excitement and adventure represented by the idea of escape.' This is a conflict familiar enough in the lives of small-town boys who intend not so much to move into the big city as to invade and conquer it. Many of them who make it resolve the conflict – or mask it – in uneasy comfort or fussy spending (what the food and fashion editors call 'sophistication'). Few of them resolve it, as Nunnally did, in engaging self-mockery. He was too intelligent to pretend to a cosmopolitanism he was uncomfortable with: he was suspicious of what he called 'highbrow' literature, and on the plane of day-to-day living he never quite got over the riches and the big house. And his observation was too ruthless to let him fall back on sentimental comparisons between the old fish-fry and the Hollywood bash.

Like many another Southerner, he maintained a surface courtesy and tact behind which glowed an owl-like scepticism about human motives, whether in Columbus, Georgia, or Beverly Hills, California. With a slight shift in his genes, he could have been a bitter man. But he had the luck of his inheritance and his gifts: a wry, uninhibited humour from his father, and a prose style of great clarity he developed on his own. He relaxed Stempel's 'tension' by the highly successful device of adopting, in a flashy and cynical society, a pose not very different from that with which two other small-town boys, Mark Twain and James Thurber, were able to cope with rich and complicated people and also to earn their applause. Nunnally rendered himself no threat to anybody by adopting, as a second nature, the air of a bewildered mouse in a world of tigers and jaguars. I believe this book will reveal him, to an audience much larger than that of his fortunate cronies, as a remarkable American humorist.

¶ Reviewing *Bringing Up Baby*, AC had said: 'Gaiety's good when it's a grace note to living. It's awful as a profession.' Reason enough, perhaps, for him to dislike the full-tilt crazy comedy of the writer-director Preston Sturges, even when typing his obituary.

*　　　*　　　*

Preston Sturges: The Man Who Succumbed to Hollywood

Manchester Guardian, 8 August 1959

New York, 7 August. When the word got around town last night that Preston Sturges, like so many of his brother wits of the 20s, had come to his end in a room at the Algonquin, there were as many shaking heads as sighs. For here was a man who never fulfilled the devastating promise of his best, who never recovered from the discovery that life in Southern California can cheat art of its most outrageous fantasies.

Few Americans born with brains and wit have had a more privileged upbringing. His mother sent him for six months every year to Europe, where he was put on an exhausting but congenial diet of museums in the afternoon and opera in the evening. He was temperamentally the antithesis of a culture-vulture, and by the time he returned to New York and wrote the play *Strictly Dishonorable*, which served as a passport to Hollywood, he was an accomplished linguist, a canny art critic and an ironist with a Martian's eye for the oddity and vitality of American life. He was ready to storm Hollywood.

But he had the misfortune to be a social satirist in Hollywood, which is to say a man trying to make a rapier felt in a blitzkrieg. After one savage success with *The Great McGinty*, a burlesque of American machine politics, he threw away his personal weapon, with indelicate accoutrement of irony, compassion and the rest, and fitted himself out in the more acceptable costume of bladder, cap and bell. His movies – *The Miracle of Morgan's Creek*, *Hail the Conquering Hero*, *The Beautiful Blonde from Bashful Bend* – inflated their humours until they were indistinguishable from the absurdities of Southern California itself.

Hollywood, he once said, 'is a comic opera in which fat businessmen, good fathers, are condemned to a conjugal existence with a heap of drunkards, madmen, divorcees, sloths, epileptics and morphinomaniacs who are – in the considered opinion of the management – artists'. The bitterness of this verdict was salted by his own inability to stand apart from the community he despised.

For he was an open-handed man, an epicure of extravagant tastes who could envy but never achieve the sort of financial independence which made Bogart, another shrewd cynic, able to say aloud with impunity: 'The only point of earning a million dollars in this town is to be able to tell some fat slob to go to hell.'

¶ AC became friends with Groucho Marx in the 1950s after trying unsuccessfully to get him to appear on the *Omnibus* television arts series. During a trip to California in April 1960, ten weeks before the Democratic Party convention that chose the Catholic John F. Kennedy as its Presidential candidate, Alistair visited Groucho in Los Angeles on the set of NBC's television version of *The Mikado*, transmitted live later in the day.

*   *   *

The Positive Demise of G and S

Guardian, 5 May 1960

Just as Sir Arthur Sullivan had a dreadful urge to write oratorios of stupefying solemnity, so the man who has made a comfortable fortune by insulting the human race has nursed a lifelong desire to sing. On the last Friday in April he made it; and a formidable cast that included Helen Traubel as Katisha, Dennis King as the Mikado and Stanley Holloway as Pooh-Bah was topped by Julius (Groucho) Marx as Ko-Ko. The original operetta, which runs to a bothersome two and a half hours, was compressed for television into a tight, not to say breathless, hour, which is par for the course in all television adaptations, whether they be of *King Lear* or the *Ring* cycle.

I heard this alarming news at breakfast-time of the day the show was to be taped and lost no time phoning Groucho, who was 'in make-up' and, judging from his rotund tones, had his customary ten-inch Dunhill lodged between his teeth.

'Grouch,' I cried, 'this is Alistair!'

'What a ridiculous name – Alistair.'

'How about Julius?'

'That's ridiculous, too. But they call me Groucho. I'll call you Groucho if you like.'

'It won't do you any good, besides I'm too big for Ko-Ko.'

'Cut out the grandiosity, Cooke, and get the hell over here and see the positive demise of G and S.'

'Just a moment. Let me check with my room-mate.'

'What *is* this? You got a dame up there? You'd be mad, mad, to leave her for me. Better still, bring her over and you can go.'

'No, he's a navy commander, a submarine salesman to be exact.'

'Do I salute or submerge? – remember I'm only a civilian.'

'The question is, may I bring him along?'

'Cut out this nonsense and run over to Highland, on to the freeway, drive past Warner Brothers – quickly – and you'll make the dress rehearsal.'

We were blinded by the big studio, where every set detail was in three colours and every costume in four (it was a colour telecast) and came in just as the chorus was hailing the Lord High Executioner. Their ranks divided and a small, loping character appeared in a patchwork costume of purple and red and black and green. He had big flouncing sleeves and a peaked coat and was totally unrecognizable between the mouth and the toes. But he wore black horn-rimmed glasses and behind them rolled the liquid brown eyes as big as ping-pong balls. Sullivan was about to receive the supreme sacrifice. His voice, if that's what it was, was too reedy to register in the great cavern of the studio, but by the magic of electronic amplification it could be heard in the control room and would no doubt be audible on the air. Anyway, he went through the motions of singing and pattered off and headed through the gloom for our chairs, which were up-front at the elbows of the string section.

'Grouch,' I said, 'meet Commander Russell.'

'At ease, Commander,' he nodded. He sat down and turned his

saddest look on his daughter, kneeling a few yards away, the smallest of the Three Little Girls.

'She's grown,' I noticed.

'She's still short,' said Groucho. 'Of course, the Japs are short. If the Mikado was a Norseman, she'd never have made it.'

There was a swift, professional 'hush' from an assistant stage manager. Groucho leaned over. 'You know how this thing comes out, don't you?' he hissed. 'I wind up with Katisha – that's always been my fate, on and off the stage.'

A stage manager tiptoed over and beckoned Groucho. He disentangled the rooster's tail of his skirt from the chair and pulled a hand out of his sleeve. 'How the Japs,' he mumbled, 'ever attacked Pearl Harbor in these outfits is something I'll never know.'

Every time he had a bit to do (and in a fifty-four-minute opera, six minutes out for commercials, all the bits are bits) he would be led away sighing that 'if this doesn't kill Gilbert and Sullivan, nothing will', and pad back to his chair again and receive a sympathetic pat from an assistant half his age. Groucho is crowding seventy, though not very hard, but his energy belies and makes more touching the extreme frailty of his body.

'You're going good, Groucho,' the young man would whisper.

'Yes, after the show I'm going good – to Canada or any place they can't extradite me. By the way, meet Captain Bradford.' (From old acquaintance, I knew better than to say 'Russell'.)

It was the end of an act and a make-up man came over and scrutinized Groucho's face like a surgeon looking for the place to make the incision. There is not much you can do with Groucho's face, and the man simply powdered the great man's forehead and kneaded the bald wig firmly over the bald head – a curious convention of make-believe. Groucho stroked his chin, in the waggish way he used to do before he proposed to Margaret Dumont, but all the waggery had gone from his voice and his eyes were more liquid-melancholy than ever.

'So,' he said, 'tell me, what are we gonna do about the White House? You think we'll have the Pope in there?'

'I doubt it very much,' I said, 'Taft won every primary in sight. People forget about the enmities a front-man builds up. I think the important issue with Kennedy is that he's the front-runner. One way or another I think they'll use the religious issue to confuse all the issues and kill him off on the early ballots. He's very able, though, and a wonderful campaigner.'

'In that case,' said Groucho, 'he'll never make it. You see, people are looking for a colourless candidate. They're not looking for an able man. They want a guy there's nothing wrong with. Of course, that doesn't mean there has to be anything right with him either. I'd like to think that Stevenson would get it again, but he's not changed and I guess the voters haven't changed either.'

The next act was the last, and when the last chord of the orchestra had crashed, and the camera had panned lovingly across a tableau of the Mikado and the Three Little Girls and faded out on Katisha dragging a doleful Groucho across the standard Japanese bridge, he dropped his owlish look and strolled over to say goodbye. 'So glad you could be with us, Admiral Radford,' he said, 'and, well, friend, take it easy. You see, the trouble with Stevenson is the fact that he talks the English language. That's a terrible indictment against any man running for the Presidency.'

¶ 'Pretty Mr Gary Cooper,' AC wrote in 1929 in an undergraduate review of *Beau Sabreur*. But in talkies he soon appreciated Cooper's natural, laconic screen presence and mythic status as America's 'taut but merciful plainsman'.

*   *   *

Archetype of the Hemingway Hero

Guardian, 15 May 1961

When the word got out that Gary Cooper was mortally ill, a spontaneous process arose in high places, not unlike the first moves to sanctify a remote peasant. The Queen of England dispatched a sympathetic cable. The President of the United States called him on the telephone. A cardinal ordered public prayers. Messages came to his house in Beverly Hills from the unlikeliest fans, from foreign ministers and retired soldiers who never knew him, as also from Ernest Hemingway, his old Pygmalion who had kept him in mind, through at least two novels, as the archetype of the Hemingway hero: the self-sufficient male animal, the best kind of hunter, the silent infantryman padding dutifully forward to perform the soldier's most poignant ritual in 'the ultimate loneliness of contact'.

It did not happen to Ronald Colman, or Clark Gable, or – heaven knows – John Barrymore. Why, we may well ask, should it have happened to Frank James Cooper, the rather untypical American type of the son of a Bedfordshire lawyer, a boy brought up in the Rockies among horses and cattle to be sure, but only as they compose the unavoidable backdrop of life in those parts; a schoolboy in Dunstable, England, a college boy in Iowa, a middling student, then a failing cartoonist, failed salesman, an 'extra' in Hollywood who in time had his break and mooned in a lanky, handsome way through a score or more of 'horse operas'? Well, his friends most certainly mourn the gentle, shambling 'Coop', but what the world mourns is the death of Mr Longfellow Deeds, who resisted and defeated the corruption of the big city; the snuffing out of the sheriff in *High Noon*, heading back to duty along the railroad tracks with that precise mince of the cowboy's tread and that rancher's squint that sniffs mischief in a creosote bush, sees through suns and is never fooled. What the world mourns is its lost innocence, or a favourite fantasy of it fleshed out in the most durable and heroic of American myths: that of the taut but merciful plainsman, who dispenses justice with a worried conscience, a single syllable, a blurred reflex action to the hip, and who must face death in the afternoon as regularly as the matador, but on Main Street and for no pay.

Mr Deeds Goes to Town marks the first gelling of this fame, and *The Plainsman* the best delineation of the character that fixed his legend. These two films retrieved Cooper from a run of agreeable and handsome parts, some of them (in the Lubitsch films for instance) too chic and metropolitan for his own good. At the time of *Mr Deeds*, an English critic wrote that 'the conception of the wise underdog, the shrewd hick, is probably too Western, too American in its fusion of irony and sentimentality to travel far'. He was as wrong as could be, for the film was a sensation in Poland, the Middle East and other barbaric regions whose sense of what is elementary in human goodness is something we are just discovering, perhaps a little late.

It is easy to forget now, as always with artists who have matured a recognizable style, that for at least the first dozen years of his film career Gary Cooper was the lowbrow's comfort and the highbrow's butt. However, he lasted long enough, as all great talents do, to weather the four stages of the highbrow treatment: first, he was derided, then ignored, then accepted, then discovered. We had seen this happen many times before; and looking back, one is always shocked to recognize the people it has happened to. Today the intellectual would deny, for instance, that Katharine Hepburn was ever anything but a lovely if haggard exotic, with a personal style which might enchant some people and grate on others, but would insist she was at all times what we call a serious talent. This opinion was in fact a highly sophisticated second thought, one which took about a decade to ripen and squelch the memory of Dorothy Parker's little tribute to Miss Hepburn's first starring appearance on Broadway: 'Miss Hepburn ran the gamut of human emotions from A to B.'

Marilyn Monroe is a grosser example still. Universally accepted as a candy bar or cream puff, she presented a galling challenge to the intelligentsia when she married Arthur Miller, a very sombre playwright and indubitably *un homme sérieux*. The question arose whether there had been serious miscalculation about a girly calendar that could marry a man who defied the House Un-American Activities Committee. The doubt was decided in Miss Monroe's favour when she delivered pointed ripostes to dumb questions at a London press conference.

At least until the mid-1930s there was no debate about Gary Cooper because he presented no issue. He belonged to the reveries of the middle-class woman. He reminded grieving mothers of the upright son shot down on the Somme; devoted sisters of the brother sheep-ranching in Australia; the New York divorcee of the handsome ranch hand with whom she is so often tempted to contract a ruinous second marriage in the process of dissolving her first. To the moviegoer, Cooper was the matinee idol toughened and tanned, in the era of the outdoors, into something at once glamorous and primitive. He was notoriously known as the actor who couldn't act. Only the directors who handled him had daily proof of the theory that the irresistible 'stars' are simply behaviourists who, by some nervous immunity to the basilisk glare and hiss of the camera, appear to be nobody but themselves. Very soon the box-offices, from Tokyo to Carlisle, confirmed this theory in hard cash. Then the intellectuals sat up and took notice. Then the Cooper legend took over.

For the past quarter-century, Cooper's worldwide image had grown so rounded, so heroically elongated rather, that only some very crass public behaviour could have smudged it. There was none. After a short separation he was happily reunited with his only wife. He spoke out, during the McCarthy obscenity, with resounding pointlessness and flourished the banner of 'Americanism' in a heated way. Most recently, there has been a low-pressure debate in progress in fan magazines and newspaper columns about whether his 'yup-nope' approach was his own or a press agent's inspiration, like the malapropisms of Sam Goldwyn, another happy device for blinding mockers to the knowledge that they were losing their shirts. This was decided a week or two ago by the *New York Post*, which concluded after a series of exhaustive interviews with his friends that Cooper's inarticulateness was natural when he was in the presence of gabby strangers, that gabbiness was his natural bent with close friends.

He could probably have transcended, or dimmed, bigger scandals or more public foolishness than he was capable of, because he was of the company of Chaplin, Groucho Marx, W. C. Fields, Bogart, Louis Jouvet, two or three others, give or take a personal favourite. He filled an empty niche in the world pantheon of essential gods. If no cowboy was ever like him, so much the worse for the cattle kingdom. He was Eisenhower's glowing, and glowingly false, picture of Wyatt Earp. He was one of Walt Whitman's troop of democratic knights, 'bright-eyed as hawks with their swarthy complexions and their broad-brimmed hats, with loose arms slightly raised and swinging as they ride'. He represented every man's best secret image of himself: the honourable man slicing clean through the broiling world of morals and machines. He isolated and enlarged to six feet three an untainted strain of goodness in a very male specimen of the male of the species.

FREE access to over 8 million songs

From over 28,000 labels including the Sony Music catalogue UK

Stream 3 hours of music every day

Download 3 music tracks or 1 music video per week

You will need internet access, your library card number and PIN. Enjoy!

http://aberdeenshireuk.freegalmusic.com/index

Aberdeenshire
COUNCIL

Marilyn Is Dead. A Woman
of Integrity

Guardian, 6 August 1962

New York, 5 August. Marilyn Monroe was found dead in bed this morning in her home in Hollywood, only a physical mile or two, but a social universe, away from the place where she was born thirty-six years ago as Norma Jean Baker. She died with a row of medicines and an empty bottle of barbiturates at her elbow.

These stony sentences, which read like the epitaph of a Raymond Chandler victim, will confirm for too many millions of movie fans the usual melodrama of a humble girl, cursed by physical beauty, to be dazed and doomed by the fame that was too much for her. For Americans, the last chapter was written on the weekend that a respectable national picture magazine printed for the delectation of her troubled fans a confessional piece called 'Marilyn Monroe Pours Out Her Soul'.

The plot of her early life is as seedy as anything in the pulp magazines, and to go into the details now would be as tasteless as prying into the clinical file of any other pretty woman whose beauty has crumbled overnight. It is enough, for summoning the necessary compassion, to recall her miserable parents, her being shuttled like a nuisance from foster home to orphanage, the subsequent knockabout years in a war factory, her short independence as a sailor's wife, the unsuspected first rung of the ladder provided by a posing job for a nude calendar.

She talked easily about all this, when people had the gall to ask her, not as someone reconciled to a wretched childhood but as a wide-eyed outsider, an innocent as foreign to the subject under discussion as Chaplin is when he stands off and analyses the appeal of 'the little man'.

Then she wiggled briefly past the lecherous gaze of Louis Calhern in Huston's *Asphalt Jungle*, and his appraising whinny echoed round the globe. Within two years she was the enthroned sexpot of the Western world. She completed the first phase of the American dream by marrying the immortal Joe DiMaggio, the loping hero of the New York Yankees; and the second phase by marrying Arthur Miller, and so redeeming his suspect Americanism at the moment it was in question before a House committee.

To say that Marilyn Monroe was a charming, shrewd and pathetic woman of tragic integrity will sound as preposterous to the outsider as William Empson's Freudian analysis of *Alice in Wonderland*. It is nevertheless true. We restrict the word 'integrity' to people either simple or complex, who have a strong sense of righteousness or, if they are public men, of self-righteousness. Yet it surely means no more than what it says: wholeness, being free to be spontaneous, without reck of consistency or moral appearances. It can be as true of forlorn and bewildered people as of the disciplined and solemn.

In this sense, Marilyn Monroe was all of a piece. She was confused, pathologically shy, a straw on the ocean of her compulsions (to pout, to crack-wise, to love a stranger, to be six hours late or lock herself in a room). She was a sweet and humorous person increasingly terrified by the huge stereotype of herself she saw plastered all around her. The exploitation of this pneumatic, mocking, liquid-lipped goddess gave the world a simple picture of the Lorelei. She was about as much of a Lorelei as Bridget, the housemaid.

This orphan of the rootless City of the Angels at last could feel no other identity than the one she saw in the mirror: a baffled, honest girl forever haunted by the nightmare of herself, sixty feet tall and naked before a howling mob. She could never learn to acquire the lacquered shell of the prima donna or the armour of sophistication. So in the end she found the ultimate oblivion, of which her chronic latecomings and desperate retreats to her room were token suicides.

¶ Lauren Bacall took New York by storm when the stage musical *Applause* opened on Broadway on 30 January 1969. AC, friend and fan, was there.

*　　　*　　　*

The Bacall of a Wild Martini

Guardian, 2 April 1970

The movie queen who decides too soon to take Broadway in her stride can invite a cruel fate: simply the inevitable comparison between her – possibly haunting – presence on the screen and her ineptitude in the different craft being expertly practised all around her.

Connoisseurs of theatrical disasters still recall the night, thirty-seven years ago, that Katharine Hepburn drifted airily on stage (in an appalling play called *The Lake*) in the fatal hope of mingling easily with such old stage pros as Blanche Bates. Everyone remembers Dorothy Parker's judgement that Miss Hepburn then proceeded to 'span the human emotions from A to B', though oddly fewer people recall Miss Parker's later explanation of why Miss Hepburn regularly retreated upstage left whenever Miss Bates appeared: 'she was evidently afraid of catching acting from Blanche Bates'.

These mean lines can be recalled in all Christian charity, for Miss Hepburn has burnished, down the decades, a theatrical talent as unforgettable as her beauty. And in the current *Coco* she has taken a long lovely revenge on the Parker attack. Troops of worshippers nightly attest to the fact, proclaimed by the sourest critics, that this season, Miss Hepburn exhibits a theatrical presence that is unsurpassed.

Rather, she was unsurpassed until a second lady, long mistaken for a steady star hanging over Beverly Hills, hurtled into New York, to be recognized as a comet: that is to say, according to the best definition, as 'a body with a star-like nucleus and a train or tail of light moving around the sun in an elliptical course or towards and from it in a parabola'.

Nobody who has watched the stars in their courses needs reminding of the enchanting arrival on the screen of a flaxen-haired girl with a body as trig as a fish and a come-hither look that, unique among all previous come-hither looks, could invite its victims either to bed or butchery. Lauren Bacall, of course.

After the early celebration, in the Bogart years, of her lynx-like glances, her mocking whistle and her youthful beauty, Miss Bacall suffered an embarrassing decade or so during which she was regularly required to be a romantic and fragile figure. Now, as her authors remark, 'she is as fragile as a moose', and for too many years she withstood prodigies of miscasting. In the Hollywood casting directory, nubile girls with flaxen hair and yellow eyes must be either sirens or helpless fawns. Bacall was too young for a siren, unlikely to threaten Gale Sondergaard. So, how often did we watch strong males, from John Wayne to Kenneth More, attempt to be tender with Miss Bacall, who is as susceptible of protection as a tornado and as easy to embrace as a swordfish. It took a close friend, happily also a famous humorist and then a director, to recognize that Lauren Bacall is a first-rate clown, as malleable, as funny, as a monkey in a barrel. Nunnally Johnson cast her as the toughest of the three tough babes in *How to Marry a Millionaire*, and it could be only a matter of time before somebody saw that for the full swinging of her train or tail of light she needed not a wide screen but a wider stage.

She has appeared on Broadway before. She was again miscast as a hermaphrodite (help!) in a woeful and short-lived play. Three seasons ago she became a promising parody of herself in the Broadway version of *Cactus Flower*. It was generally conceded to be a 'smash', but was a mere rehearsal for the blinding triumph of *Applause*, which has now burst on Broadway and which may well outshine any other terrestrial explosion until the crack of atomic doom.

Applause is neatly based, by the foxy old team of Betty Comden and Adolph Green, on the best Joseph Mankiewicz movie, *All About Eve*, the story of an ageing actress adored by a stage-door slip of a girl who comes in like a waif and goes out like a werewolf. It is the old story, as durable as a Groucho–Chico vaudeville routine, of the old witch out-bitched by the new. It would be nice to say that the young girl puts up, as Anne Baxter did against Bette Davis, menacing competition. The truth is that Miss Bacall defuses and obliterates every other talent on stage. She can toss a line like a dart and leave it twanging in the bull's-eye, as the audience roars its applause. She sings in a Bankhead growl but with a blissful confidence which implies Ella Fitzgerald is a pedant for singing on pitch. She dances, through an anthology of every popular dance of the last thirty years, with her train or tail of light moving in a parabola that leaves the audience with the breathless impression that Florence Mills, Adele Astaire and Isadora Duncan are returned in one flashing body.

It is academic to mention the modesty of the music, the inaudibility of the lyrics and the mere adequacy of the rest of the cast, gasping to stay above water. The theatre is Bacall's private heaven. And who asks that the Florida sky should be studded with stars when Apollo is launched? It is enough that there should be no distracting clouds, no drizzle, no high wind.

At the end, the lovely rascal threw her head up and arms high, and the Palace Theatre resounded with a tumult unlike anything heard in this town since Laurence Olivier wiped the red paint from his eyes and bowed himself out as Oedipus. Lauren Bacall has achieved her reincarnation: Groucho reborn as Dietrich, Judy Garland as Monroe. Better, Lauren Bacall as her true self.

¶ *Applause* ran for 896 performances. Bacall later beat Katharine Hepburn to the Tony Award for Best Actress in a Musical. The 'hermaphrodite' play was George Axelrod's *Goodbye, Charlie* (1959).

¶ AC was a regular fan of Warner's crime dramas in the 1930s, partly because of James Cagney's cocky persona and machine-gun speech. In this tribute, written in 1986 after Cagney's death, he looked underneath the actor's surface to find the 'candid, decent Everyman'.

*   *   *

Genius as an Urchin

Fun and Games with Alistair Cooke, 1994

Only three blocks east of Fifth Avenue's elegant museums, 96th Street takes a social dive and becomes a thoroughfare for the working class and its daily needs. There is on the south side a row of grimy, five-storey Victorian houses, shades permanently down, some of them perhaps permanently abandoned. On the north side, a corner lunch counter, basement locksmith, shoe repair shop, laundry, flower shop, hemmed in to the west by the slab of a high-rise apartment building. In the middle of the north block, planted deep and flat alongside the seedy or garish little stores is a church in sombre grey stone. It is the church of St Francis de Sales.

Here on a mild morning in April, the sidewalk opposite the church was lined with neighbours fenced in by a police cordon. They had come to see a rare event, the funeral of a film star. An old man, evidently not a local but a puzzled passerby, wondered what it was all about. 'Which film star?' James Cagney. '*The* James Cagney?' The same. Humph! (St Francis de Sales became the Cagneys' church when, in the boy's teens, they had moved across town from his slummy birthplace to the still German-Hungarian section known as Yorkville.)

The old man mused for a moment. 'Was that his real name?' A nod was the polite response. The rude answer would have been: 'Of course it was his real name, he was an Irishman.'

When Cagney came along in Hollywood in the early 30s, the original film tycoons – the Mayers, Goldwyns, Zukors, the young Thalberg – were still very much in charge and had for long dictated the mores and folkways, among which was the custom of looking over a new name and if it was not an Anglo-Saxon name, making it one. They had flirted in the silent days with the notion of French and Spanish names as romantic magnets and, for native sexpots, anything wildly exotic (Theodosia Goodman, of Cincinnati, was set up in a house with snakes and incense and rechristened Theda Bara, an acronym for Arab Death!). But with the sound films and the requirement to speak literate or at least intelligible English, the old immigrants reverted to the Anglo-Saxon prejudice that the United States was an Anglo-Saxon culture, at least that the toniest stratum of its society had English names. Any arriving actor with a Russian, Polish, German or Lithuanian name had it promptly changed, by producers who themselves were Russian, Polish, German or Lithuanian. And because of the strong, if sometimes tacit, anti-Semitism (when I shopped around for a New York apartment in 1937, every building I looked at had a handsome sign posted outside the entrance with the warning word – 'Restricted') all Jewish names were changed at once. Hence, Emmanuel Goldenberg became Edward G. Robinson, Marion Levy turned into Paulette Goddard, Issur Danielovich Demsky into Kirk Douglas.

I can think of no Irishman, or woman, who was ever given a change of name. There was for the longest time almost as much social prejudice against the Irish ('No Irish Need Apply') as against the Jews. But the first producers were canny enough to know that in the cities where they picked up the most substantial revenue – in New York, Boston, Philadelphia, Chicago – the Irish might be the majority immigrant group and, in any case, were stalwart movie fans, particularly proud of their own. The day it got out that Paddy O'Neill had had his name changed to – say – Derek Wakefield, there would be a hot time in his old home town that night. So no changes were anticipated or attempted when there appeared at the studios George Murphy, Maureen O'Sullivan, Ronald Reagan and all the O'Briens from Edmond to Virginia. And James Cagney.

He was born and brought up on the Lower East Side, the son of a bartender who died, when Cagney was still in his teens, in the flu pandemic of 1918–19. It was a poor family of five children, and long before his father's death, Cagney was automatically expected, as soon as he could use his fists and jump to attention, to support his mother and the other children. The biography of his early manhood reads like a resumé of his early parts. He worked through several lowly occupations: waiter, office boy, poolroom racker. He made it through high school, but the Army Training Corps at Columbia paid no wages and he descended to a department-store basement as a daytime package wrapper. By night, he watched all the current vaudeville dancers and decided to be one himself. Which – if I had a thesis, it would be mine to maintain – he remained all his life, in all his movies. (This judgement contradicts my pet theory that the best film acting is done with the face only. There must be glaring exceptions: Chaplin, Astaire, Cagney require the whole screen – the full proscenium – to show how swiftly and subtly and fluidly emotion can be expressed with the whole body – whether or not there is any accompanying music.)

He went into a Broadway chorus, he toured in vaudeville. Married at twenty-two and just getting by, he grabbed a modest Hollywood offer and made seven inconsequential films in two years. But in one of them (*The Public Enemy*) he signalled his arrival as a tough guy, what was known at the time as a woman's man (later, more pejoratively, a male chauvinist), by shoving a grapefruit into the face of his complaining girlfriend, Mae Clarke. This outrage, *Variety* wrote, 'sent his stock soaring 100 percent as a heart palpitator among femme fans'. At any rate, that single scene, remembered by old folks who could recall nothing else of Cagney's career, guaranteed his continued stardom, and a life of wealth and fame, throughout thirty years and fifty films. (The scene did nothing for Mae Clarke, who rapidly declined into bit parts and what are fancifully known as cameos.)

In all the gangster and street-smart parts, while frighteningly true to type, he always had a documentary honesty about him, as if he had stalked into the picture by mistake to embarrass the fancy actors trying to impersonate people like him. This intrusion of actual street life into the filmed fantasies of it was often almost literally true, for Cagney was a born mimic and, from boyhood on, whether by intention or simple symbiosis, had observed and memorized in the flesh the physical gestures of the sailors, conmen, bums, thieves and layabouts he had known. At one time, he went up to Sing Sing to entertain five of his old pals who were doing time, one of whom was subsequently executed.

It is a tribute to the verisimilitude of the low-life parts that so many moviegoers, otherwise intelligent and perceptive, disliked him for the oldest, as also the most flattering, reason – the first critical blunder: disliking the exponent of a milieu because you're uncomfortable with the milieu itself. (I once knew a man who couldn't abide the television series *Upstairs, Downstairs* because, it eventually came out, he didn't like rich people with servants!)

Everyone will have lasting memories of Cagney. Mine are not the more explicit gangster impersonations. They are what you might call the intervals of shameful self-knowledge in between the spasms of violence and meanness: his gratitude to the old saloon madam for taking him in when his self-respect was in shreds (*The Roaring Twenties*); his fusion of pride and embarrassment in seeing how right it is that his old girlfriend, Priscilla Lane, should be married to the clean-cut DA; the hoodlum storming through *Love Me or Leave Me*, as the husband of Doris Day, seething with jealousy he is trying and failing to contain. And there is, finally, the time he emerged from the chrysalis – or closet – where he had stealthily choreographed all the Hell's Kitchen gestures, of defiance, affection, belligerence, pathos, and was finally revealed (in *Yankee Doodle Dandy*) as the dazzling song-and-dance man he had been all along.

Nothing much can be done for those people, a considerable faction, who saw nothing more in Cagney than the vulgarity and general offensiveness of much of his material. But to anyone who saw the good man inside whatever he played, however malign, it was no surprise to discover from the obituaries that he was a man of principle (what we now call 'values'), a non-smoker, a rare, mild drinker, a lifelong Catholic living by fidelity (one wife for sixty-one years), thrift, his family and one or two close friends; and that he rarely if ever intruded into Beverly Hills, or any other chic society, having a natural indifference or allergy to the whole *Vogue* view of life.

There are one or two surprises. He had seen, in his scraping urban youth, a big patch of Brooklyn where, indeed, grew many trees. He saw himself as a displaced countryman. He bought a farm, when he was in his thirties, in the beautiful Amenia Valley, at Millbrook up the Hudson, where he raised horses and – for the last twenty-odd years of his life – was a working farmer. Outside his family, he said in a rare interview, 'the prime concern of my life has been nature and order, and how we've been savagely altering that order'. He could be quite sententious about what he saw as the decline of American life. A former enthusiastic New Dealer, he admitted to turning more and more conservative in old age because he saw his country 'threatened by moral confusion'.

So it was entirely right and characteristic that he should come back to that frowzy stretch of 96th Street to be honoured in the church of St Francis de Sales. He knew where he came from, and he went back to it at the end.

If there is a wishful strain in this catalogue of virtues, it may spring simply from a romantic desire to make the ideal, at the core of the Cagney character, realize itself in the flesh. At any rate, I am one who cannot lose the sharp image of that jaunty, bouncing, forever cocky little figure, successfully pretending, through so many rowdy films, to be a scamp but rarely managing to conceal the candid, decent Everyman underneath. A *brave homme*!

¶ Not all of AC's movie tributes celebrated the names above the title.

*   *   *

Yakima Canutt Is Dead

Letter from America, BBC, 30 May 1986

Yakima Canutt is dead. In case anyone is saying, 'How's that, again?' or 'Would you please speak distinctly?', I will repeat: Yakima Canutt is dead.

And it's a reflection on the sad fate of the people who really make the wheels go round in the world of make-believe, in the movies particularly, that for every moviegoer who knew and honoured the hair-raising courage of Yakima Canutt, there were a 100,000 fans who knew the handsome boys up front whose appearance of courage and selflessness, whose very reputation as Western heroes, was made possible by Mr Canutt's dirty work.

He was, to put it simply, the most famous 'stunt man' in the history of Hollywood. And anyone familiar with the Western or swashbuckling stars must have seen Yakima Canutt a hundred times – usually in a blur of horses run wild, or burning motor cars spinning over, or even in long shots of superb horsemanship through the Indians' enemy lines.

The first name – what in officially Christian countries is called the Christian name – may puzzle you. And I don't wonder. Canutt was christened Enos Edward Canutt and was born in Colfax, in the north-western state of Washington in November 1895. Though, like the rest of us, he had only two parents, he was said to be of Irish–Scotch–Dutch parentage. As a boy he became a ranch hand, and very soon entered local rodeos and won prizes for roping and riding. He was so much better than anyone around, even in his teens, that it was a matter of only a year or two before he won the world's rodeo championship at a rodeo staged in the – ah ha! – Yakima Valley, a huge half-million acre high-plateau stretch – once of sagebrush, now of prosperous fruit-growing – that lies just east of the Cascade Mountains. It was here that Canutt became known as 'The Cowboy from Yakima', and thereafter few people knew his given names.

In the early 1920s, with Western movies beginning to hit their stride, inevitably a call came from Hollywood, for there was already a generation of dashing young movie actors who itched to become cowboy stars but who naturally preferred not to make it by breaking their backbones. Canutt had the same ambition – I mean, he too wanted to be a movie star, and by 1924 became one, playing the lead in *Romance and Rustlers*, *Ridin' Mad*, *White Thunder*, *The Human Tornado*, *The Fighting Stallion*, and other minor epics unknown today even to the most earnest film libraries. The fact is, Canutt didn't quite have the looks, and when the talkies – remember? – came in, his voice didn't have an agreeable sound. But he was not on that account to be pitied, like other silent actors – John Gilbert, for instance. The glamour boys beat a path to his door, since he was the only rough rider in the business who did all his own stunts, never used a double. Hence, the urgent applications of some of the upcoming cowboy stars – Gene Autry, Roy Rogers – to hire Canutt to be their heroic selves.

Well into the late 30s, he substituted for the stars I've mentioned, and many others, in any and every sequence that offered a risk to life and limb. He was loose-limbed and average tall, and in long-shot could be easily made to look like the dauntless star, who in fact could sit sipping a drink in a director's chair and watch his fearless alter ego leap from one railroad car to another, break a wild horse from the pack – in one of John Wayne's breathtaking scenes, jump from a stagecoach, hop from one bareback to another of a flying team and fall under the lead horse, be dragged along the road through the flying hooves of the rest, and be tossed by the galloping steeds on to the desert floor and left for dead. When the director yelled 'Cut', there was always the awful moment, the very anxious moment for the onlooking star, when it was not certain whether Canutt was in fact dead or not. To everyone's relief, and a patter of grateful applause from the crew and the star, Canutt usually got up and strolled back to announce either that 'everything was Jake' (a long-gone term for okay) or to announce that he thought he'd broken an ankle, an elbow, a thigh bone or a couple of ribs. Before he switched to directing stunt sequences and chariot races with other stunt men he'd trained, Canutt had broken just about every bone in his body, arms, legs, ribs, pelvis, internal injuries, whatever. It must be a matter of puzzlement to the doctors, and pride to the orthopaedic surgeons especially, that this week he died in his bed, of natural causes, in his ninetieth year. All hail Yakima Canutt, who risked his life hundreds of times that millions around the world might marvel at the manliness and audacity of Errol Flynn, John Wayne, Clark Gable, Roy Rogers, Gene Autry, Henry Fonda and Randolph Scott.

His career, and the star-spangled fame of the good lookers who stood in for him in the romantic and other harmless sequences, was made possible by the essential and delightful fraudulence of the motion picture. Nobody has ever put better, or more simply, the unique trickery of the movie method than the early Russian director Eisenstein, who wrote that the making of a movie is in essence an act of deceit. You show, he said, a picture of a keyhole. You then, in a fraction of a second, show a picture of a girl taking a bath. The keyhole may have been shot in Leningrad and the girl in the bath in Moscow. But the lightning blend of images convinces the audience that it is peering through the keyhole of a door beyond which a girl is taking a bath.

You may have noticed that there is one famous name missing from that roster of seeming movie heroes. It is the name of Gary Cooper, who was himself a splendid horseman and the best man with a revolver that his friend Ernest Hemingway had ever seen. I remember, sometime – it must have been – in the late 1930s, when Cooper was at his peak, *Life* magazine showed a set of what were then called stroboscopic pictures – a running sequence of images shot a twenty-fourth of a second apart. As you know, in a sound film, twenty-four still pictures a second run through the projector and so give the illusion of movement. This *Life* sequence, as I recall, had seventy-two pictures of Cooper twirling a revolver in one hand, then reaching for another revolver with the other hand, and firing at the bad guy with both barrels. The whole thing took three seconds, and even in one run of a dozen pictures or so, Cooper's hands were a blur. It will redeem, I hope, the true memory of the greatest of all cowboy stars to know that he, at least, was most often what he appeared to be.

¶ After Greta Garbo died in 1990, AC recollected the only time, in 1952, when he had actually seen the screen divinity who had prompted many paragraphs in his film critic days and inspired the title of his first book. They watched a film together, Chaplin's *Limelight*, not yet released; the location was the ballroom at 19 Gramercy Park, home of AC's friend Ben Sonnenberg, PR chief for the elite.

*　　　*　　　*

Garbo and the Night Watchman
Unidentified media interview, 1990

Q: Did you ever meet her?
A: Yes, once. In a rich man's house. He used to show movies on Sunday nights, and brighten up his friendships with a sprinkling of famous people of all sorts. That evening I saw Garbo, in the sense of being put next to her on a love seat, which, as you know, is made for two. No sniggering inferences should be drawn from that. In the first place, she was about as approachable as an iceberg – very lofty and shiningly beautiful, and daunting. I soon realized, from the very remarks – single words, really – that she was pathologically shy. I spent the evening – it was a very long film – just keeping lit the chain of her cigarettes. So, about every ten minutes I had the odd pleasure of lighting up her breathtaking profile in the surrounding darkness. I've never forgotten it. Afterwards, there was a small pathetic attempt at conversation. She had only one thing on her mind: the awful price of vegetables.

¶ In his ninety-fifth year, still delivering the BBC's *Letter from America*, AC continued to look back at cinema's past and his own film experiences. In April 2003 he saluted the passing of MGM's long-serving editor, Margaret Booth, aged 104. Two months later he said farewell to a closer contemporary, Katharine Hepburn, and summoned up for one last time his interview spree in Hollywood seventy years before. The following year, from his bed, he made his final broadcast, first transmitted on 20 February 2004.

*   *   *

Longevity

Letter from America, BBC, 11 April 2003

Here I find a faded snippet from the *New York Times*, datelined Los Angeles, and the lead sentence carries the astounding news that Margaret Booth, a film editor, had died at the age of 104 [on 28 October 2002]. She was a top-flight, greatly admired film cutter. She started film editing with D. W. Griffith, the inventor of the cinema's grammar – fade-in, fade-out, dissolve – those simple devices to show the end of a scene, a mood, a year, which now you have to guess at, from the universal practice of what they call a 'jump cut' from one scene, one continent, one mood, to another in one twenty-fourth of a second.

Miss Booth polished up the fame of many directors and stars. I put it that way because I hope the day is coming when the moviegoing public will become as sensitive to the editing of a film as in the past forty years or so it has pretended to be about directors, whose names in the early days we scarcely knew. The actors were the stars. I say this for a simple reason known to everybody in the movie industry but practically nobody outside it: the person who makes or breaks a film is not the scriptwriter or the director, but the film editor.

What is astonishing about Miss Booth's obituary is her longevity. Of all the unhealthy, bent-over occupations likely to produce hunchback, anaemia and an early end, I would until now have chosen sitting in a small dark cell with your shoulders permanently rounded, your hands trying to gum together twenty strips of film into a continuous sequence of action that is dramatic, lucid and moving. Let's hear it then for Margaret Booth, who whatever her theory of longevity beat all the odds, and remains the real creator of Garbo's *Camille*, *The Red Badge of Courage* and the original, unbeatable *Mutiny on the Bounty*.

Meeting the Stars

Letter from America, BBC, 4 July 2003

Last Monday morning, her picture, accompanying a huge obituary, took up a page and a half of the *New York Times*. When I saw the photograph, I realized, from the calendar, that it was exactly seventy years ago that, visiting Hollywood for the first time (as a student/tourist), I had the august sensation of being picked up at my humble hotel by a studio limousine – a limousine sent expressly for me, a totally anonymous student driving round the country, the USA, in a second-hand, $45 Ford. It came about this way.

During the previous winter and spring, I had sent to one of the two distinguished English Sunday papers a few theatre reviews of a new O'Neill play (Nobel Prize playwright), and a play by one Noël Coward (then the chicest of English playwrights). Out of what in New York is called chutzpah, I had the audacity to write to the editor of this Sunday paper, an awesomely famous man, suggesting that, on my summer trip – since I should be stopping by Hollywood – how about my writing a series of six pieces on the movies, beginning with an interview with Charlie Chaplin, then with the celebrated German director Ernst Lubitsch, with an English star (how about the monumental C. Aubrey Smith?), an Oscar-winning cameraman and so forth? Of course, I knew none of these magnificos. But when, to my astonishment, the awesome editor wrote back and said it just so happened that their film critic, Miss Lejeune, was taking off for just six weeks, I might submit the pieces. This made it automatic for me then, swollen with chutzpah, to write to all the stars and say, 'On behalf of the London *Observer* . . . I have been commissioned, etc . . .' Not one refused to set a date. On the contrary, before they'd even glimpsed this brash 24-year-old, several of them wrote back to be sure a day could be set apart at *my* convenience. I remember an ingratiating letter from Mr Chaplin, the beginning of a beautiful friendship.

When I got out there, I started my grand tour by deciding to write first about a famous director at work. The man I chose, then in the first flush of great success, was one George Cukor. He had just started shooting the immortal Louisa May Alcott's *Little Women*. Why not come out and spend the day with the cast, in a stretch of what they had turned into a New England landscape, about twenty miles out from Beverly Hills? And so I was driven off and greeted in the warmest way (after all, I represented the *Observer*, owned by the Astors, no less) by Mr Cukor and the cast. I'll call off their names without further definition – you may take my word for it, it was a very starry cast, palpitating in the wake of the veteran actors Paul Lukas and Henry Stephenson and Edna May Oliver, Joan Bennett, Jean Parker, Frances Dee *and* Katharine Hepburn. Of course you know her (thanks to television re-runs).

Katharine Hepburn was, indeed, the subject of the *New York Times* obituary. And it was not a lament. She was ninety-six, and long a martyr to an embarrassing trembling of the head and hands, which she swore to the end was not Parkinson's disease.

Back there (seventy years ago in that California valley), what struck me, in watching the shooting of this famous story of four young sisters growing up in New England before the Civil War, was nothing about the play or the shooting of it, but the – how shall I put it? – the social oddity of this girl Hepburn. She stood out, as a kind of attractive freak. All because of her accent, which was that of a well-schooled, upper-middle-class New England girl just out (she was four years out) of Bryn Mawr (a college of high academic standing but also notable for breeding well-bred, upper-class young women). It had its own distinct variation of an upper-crust New England accent, which is not, by the way, anything like British English of the same class. Miss Hepburn had it, and, in that time and place, it was quite strange.

I don't believe it will be news to older listeners to hear that the majority, maybe a large majority, of American screen actors and actresses in those days – whatever parts they became trained to play – came from humble immigrant South and Eastern European backgrounds. Since the top producers who founded Hollywood had also that background (most of them pedlars who had fled from Jewish pogroms in Europe), one of the notable signs of their feelings of social inferiority, throughout the 1920s into the 50s, was the alacrity with which they rushed to change the given names of rising stars to English names, since, way back then, those cunning but simple Russian and Lithuanian and German producers thought, wrongly, that the absolutely top social class in the United States was English. Hence, Emmanuel Goldenberg became Edward G. Robinson, Bernard Schwartz – Tony Curtis, Frances Gumm – Judy Garland, Allen Konigsberg – Woody Allen, Issur Danielovich Demsky – Kirk Douglas, Marion Levy – Paulette Goddard, and so on and so on.

Katharine Hepburn was born and stayed Katharine Hepburn, daughter of a distinguished surgeon in Connecticut and a mother who was, as in England, a fervent socialite suffragette. This rationalization of mine, of course, came to me later, during a period of Hepburn's life, in her late twenties, early thirties, when she made some indifferent movies and was famously dubbed 'box-office poison' because, I now think, the movies she was making then were not good enough to overcome the general popular dislike of what was called her fancy accent. In that summertime, all I noticed was that the rest of the cast treated her with particular respect not usually due a young actress. She had, however, won an Oscar the year before. But the three other sisters somehow gave off the feeling that she was not the normal Hollywood product. But she was totally unaffected, she was who she was: an upper-class Yankee of character. They took to her simply because of her character. And what a character. She refused to be bought and sold by a studio, no matter how tyrannical and fearsome a Zukor, a Goldwyn, might be. She had a play written for her by a famous Philadelphia playwright, bought the play, acted in it, and then sold it to a Hollywood studio to be made *her* way on *her* terms. They hated her but the actors (slaves to anything the studio picked for them) cheered her. And for the rest of her screen life she ran things her way, and made tyrants say, 'Yes, Miss Hepburn.' 'Well, Kate. Okay.'

Late in life she said flatly that she had been born of a well-to-do family and felt an obligation to live up to its responsibilities. 'I was not,' she wrote, 'a poor little thing. I don't know what I'd have done if I'd come to New York and had to get a job as a waiter or something.' She added she was a success, not because of any great individual talent; 'I had advantages,' she said, 'I had *better* be a success.'

¶ Alistair Cooke's fondness for cinema continued until the end, though he had stopped being a practising film critic some sixty years before. In 1971, introducing a new edition of *Garbo and the Night Watchmen* (1937), his anthology of film reviews by nine critics (Robert Herring, Don Herold, John Marks, Meyer Levin, Robert Forsythe, Graham Greene, Otis Ferguson, Cecelia Ager, and himself), he crisply summarized the critical qualities he admired, and put a revealing perspective on his own years spent at the movies, hat and notebook in hand.

*   *   *

Envoi

'Preface to 1971 Edition', *Garbo and the Night Watchmen*, 1971

What I admired, and admire, most in a critic is a personal point of view and the ability to express it crisply, or passionately, or drolly or entertainingly, but above all intelligibly ... If I had a prejudice, then, in choosing my co-authors it was for people who showed, first, an appetite for life and second, a liking for the movies as a warming part of it. Each of the nine was true to a different background and so had an honestly different point of view. They all loved the movies yet did not feel called on to claim for their love that it was about to replace religion, sex, and Supreme Court or interstate commerce. They were all gifted and intelligent people, none of them educated to compulsory polysyllables, all of them with their own brand of humour ... Yours truly is happy indeed that he gave only a little of his life to the movies and most of it to American politics, the landscape of the West, music, golf, fishing, and every known indoor game excepting only bridge.

Acknowledgments

Without the Estate of Alistair Cooke and Colin Webb, his Literary Executor, and of course Penguin Books, this anthology would never have happened; I am most grateful for their support. Patti Yasek, in New York, deserves particular thanks for her enthusiasm and tenacity in locating material. Alex Rankin and Jennifer Pino were of great assistance at the Howard Gotlieb Archival Research Center, Boston University, splendid home of the Alistair Cooke papers. I am equally grateful for the support of Louise North and Erin O'Neill at the BBC Written Archives Centre in Reading, and Ron Magliozzi at Research and Collections, Department of Film, the Museum of Modern Art in New York. Crucial research was also conducted at the British Library, Birmingham City Library, and the BFI National Library. Kevin Brownlow, Tony Aspler, and Eamon Dyas, the *Times* archivist, gave friendly assistance, and Tara McCabe offered warm hospitality in Boston. And a special bouquet to my wife Catherine Surowiec for her love, her eagle eye, and for being an American.

For permission to reprint material, I am most grateful to the following publishers, newspapers and magazines:

Atlantic Monthly, for material extracted from the essay 'Charlie Chaplin' (August 1939)

Guardian News and Media, for 'Charlie Chaplin Talks' and 'Messrs George Cukor and C. Aubrey Smith', from material first published in the *Observer* series 'Hollywood Prospect' (10 September and 15 October 1933), and the following material filed for the *Guardian*: 'Mr Bogart Defends His Own' (1 October 1949), 'A Hollywood

Ex-Communist' (9 May 1953), 'The French Line' (31 December 1953), 'Will Hays' (9 March 1954), 'A McCarthy Legacy' (26 June 1956), 'Bogart and the Age of Violence' (16 January 1957), 'Hollywood Stars on the Rack' (21 August 1957), 'Annual Parade of Leading Film Stars' (28 March 1958), 'Preston Sturges' (8 August 1959), 'Showing Mr K the "Real America"' (12 September 1959), 'The Script that Got Away' (21 September 1959), 'First Night for Doomsday' (17 December 1959), 'The Positive Demise of G and S' (5 May 1960), 'Archetype of the Hemingway Hero' (15 May 1961), 'Marilyn Is Dead' (6 August 1962), 'Dignified Hollywood Awards its Oscars' (10 April 1963), 'Mr Zanuck Triumphs' (24 May 1963), 'Cleopatra, a Working Girl's Dream' (14 June 1963), 'The Bacall of a Wild Martini' (2 April 1970), 'Men Zsa Zsa Did Not Want to Meet' (21 August 1970)

The Museum of Modern Art, New York, for material extracted from *Douglas Fairbanks: The Making of a Screen Character* (1940). © The Museum of Modern Art. All rights reserved

The New York Times, for 'To Iris Barry (1895–1969)' (18 January 1970)

Sight and Sound and the British Film Institute, for material extracted from the articles 'Films of the Quarter' (Winter 1934/5 and Summer 1936) and AC's review of *The March of Time* (Autumn 1935)

The Spectator, for 'A Gift from the Gods', 'Technicolor versus Monochrome' and 'The Night I Saw *Ernte*', from AC's film columns of 8, 15 and 27 January 1937

The Times, for 'Mr Chaplin as Dictator' (16 October 1940)

World Book Inc., for 'The End is Nigh', extracted from 'Alistair Cooke on the Arts' by Alistair Cooke. THE 1963 WORLD BOOK YEAR BOOK © 1977 Field Enterprises Educational Corporation. By permission of World Book, Inc. www.worldbookonline.com. All rights reserved. 'Festival of Blood and Guts', extracted from 'Focus: The Arts' by Alistair Cooke. THE 1977 WORLD BOOK YEAR BOOK © 1977 Field Enterprises Educational Corporation. By permission of World Book, Inc. www.worldbookonline.com. All rights reserved. 'The Video-cassette Recorder', extracted from 'Focus: The

Arts' by Alistair Cooke. THE 1978 WORLD BOOK YEAR BOOK © 1978 Field Enterprises Educational Corporation. By permission of World Book, Inc. www.worldbookonline.com. All rights reserved.

Index

PENGUIN LETTERS

LETTER FROM AMERICA 1946–2004
ALISTAIR COOKE

'A chronicler of amazing times … There is never going to be anyone like Cooke'
Daily Telegraph

'Cooke's Letters are more than mere journalism: they are a moving picture of
Anglo-American relations – a piece of history in their own right' *Daily Mail*

For over half a century Alistair Cooke entertained millions of listeners across the
globe with his weekly BBC radio programme *Letter from America*. An
outstanding observer of the American scene, he became one of the world's best-
loved broadcasters and achieved the longest running one-man show in radio
history.

Here, published for the first time, is a selection of the finest of Alistair Cooke's
2,869 broadcasts, which celebrates the inimitable style of this wise, witty and
acute reporter. Presented chronologically, these famous letters span Cooke's
extraordinary career, beginning with a powerful description of American GIs
returning home in 1946, and ending with his last broadcast in February 2004
discussing the US presidential campaign.

Imbued with Alistair Cooke's special brand of good humour, elegance and
understanding, *Letter from America 1946–2004* is a captivating insight into the
heart of a nation, and a fitting tribute to the man who was for so many the most
reassuring voice of our times.

'No one succeeded in explaining to the English-speaking world … the
idiosyncrasies of a country at once so familiar, and yet so utterly foreign'
Independent

'An enchanting volume … A remarkable, perhaps unique transatlantic diary …
what stories he has to tell … Cooke expressed a mutual affection between two
nations which radiates from these debonair pages' *Sunday Telegraph*

ALISTAIR COOKE

AMERICAN JOURNEY
ALISTAIR COOKE

'I could quote Cooke forever; his phrasing is so elegant, his images are so evocative and moving' Miranda Sawyer, *Observer*

Then a Washington correspondent for the *Guardian*, Alistair Cooke recognized a great story to be told in investigating at first hand the effects of the Second World War on America and the daily lives of Americans as they adjusted to radically new circumstances. Within weeks of the Pearl Harbor attack, Cooke set off with a reporter's zeal on a circuit of the entire country to see what the war had done to people. This unique travelogue celebrates an important American character and the indomitable spirit of a nation that was to inspire Cooke's reports and broadcasts for some sixty years.

'Exceptionally interesting, reflective and informative as well as personal, quirky and sometimes very funny' Selina Hastings, *Daily Telegraph*

ALISTAIR COOKE

SIX MEN
ALISTAIR COOKE

'A rare delight … he has that priceless gift of the gods, irresistible readability'
Spectator

During his broadcasting career Alistair Cooke met and knew some of the twentieth century's most fascinating and legendary figures. Here are candid portraits of Humphrey Bogart; the lovable yet unreliable Charlie Chaplin; the charming yet childlike 'golden boy', Edward VIII; Cooke's friend and mentor, H.L. Mencken; the larger-than-life liberal politician, Adlai Stevenson; and the heroic social reformer, Bertrand Russell. Each superbly realized portrait gives us an insight into a golden age of 'great men', and is a masterpiece of observation, warmth and humour.

'Six Men is the journalist's memoir par excellence' *Newsweek*

ALISTAIR COOKE

THE MARVELLOUS MANIA: ALISTAIR COOKE ON GOLF

'Wonderful … something to treasure' Jack Nicklaus

Although Alistair Cooke called golf 'a method of self-torture, disguised as a game', from the first time he swung a club at the age of fifty-five, he was hooked for the rest of his life. This book brings together the best of Cooke's writings about his greatest sporting passion, which display the incomparable wit, the unexpected insights, the mischievous charm, the elegance and enchantment which made him famous for over sixty years as a broadcaster.

'The master of avuncular fireside chat' *Daily Telegraph*

ALISTAIR COOKE

REPORTING AMERICA: THE LIFE OF A NATION 1946 - 2004

This book presents the cream of Alistair Cooke's writings on the events that shaped modern American history, from the end of the Second World War through to the assassination of John Kennedy and of Bobby Kennedy (Cooke was actually present), the moon landings and the Monica Lewinsky scandal. Almost all the material is previously unpublished in book form – transcripts of his legendary Letters from America, long-forgotten reports in the Guardian (whose correspondent in New York he was for twenty-five years) and other freshly discovered writings. The book is illustrated throughout in full colour with iconic photographs of the events Cooke is describing.

'Cooke *was* the special relationship' *Daily Mail*

PENGUIN HISTORY

AMERICA, EMPIRE OF LIBERTY: A NEW HISTORY
DAVID REYNOLDS

'An enthralling tale' *Daily Telegraph*

It was Thomas Jefferson who envisioned the United States as a great 'empire of liberty.' David Reynolds takes Jefferson's phrase as a key to the saga of America, bringing to life presidents from Washington to Obama, whilst also drawing on the voices of settlers and immigrants, factory workers and suburban housewives. He examines how the anti-empire of 1776 became the greatest superpower the world has seen, how the country that offered liberty and opportunity on a scale unmatched in Europe nevertheless founded its prosperity on the labour of black slaves and the dispossession of the Native Americans.

Written with verve and insight, this extraordinary history reveals the grandeur and paradoxes of the world's great superpower.

'Readable, full of anecdotes, mini-biographies and arresting juxtapositions. Reynolds sprinkles his text with humour' *Independent*

'Let us not mince words. This is the best one-volume history of the United States ever written' *The National Interest*

www.penguin.com

He just wanted a decent book to read ...

Not too much to ask, is it? It was in 1935 when Allen Lane, Managing Director of Bodley Head Publishers, stood on a platform at Exeter railway station looking for something good to read on his journey back to London. His choice was limited to popular magazines and poor-quality paperbacks – the same choice faced every day by the vast majority of readers, few of whom could afford hardbacks. Lane's disappointment and subsequent anger at the range of books generally available led him to found a company – and change the world.

'We believed in the existence in this country of a vast reading public for intelligent books at a low price, and staked everything on it'
Sir Allen Lane, 1902–1970, founder of Penguin Books

The quality paperback had arrived – and not just in bookshops. Lane was adamant that his Penguins should appear in chain stores and tobacconists, and should cost no more than a packet of cigarettes.

Reading habits (and cigarette prices) have changed since 1935, but Penguin still believes in publishing the best books for everybody to enjoy. We still believe that good design costs no more than bad design, and we still believe that quality books published passionately and responsibly make the world a better place.

So wherever you see the little bird – whether it's on a piece of prize-winning literary fiction or a celebrity autobiography, political tour de force or historical masterpiece, a serial-killer thriller, reference book, world classic or a piece of pure escapism – you can bet that it represents the very best that the genre has to offer.

Whatever you like to read – trust Penguin.